The
REGISTER
of the
GEORGE
CROSS

THE REGISTER OF THE GEORGE CROSS

First published in 1985
by This England Books
73 Rodney Road, Cheltenham, Gloucestershire.

Second edition (revised) 1990
Printed in Great Britain by
BPCC Wheatons Ltd, Exeter, Devon.

ISBN 0 906324 17 3

Companion Volume: *The Register of the Victoria Cross*
First published by This England in 1981. Revised and
enlarged edition published 1988. (ISBN 0 906324 07 6)

Contents

His Majesty
KING GEORGE
THE SIXTH

CLARENCE HOUSE
S.W. 1

In the early days of the war The King was impressed by some very heroic deeds in mine and bomb disposal: deeds performed far from any human enemy but requiring the peak of courage for a considerable time. He felt that no existing award for gallantry reflected such an impersonal bravery.

In the following months there were more deeds of great courage when no enemy was present: more bombs and mines made safe, rescues after bombing, accident and disaster in truly terrifying circumstances.

In a broadcast to the nation in September 1940 The King announced the institution of the George Cross for the most courageous acts performed away from the heat of battle, and in November decorated the first recipients at an Investiture in Buckingham Palace.

As President of the Victoria Cross and George Cross Association I am glad that the names of all those men and women who have been awarded the George Cross, together with those formerly holding other decorations since gazetted George Cross, should be here collected in one volume.

ELIZABETH R
President

A Short History of the George Cross

Medals — and in particular medals for gallant actions — have a long and honourable history in our land. In the civilian field pride of place is held by the George Cross.

There are those in the gift of societies, such as The Royal Humane Society, The Royal National Lifeboat Institution, and also the Board of Trade — to name some whose records are filled with details of outstanding courage and devotion in circumstances of great danger in civilian life. Then there are those which have been awarded by the nation for similar acts, among which are the Albert Medal for saving life at sea and on land, always justly accorded second place only to the military award of the Victoria Cross, and in later times the Edward Medal, granted for bravery in industrial accidents.

In 1922, the Order of the British Empire having been instituted in 1917, there was included among its several grades a medal for gallantry, which became known as the Empire Gallantry Medal and was awarded for both civil and military actions, many retrospectively. The records and citations of awards by societies were published in the journals of these societies: those of national awards appeared in the issues of the *London Gazette*.

When, in 1940, King George the Sixth instituted the Cross and Medal which bear his name the total nature of World War Two had brought war into all civilian life, and there were many acts of outstanding gallantry for which the terms of award of the existing non-military medals were deemed to be inappropriate. In place of these national medals, therefore, awards were to be made of the George Cross or the George Medal (which would be awarded more freely, although the standard would be high). The George Cross could be awarded posthumously, but awards of the George Medal could be made only to living men and women until 1978 when a new warrant for the George Medal extended its availability for posthumous awards.

Every living recipient of the Empire Gallantry Medal at the date of the George Cross warrant (24th September, 1940), was required to return that medal to the Central Chancery of the Orders of Knighthood at St. James's Palace and receive a George Cross in exchange. Later, on 21st October, 1971, every living recipient of the Albert Medal or the Edward Medal, might, in like manner, exchange his or her medal for a George Cross. In this case, however, unlike that of the Empire Gallantry Medallists where the exchange was compulsory, some opted to retain their original medals while being accorded the title of George Cross winner.

As a result of these several arrangements, the total number of men and women on the George Cross roll, up to the present time, is:

By direct award (82 posthumously)	152
Eligible Empire Gallantry Medallists	112
Eligible Albert Medallists	64
Eligible Edward Medallists	68
Total	396

During World War Two there were instances when it was not easy to decide whether a Victoria Cross or a George Cross was the more proper award. The George Cross was intended to be an award for outstanding civilian bravery, but as many people in the armed services were unavoidably engaged in work not appropriate for strictly military awards (that is, under direct orders of commanders in the battlefield) they became eligible for recommendation for the George Cross equally with civilians. Consequently, 76 of the first 100 awards were made to members of the armed forces. A complete tally of the 152 direct awards of the George Cross up to the date of publication (Jan. 1985) shows that only 49 have gone to civilians.

It may be that men and women in civilian life who are personally aware, as witnesses, of brave deeds do not know of the channels of recommendation so that deserving cases go unrewarded. It may also be that the authorities who do make final recommendations set such a demanding standard that a candidate who survives his action may be deemed only to deserve the lesser award of a

George Medal. Awards of a George Cross have now become so rare that few people are ever likely to see one, or its recipient.

The George Cross is of silver, with the words *"For Gallantry"* as described in the warrant, and is suspended from a dark blue ribbon one and a half inches wide (it was originally one and a quarter inches, but this was increased to the present width by the Royal Warrant of 8th May, 1941), and is worn on the left breast before all other medals and orders except the Victoria Cross. Ladies not in uniform wear the Cross, suspended from a wide bow of the blue ribbon, below the left shoulder. Each Cross is made by the Royal Mint and engraved on the reverse with the recipient's name and date of the *Gazette* in the case of direct awards and for exchanged Empire Gallantry Medals, and the date of the action for exchanged Albert and Edward Medals. They are supplied to the appropriate ministry — Home Office for civilians and the Ministry of Defence (in earlier days its separate parts) for the armed services. Where possible they are presented at Royal Investitures to living recipients and to the next of kin of those who have not survived.

As with the Victoria Cross, bars may be awarded, but so far no one has been so honoured and the approved design for such a bar has not been included in the descriptive warrant.

In the following pages are the accounts of the actions which have led to the ultimate awards of George Crosses. In reading them it must be realised that they were not all awarded within the terms of the same warrant. Those originally made of the Albert Medal and the Edward Medal were, like those of the Victoria Cross, in limited fields of human activity. The awards of the Empire Gallantry Medal were, like those of the George Cross itself, in an unlimited field and some of the accounts are not very informative. While comparisons are unavoidable, one must remember that in all cases the man or woman involved did all, and often more than the situation demanded without thought of self. To use a phrase from John Drinkwater's play *"Abraham Lincoln"*, each was the "lord of his event", and if the need had been greater it is not unreasonable to think that every one of them would have matched the demand with their actions. They did not count the cost to themselves of the risks they took and accepted.

FREDERICK G. CARROLL

The
REGISTER

NOTE: In the following entries, former Empire Gallantry Medallists, Albert Medallists and Edward Medallists are indicated by the initials EGM, AM or EM in brackets under "Remarks".

ABBOTT 1

Edmund Geoffrey
Rank/Title: Lieutenant (later Captain)
Unit/Force/Occupation: Royal Navy
Other Decorations: —
Date of Gazette: 12 Mar. 1920
Place/Date of Birth: — 20 Jul. 1895
Place/Date of Death: Crowthorne, Berkshire — 3 Apr. 1974
Place of Memorial: —
Town/County Connections: Crowthorne, Berkshire
Remarks: (AM); served in Second World War, retired in 1948.

Account of Deed: On 5th August, 1919, an explosion occurred on board the ex-German battleship *Baden*, whilst in dry dock at Invergordon. Lieutenant Abbott immediately went down to the main deck and saw that smoke was coming from the ladder way tunnel leading down to the shaft passage and after-room containing the cooling plant. First efforts proving useless, he went to the corresponding tunnel on the starboard side, to see whether it was possible to get below and work up to the scene of the explosion from that side. The starboard tunnel was practically clear of smoke, so he collected a party, and went down again through the tunnel to the room containing the cooling plant. He made his way to the port side and found a dockyard workman lying unconscious. Lieutenant Abbott and his helpers got the body to the upper deck, but the man was already dead. Although greatly affected by the fumes, Lieutenant Abbott called for further volunteers and again went to the rescue of a second man whose groans had been heard, and succeeded in removing him from danger. Throughout the proceedings this officer showed an utter disregard for his own safety.

ABBOTT 2

George Fawcett Pitts
Rank/Title: Mr.
Unit/Force/Occupation: Deckhand, Royal Naval Reserve
Other Decorations: —
Date of Gazette: 12 Dec. 1917
Place/Date of Birth: Nelson, Lancashire — 18 Sep. 1897
Place/Date of Death: Nelson, Lancashire — 10 Jun. 1977
Place of Memorial: —
Town/County Connections: Nelson, Lancashire
Remarks: (AM)

Account of Deed: On 14th September 1917, on Hornsea Island, a seaplane collided with a Poulsen mast and remained wedged in it; the pilot was unconscious and had been thrown out of his seat and on to one of the wings. Deckhand Abbott, together with two other seamen, at once climbed up the mast for 100 feet, when one of them, making use of the boatswain's chair, was hoisted up by men at the foot of the mast to the place, over 300 feet from the ground, where the seaplane was fixed. He then climbed out on to the plane and held the pilot until the arrival of Deckhand Abbott and the third seaman.* A gantline was then secured round the pilot who was safely lowered to the ground. All three men were very well aware of the damaged and insecure condition of the mast, which was bent to an angle where the seaplane had become wedged. One of the three supports of the mast was fractured, and so far as the men knew, the mast or seaplane might at any time have collapsed. (*See also entry for KNOWLTON, R.J.)

ADAMSON 3

George John
Rank/Title: Inspector
Unit/Force/Occupation: River Traffic Police, Calcutta, Bengal
Other Decorations: King's Police Medal for Gallantry & Bar, Indian Police Medal for Gallantry
Date of Gazette: 1 Feb. 1937
Place/Date of Birth: — 4 Mar. 1896
Place/Date of Death: — 14 Mar. 1976
Place of Memorial: —
Town/County Connections: Penge, London
Remarks: (EGM); served with The Leicestershire Regiment prior to 1920; served in Second World War; retired from the police 1950.

Account of Deed: On 6th May 1936 Inspector Adamson, with the Assistant River Surveyor* as pilot, was in charge of two Port Police launches escorting a cargo of defective dynamite. This cargo was being taken for destruction up the Hoogly river in a barge towed by a launch. The barge proved quite unseaworthy and, after a journey of 15 miles, was sinking. Inspector Adamson and his assistants had no responsibility except for escorting the cargo; but in spite of this they tried at great personal risk to keep the barge afloat by bailing from 7am until midnight, when it was found necessary to beach the barge on the bank near a large jute mill. In spite of the dynamite exuding nitro-glycerine the inspector, with two sergeants, worked indefatigably in the water and in the dark to help to guide the barge ashore by hand. The beaching took 5½ hours. The barge was partially unloaded but it was found impossible to remove the 2½ tons at the bottom owing to its dangerous condition, and then it had to be refloated, towed into deep water and sunk. The smallest accident during these operations would have resulted in certain death to those working and a disaster of the first magnitude to the surrounding mills. (*See also entry for KELLY, C.F.)

ALDER 4

Thomas Edward
Rank/Title: Lance-Sergeant
Unit/Force/Occupation: 2nd Bn., The Green Howards
Other Decorations: —
Date of Gazette: 4 Aug. 1931
Place/Date of Birth: Sunderland, Co. Durham — 20 Jan. 1907
Place/Date of Death: Sunderland, Co. Durham — 5 Mar. 1973
Place of Memorial: —
Town/County Connections: — Sunderland, Co. Durham
Remarks: (EGM); served in Second World War.

Account of Deed: In November 1930 The 2nd Bn. The Green Howards were employed on anti-piratical duties on the Yangtse-Kiang River. On 14th November Lance-Sergeant Alder, in charge of a party of three other ranks, arrived at Hankow and embarked on the *SS Wuhu.* At 4.30pm on the 16th, hearing that the *SS Kiatung* had run ashore and was being attacked by the Communists, Lance-Sergeant Alder and his party left the *Wuhu* and went up-river in a sampan to assist the *Kiatung.* They had to travel 2½ miles in this open boat under rifle fire from both banks all the way. Having arrived at the *Kiatung* they climbed on board and prepared for its defence. From that moment, until the *SS Kian* arrived to assist them at 12.30 next day, Lance-Sergeant Alder and his men were exposed to rifle and gun fire from both sides of the river. When they were relieved they had only 43 rounds of small-arms ammunition left between them.

ALDERSON 5

Thomas Hopper
Rank/Title: Mr.
Unit/Force/Occupation: Detachment Leader, ARP
Other Decorations: —
Date of Gazette: 30 Sep. 1940
Place/Date of Birth: Sunderland, Co. Durham — 1903
Place/Date of Death: Driffield, Yorkshire — 28 Oct. 1965
Place of Memorial: —
Town/County Connections: Bridlington, Yorkshire
Remarks: First GC to be gazetted.

Account of Deed: Bridlington, Yorkshire, suffered a number of incidents at the beginning of the Blitz in September 1940 and Mr. Alderson, together with other members of his section, rescued many people trapped under the wreckage of demolished houses. In just one of these incidents six people were trapped in a cellar beneath the debris of two five-storied buildings which had been totally demolished. Mr. Alderson worked his way into this cellar by tunnelling 13 to 14 feet under the main heap of wreckage and for 3½ hours he worked unceasingly in an exceedingly cramped position, and managed to free all the trapped people.

ALI BEY 6

Yusuf Hussein
Rank/Title: Qaid
Unit/Force/Occupation: Trans-Jordan Frontier Force
Other Decorations: —
Date of Gazette: 3 Jan. 1939
Place/Date of Birth: —
Place/Date of Death: Piki'in Village, Upper Galilee — Nov. 1985
Place of Memorial: —
Town/County Connections: —
Remarks: (EGM)

Account of Deed: On 5th July 1938, at Khirbat Samra, Qaid Yusuf Hussein Ali Bey showed great leadership and initiative. By his fine example under heavy fire and when his men were nearly exhausted by heat, he was an inspiration to further efforts which resulted in the defeat of an enemy gang and in the capture of prisoners and rifles.

ALLEN

7

Florence Alice
Rank/Title: Miss (later Mrs. F.A. ALLEN)
Unit/Force/Occupation: Children's Nurse
Other Decorations: —
Date of Gazette: 19 Nov. 1935
Place/Date of Birth: — 26 Sep. 1906
Place/Date of Death: High Wycombe, Buckinghamshire — 1 Aug. 1985
Place of Memorial: —
Town/County Connections: Marlow, Buckinghamshire
Remarks: (AM)

Account of Deed: Miss Allen was a children's nurse at Quetta, Baluchistan at the time of the earthquake on 31st May 1935. At the risk of her life, and at the cost of terrible injuries to her leg, she saved the life of the child in her charge by throwing herself across the cot.

ALLPORT

8

Ernest
Rank/Title: Mr.
Unit/Force/Occupation: Miner, Bentley Colliery, Yorkshire
Other Decorations: —
Date of Gazette: 30 Sep. 1932
Place/Date of Birth: Bolsover, Derbyshire — 10 Apr. 1893
Place/Date of Death: Doncaster, Yorkshire — 6 Oct. 1987
Place of Memorial: —
Town/County Connections: — Bentley, Doncaster, Yorkshire
Remarks: (EM)

Account of Deed: On 20th November 1931, in the afternoon, a violent explosion of firedamp, followed by fires, occurred in the North East District of the Bentley Colliery, Yorkshire. Of some 47 men working at or near the coal face, 45 were either killed or died later. A number of miners rendered heroic assistance at the work of rescue, among them Mr. Allport, who was one of those concerned with rescues from the area of the fires, where the danger was extreme. He displayed great energy, initiative and bravery and encouraged the other members of the Rescue Team. He spent over 3 hours in breathing apparatus, and during part of the night when his rescue apparatus required replenishing, he assisted in loading men on to stretchers. Subsequently, in answer to a call for volunteers after the second explosion, he seized a breathing apparatus, and joined a rescue party which penetrated past a fire to rescue two other men.(See also entries for DARKER, R.E., SOULSBY, O., SYKES, F., TEMPERLEY, S.J. and YATES, P.W.)

ANDERSON

9

Frederick John
Rank/Title: Chief Engine Room Artificer
Unit/Force/Occupation: Royal Navy
Other Decorations: DSM
Date of Gazette: 8 Jun. 1939
Place/Date of Birth: Swindon, Wiltshire — 25 Dec. 1902
Place/Date of Death: Great Sutton, Wirral — 31 Jul. 1986
Place of Memorial: —
Town/County Connections: Wirral, Cheshire
Remarks: (EGM); served in Royal Navy until 1946; became a Special Constable later.

Account of Deed: On 25th July 1938 an Inspector of the Salt Revenue Office was fired on and wounded in Shanghai by a Chinese man. Mr. Anderson, a Chief Engine Room Artificer, who saw the incident, gave chase to the gunman, though unarmed himself. Despite being shot at, he closed with the assailant and prevented him from shooting a police constable on duty, at whom the gunman had already shot once.

ANDERSON

10

Walter
Rank/Title: Flying Officer
Unit/Force/Occupation: Royal Air Force
Other Decorations: —
Date of Gazette: 12 Apr. 1929
Place/Date of Birth: — 27 Jul. 1890
Place/Date of Death: — 11 May 1959
Place of Memorial: —
Town/County Connections: Southampton, Hampshire
Remarks: (EGM)

Account of Deed: On 10th December 1928 an RAF pilot, whilst flying off Leysdown, Sheerness, crashed into the sea two hundred yards from the shore. Flying Officer Anderson, with Corporal McTeague*, at once plunged into the sea and swam to his assistance. Between them they brought the pilot safely to shore in spite of a rough and bitterly cold sea. (*See also entry for McTEAGUE, T.P.)

ANDREWS

11

Wallace Launcelot
Rank/Title: Second Lieutenant (later Major)
Unit/Force/Occupation: 22/23 Bomb Disposal Sections, Corps of Royal Engineers
Other Decorations: —
Date of Gazette: 17 Sep. 1940
Place/Date of Birth: — 13 Mar. 1908
Place/Date of Death: Ripon, Yorkshire — 30 Jul. 1944
Place of Memorial: St. Mary's Cemetery, Taunton, Somerset
Town/County Connections: Taunton, Somerset
Remarks: (EGM)

Account of Deed: At Crohamhurst Golf Course near Croydon, Surrey on 26th August 1940, Second Lieutenant Andrews was in charge of Nos. 22 and 23 Bomb Disposal Sections when a bomb which fell near the aerodrome failed to explode. It was necessary to extract the fuse if possible in order to forward it to the Department of Scientific Research, but several attempts were made to remove it without success. Lieutenant Andrews then told his men to take cover and after tying a piece of cord to the ring of the fuse discharger, pulled, with the result that the bomb exploded; he was blown a considerable distance and two of his men received splinter wounds.

ANSARI

12

Matreen Ahmed
Rank/Title: Captain
Unit/Force/Occupation: 7th Rajput Rifles, Indian Army
Other Decorations: —
Date of Gazette: 18 Apr. 1946
Place/Date of Birth: —
Place/Date of Death: POW Camp, Hong Kong — 29 Oct. 1943
Place of Memorial: Stanley Military Cemetery, Hong Kong
Town/County Connections: —
Remarks: —

Account of Deed: Captain Ansari became a prisoner of war of the Japanese when they invaded Hong Kong in December 1941. For a time he was treated reasonably well, but as he was closely related to a ruler of a great Indian State his captors tried to persuade him to renounce his allegiance to the British and help to spread subversion amongst the Indian ranks in the prison camps. When they found these approaches were useless he was thrown into Stanley Jail in May 1942, where he suffered starvation and brutal ill-treatment. On being returned to the prisoner of war camp he still proclaimed his loyalty to the British and in May 1943 he was again thrown into Stanley Jail where he was starved and tortured for five months. He was finally sentenced to death with 30 other British, Indian and Chinese prisoners and executed in October 1943. Throughout his long ordeal Captain Ansari's loyalty, courage and endurance never wavered and his example helped many others to remain loyal.

ARCHER   13

Bertram Stuart Trevelyan
Rank/Title: A/Lieutenant (later Lieutenant Colonel)
Unit/Force/Occupation: Corps of Royal Engineers
Other Decorations: OBE, ERD
Date of Gazette: 30 Sep. 1941
Place/Date of Birth: — 3 Feb. 1915
Place/Date of Death: —
Place of Memorial: —
Town/County Connections: London
Remarks: —

Account of Deed: Lieutenant Archer had been employed on bomb disposal since June 1940 and had dealt with over 200 bombs. He had enjoyed unbelievable immunity from death and shown sustained nerve and courage of the highest order. On 2nd September 1940 he was called out with his section to deal with a whole stick of unexploded bombs which had fallen in the Anglo-Iranian Oil Company's refinery at Llandarcy, near Swansea. Several tanks of oil were on fire, which added greatly to the danger and difficulty of the work. Whilst tackling the most dangerous of the bombs two of the others exploded and it was obvious that the one on which they were working might do likewise at any moment. They continued working on it, however, for several hours until Lieutenant Archer had removed the fuse and rendered the bomb harmless.

ARMITAGE   14

Robert Selby
Rank/Title: T/Lieutenant (later Lieutenant-Commander)
Unit/Force/Occupation: Royal Naval Volunteer Reserve
Other Decorations: GM
Date of Gazette: 27 Dec. 1940
Place/Date of Birth: Birling, Kent — 28 Mar. 1910
Place/Date of Death: Nettlebed, Oxfordshire — 1 Jun. 1982
Place of Memorial: —
Town/County Connections: Nettlebed, Oxfordshire
Remarks: Commanded a small coaster at the evacuation of Dunkirk.

Account of Deed: Lieutenant Armitage did a great deal of very dangerous work in disabling land mines in September and October 1940, accepting great risks in the course of his duty. One of the mines he dealt with was hanging from a tree at Orpington, Kent and could only be reached from a ladder which offered no chance of escape if the fuse had been activated. On another occasion he heard the clock ticking and was only 30 yards away when the bomb exploded. In spite of this he returned with undaunted bravery to carry on with the same work next day.

ARMYTAGE   15

Reginald William
Rank/Title: Lieutenant (later Rear-Admiral)
Unit/Force/Occupation: Royal Navy
Other Decorations: CBE
Date of Gazette: 2 Aug. 1928
Place/Date of Birth: — 18 May 1903
Place/Date of Death: Downton, Wiltshire — 9 Nov. 1984
Place of Memorial: —
Town/County Connections: Downton, Salisbury, Wiltshire
Remarks: (AM); Head of Gun Design and Senior Naval Representative at Armament Design Establishment 1946; Deputy Chief Inspector of Naval Ordnance 1949, Chief Inspector 1956; Vice-President (Naval), Ordnance Board 1959, President 1961.

Account of Deed: On 23rd May, 1928, whilst HMS *Warspite* was lying alongside Parlatorio Wharf, Malta, an examination of the bulge compartments on the port side aft was being carried out and it was found that the air was foul and poisonous. A Chief Stoker who attempted to enter the compartment, was overcome by the gas and fell unconscious to the bottom of the compartment, a distance of about 20 feet. The alarm was given and Lieutenant Armytage immediately fetched his gas-mask and with a lifeline round him entered the compartment and reached the bottom, when he was overcome and became unconscious. With great difficulty, owing to the small size of the man-hole, he was hauled to the exit. He had stopped breathing when hauled into the open air and was immediately taken to hospital. Lieutenant Armytage was aware that his gas-mask would afford little protection against the gases likely to be present in the compartment. He also realised that the delay incurred in passing a diver through the man-holes would probably prove fatal to the Chief Stoker and appreciated to the fullest extent the grave risk he ran in entering the compartment. (The Chief Stoker was subsequently rescued by another volunteer — see entry for OLIVER, D.)

ARNOLD
Walter

16

Rank/Title: Leading Aircraftman (later Corporal)
Unit/Force/Occupation: Royal Air Force
Other Decorations: —
Date of Gazette: 9 Nov. 1928
Place/Date of Birth: — 30 Aug. 1906
Place/Date of Death: Romford, Essex — 12 Mar. 1988
Place of Memorial: —
Town/County Connections: Romford, Essex
Remarks: (EGM); served in Second World War.

Account of Deed: On 20th June 1928 at Digby, Lincolnshire, Leading Aircraftman Walter Arnold was a passenger in a machine which crashed on landing and immediately caught fire. Having extricated himself from the wreckage he re-entered the blazing aircraft and succeeded in dragging the pilot, who was unconscious and very badly burnt, to a place of safety. LAC Arnold himself sustained severe burns but his courageous action saved the pilot's life.

ASHBURNHAM (later ASHBURNHAM-RUFFNER)
Doreen

17

Rank/Title: Miss (later Mrs.)
Unit/Force/Occupation: 11-year-old girl
Other Decorations: —
Date of Gazette: 21 Dec. 1917
Place/Date of Birth: — 13 May 1905
Place/Date of Death: —
Place of Memorial: —
Town/County Connections: —
Remarks: (AM)

Account of Deed: On 23rd September 1916, two children, Doreen Ashburnham aged 11 and a boy aged 8, left their homes at Cowichan Lake, Vancouver Island, to catch their ponies. When half a mile from home they were attacked by a large cougar which was crouching at a corner of the path. The little girl was first attacked; the cougar sprang upon her and she was knocked down with her face to the ground, the animal being on her back. The boy at once attacked the cougar with his fists and riding bridle and drove it off the girl; it then attacked him. His companion, getting to her feet, came to his rescue, fighting with her clenched hands and bridle, and even putting her arm into the cougar's mouth to try to prevent it biting the boy. She succeeded in getting it off him and it stood on its hind legs and fought with her, but evidently it was disturbed by some sound, for presently it slunk away and ran under a log, where it was afterwards killed. The children, though both badly injured, were able to make their way home.

ASHRAF-un-NISA

18

Rank/Title: Begum of Hyderabad
Unit/Force/Occupation: —
Other Decorations: —
Date of Gazette: 1 Feb. 1937
Place/Date of Birth: —
Place/Date of Death: — 1947
Place of Memorial: —
Town/County Connections: —
Remarks: (EGM)

Account of Deed: On 14th June 1936 Begum Ashraf-un-Nisa was responsible for saving the lives of several purdah women. A disastrous fire broke out in the Moti Mahal Cinema in Hyderabad City and the building was practically razed to the ground, twelve women and two children being burnt to death. The Begum was sitting with the fourteen victims and some thirty other women in the purdah balcony, from which both exits were cut off by the fire. The Begum, though a purdah lady, stripped off her sari, tied it to the balcony railing and lowered five women to the ground floor, whence they escaped. She left her own escape so late that she had to jump, injuring herself in the process.

ATKINSON

19

Thomas
Rank/Title: Corporal (later Sergeant)
Unit/Force/Occupation: 1st Bn., The Green Howards (Alexandra, Princess of Wales's Own Yorkshire Regiment)
Other Decorations: —
Date of Gazette: 25 Jul. 1939
Place/Date of Birth: — 27 May 1915
Place/Date of Death: —
Place of Memorial: —
Town/County Connections: Weston, Portland, Dorset
Remarks: (EGM); served in Second World War.

Account of Deed: Corporal Atkinson was in charge of the mechanised transport at Jinsafut Camp, Palestine, on 15th March 1939, when a truck caught fire. With great initiative and leadership he rallied the drivers and managed to avoid a general conflagration spreading throughout the camp. A little later Corporal Atkinson was severely burnt while endeavouring to save the life of one of his comrades. (See also entry for McAVOY, T.)

AWANG anak RAWANG

20

Rank/Title: —
Unit/Force/Occupation: Iban Tracker, Johore, Federation of Malaya
Other Decorations: —
Date of Gazette: 20 Nov. 1951
Place/Date of Birth: — 1925
Place/Date of Death: —
Place of Memorial: —
Town/County Connections: —
Remarks: —

Account of Deed: During the operations against the bandits in Malaya in May 1951 a section of The Worcestershire Regiment was ambushed by about 50 of the enemy. The leading scout was killed instantly and the Section-Commander fatally wounded. Awang anak Rawang was hit through the thigh bone; at the same time a British soldier, moving behind him, was hit below the knee, the bullet completely shattering the bone. Awang dragged him into cover and protected him. He was again wounded, the bullet shattering his right arm, but despite loss of blood from his wounds and being unable to use his rifle or parang, Awang remained guarding the wounded British soldier with a grenade in his left hand. He looked so determined that the bandits drew back.

AXON

21

John
Rank/Title: Mr.
Unit/Force/Occupation: Driver, British Rail
Other Decorations: Order of Industrial Heroism
Date of Gazette: 7 May 1957
Place/Date of Birth: Stockport, Cheshire — 4 Dec. 1900
Place/Date of Death: Chapel-en-le-Frith, Derbyshire — 11 Feb. 1957
Place of Memorial: Electric locomotive named after him
Town/County Connections: Stockport, Cheshire
Remarks: —

Account of Deed: Mr. Axon was in charge of a freight train which was running on the London-Midland region from Buxton towards Chapel-en-le-Frith. He was preparing to stop the train before going down the steep gradient, when the steam pipe feeding the brake suddenly fractured. This not only destroyed the braking system but filled the driving cab with blinding, scalding steam which was discharged at very high pressure directly at the feet of Mr. Axon who was badly burnt. He could have abandoned the train and saved his own life, but realising the danger of a runaway train, and with great bravery, he tried to get the train under control with the help of his fireman. The train was, however, now going down the gradient and could not be stopped, so Mr. Axon ordered the fireman to jump clear and apply as many wagon brakes as possible. In spite of this the train gathered speed and steam and boiling water were still pouring into the cab. Mr. Axon waved a warning to a signalman that the train was running away, and remained at his post in the hope of regaining control, but before he could manage to do this, the train crashed into the rear of another freight train travelling in the same direction and Mr. Axon was killed.

BABINGTON

22

John Herbert
Rank/Title: T/Sub-Lieutenant (later Lieutenant-Commander)
Unit/Force/Occupation: Royal Naval Volunteer Reserve
Other Decorations: OBE
Date of Gazette: 27 Dec. 1940
Place/Date of Birth: — 6 Feb. 1911
Place/Date of Death: —
Place of Memorial: —
Town/County Connections: Berkhamsted, Hertfordshire
Remarks: Later Headmaster, Diss Grammar School and then of the Royal Hospital School, Holbrook, Suffolk.

Account of Deed: Sub-Lieutenant Babington had experimented with the dismantling of all types of bombs and had worked on the first suspended parachute magnetic mines. He volunteered to deal with a very dangerous bomb in Chatham dockyard in the autumn of 1940 where an anti-withdrawal device was suspected — an RAF officer had shortly before lost his life in trying to deal with a bomb of this description. Sub-Lieutenant Babington was lowered into a 16ft. pit where he tied a line to the head of the fuse but the line broke and he again went into the pit. He had to make three attempts to remove the fuse before he finally directed the lifting of the bomb which was then taken away. At that time the Bomb Disposal Authorities had very little knowledge of the mechanism of these mines and much was learnt from this incident.

BAGOT

23

Arthur Gerald
Rank/Title: Sub-Lieutenant (later Lieutenant)
Unit/Force/Occupation: Royal Naval Volunteer Reserve
Other Decorations: DSC
Date of Gazette: 20 Aug. 1918
Place/Date of Birth: Perth, Western Australia — 26 April 1888
Place/Date of Death: Western Australia — 21 Nov. 1979
Place of Memorial: —
Town/County Connections: —
Remarks: (AM); won the DSC at Zeebrugge on St. George's Day, 1918.

Account of Deed: On 12th April 1918, an explosion occurred in the engine room of HM Motor Launch 356, and the forward tanks burst into flames. The officer and some of the crew were blown overboard by the explosion, and the remainder were quickly driven aft by the flames and were taken off in a skiff. By this time the flames were issuing from the cabin hatch aft, and there was much petrol burning on the surface of the water. It was then realised by the crews of adjacent vessels that the after petrol tanks and the depth charge were being attacked by the fire, and might explode at any moment. While others were seeking shelter, Sub-Lieutenant Bagot and another officer jumped into their dinghy, rowed to the wreck, got on board and removed the depth charge, thereby preventing an explosion which might have caused serious loss of life amongst the crowd of English and French sailors on the quay.

BAILEY

24

Eric George
Rank/Title: Sergeant
Unit/Force/Occupation: New South Wales Police Force
Other Decorations: —
Date of Gazette: 29 Oct. 1946
Place/Date of Birth: Tenterfield, New South Wales, Australia — 14 Oct. 1906
Place/Date of Death: Blayney, New South Wales — 12 Jan. 1945
Place of Memorial: —
Town/County Connections: —
Remarks: —

Account of Deed: At about 8.30pm on 12th January 1945 Sergeant Bailey was on duty in Adelaide Street, Blayney, New South Wales, when he stopped a man whose movements were suspicious. During questioning the man pulled a revolver from his pocket and fired a shot which hit the policeman in the stomach. Sergeant Bailey immediately closed with his assailant who fired two more shots. Although fast succumbing to his injuries and suffering from the effects of shock and haemorrhage, Sergeant Bailey continued the struggle with the man and held him on the ground until help arrived. Shortly afterwards he died from his injuries.

BAIN SMITH, George Stewart — see **SMITH,** George Stewart BAIN

BAKER

25

John Thomas
Rank/Title: Mr.
Unit/Force/Occupation: Pit lad, South Garesfield Colliery, Durham
Other Decorations: —
Date of Gazette: 22 Nov. 1929
Place/Date of Birth: Co. Durham — 14 Apr. 1912
Place/Date of Death: —
Place of Memorial: —
Town/County Connections: Coventry, Warwickshire
Remarks: (EM); served in RAMC in Second World War.

Account of Deed: On 17th May 1929 a colliery deputy was injured during blasting operations. An overman set off down the pit and, collecting John Baker and another lad* at the bottom of the shaft and a tram and stretcher, went in search of the deputy. They were joined by two hewers. Meanwhile five other men had attempted a rescue, but four of them were overcome by gas while the fifth managed to crawl out just in time. The overman organised his party and by repeated efforts they succeeded in extricating the five men of whom three were dead. The rescue party were all affected by the fumes. For an hour, during the whole of which time the atmosphere was thick with smoke and gas, the overman with John Baker and his other three helpers, knowingly and repeatedly risked their lives in determined efforts to save the lives of their fellows, and there is no doubt that but for their courageous action the death-roll would have been heavier than it was. (*See also entry for PURVIS, J.S.)

BALDEV SINGH

26

Rank/Title: Sub-Inspector
Unit/Force/Occupation: Punjab Police Force
Other Decorations: —
Date of Gazette: 1 Jan. 1932
Place/Date of Birth: —
Place/Date of Death: — Nov. 1983
Place of Memorial: —
Town/County Connections: —
Remarks: (EGM)

Account of Deed: In June 1931 Baldev Singh, a Sub-Inspector of Police in the Punjab, displayed great bravery in organising and leading an attack under fire on a dangerous gang of offenders in the Ferozepore District. In addition he narrowly escaped death in the next month, in a raid on a house occupied by armed men

BALDWIN

27

Wilson Charles Geoffrey
Rank/Title: Dr.
Unit/Force/Occupation: Assistant Works Manager, munition factory
Other Decorations: Bronze Medallion of Carnegie Hero Fund Trust
Date of Gazette: 16 Apr. 1943
Place/Date of Birth: Dovercourt, Essex — 9 Apr. 1912
Place/Date of Death: —
Place of Memorial: —
Town/County Connections: Dovercourt, Essex; Cambridge, Cambridgeshire
Remarks: (EM); member of Executive Committee of VC & GC Association for many years.

Account of Deed: On 20th November 1942 a violent explosion occurred in a building in Essex in which explosives were being mixed, and resulted in the immediate death of the two occupants of the building, the complete destruction of the building itself, and considerable damage to adjacent structures. In one of these, a Nitrating House, a charge of 1,800 lbs. of nitro-glycerine was in the pre-wash tank, and in another nitration was about half completed. Although the building became filled with fumes and steam, the operator and his assistant remained at their posts and took prompt steps to control the nitration and render the chemicals harmless. They were assisted by Dr. Baldwin, the Assistant Works Manager, who arrived on the scene shortly after the explosion. He noticed that about three square feet of wood above the pre-wash tank was smouldering vigorously and throwing off sparks. With the operator's assistance Dr. Baldwin extinguished this very dangerous outbreak. The danger which these three men averted was a very real one since there is little doubt that if the necessary steps had not been taken, a further explosion would have occurred injuring the many workers who were still in the danger area after the first explosion. All three men acted without thought of their own safety in circumstances of considerable danger of which they were fully aware.

BAMFORD

28

John
Rank/Title: Mr.
Unit/Force/Occupation: Colliery Worker (aged 15)
Other Decorations: —
Date of Gazette: 16 Dec. 1952
Place/Date of Birth: Newthorpe, Nottinghamshire — 7 Mar. 1937
Place/Date of Death: —
Place of Memorial: —
Town/County Connections: Newthorpe, Nottinghamshire
Remarks: The youngest recipient of the direct award of the George Cross to date (1984) — 15 years, 7 months.

Account of Deed: In the early hours of the morning of 19th October 1952 a fire started in the living room in the Bamford home in Newthorpe. John, the eldest of the six children, and his father managed to get Mrs. Bamford and three of the children out, but two of the boys, aged six and four, were trapped in their bedroom. The wooden stairs of the house had burst into flames and it seemed impossible to get through to the boys, but John fought his way into the room through the flames and found the little boys huddled together, petrified with fright. He put an arm round each and dragged them to the window where he managed to push the younger child out to his father standing below, who partially broke his fall. The older boy had panicked and rushed back into the burning room, so John had to catch him, drag him to the window and throw him out to his father. By this time John himself was fast losing consciousness — he was terribly burnt on the top part of his body — but somehow got his leg over the window-sill and forced himself out. All three boys were taken to hospital, where the two youngest were soon off the danger list, but John did not go home until February 1953, after many skin-grafting operations.

BANKS

29

Arthur
Rank/Title: Sergeant
Unit/Force/Occupation: 112 Squadron, Desert Air Force, Royal Air Force Volunteer Reserve
Other Decorations: —
Date of Gazette: 5 Nov. 1946
Place/Date of Birth: Llandulas, Abergele, Wales — 6 Oct. 1923
Place/Date of Death: Ariano Polesine, Italy — 20 Dec. 1944
Place of Memorial: Argenta Gap War Cemetery, Italy
Town/County Connections: Llandulas, Abergele, Wales; Cheltenham, Gloucestershire
Remarks: —

Account of Deed: On 27th August 1944 Sergeant Banks was one of the crew of an aircraft which was on an armed reconnaissance of the Ravenna and Ferrara area in Italy when it was so badly damaged by anti-aircraft fire that it was compelled to make a forced landing. After the aircraft had been destroyed Sergeant Banks tried to reach Allied lines. He made contact with a group of Italian partisans and, during the following months, he became an outstanding figure amongst them, advising and encouraging them in action against the enemy. Early in December 1944 an attempt at crossing into Allied territory by boat had been planned, but the whole party was surrounded and captured. Sergeant Banks was handed over to the German commander of the district, at whose hands he was cruelly tortured to make him give information. At one point he managed to get hold of a light machine-gun with which he might have killed most of his captors, but one of the partisans, fearing reprisals, held his arms and he was re-captured. He was put in prison, first in Adria and then in Ariano Polesine and was again tortured to make him talk, which he refused to do. He was then stripped, bound and thrown into the River Po, from which he managed to escape, was recaptured, taken back to prison and shot.

BAREFOOT

30

Herbert John Leslie
Rank/Title: A/Major
Unit/Force/Occupation: Corps of Royal Engineers
Other Decorations: —
Date of Gazette: 22 Jan. 1941
Place/Date of Birth: — 15 May 1887
Place/Date of Death: Ipswich, Suffolk — 23 Dec. 1958
Place of Memorial: Portrait in Lower Hall, Dulwich College
Town/County Connections: Ipswich, Suffolk
Remarks: Served in First World War in RNVR and also RAMC.

Account of Deed: During the early days of the Blitz, in September and October 1940, Major Barefoot, who was a pioneer in bomb disposal, dealt with some of the first unexploded bombs which fell in Britain. He worked on the first suspended parachute magnetic mine, as a result of which he was able to put invaluable information at the disposal of the authorities. His bravery and devotion to duty were an inspiration to the men under him.

BARKAT SINGH

Rank/Title: Naik (later Jemadar)
Unit/Force/Occupation: 10th Bn., 2nd Punjab Regiment, Indian Army
Other Decorations: —
Date of Gazette: 1 Jan. 1938
Place/Date of Birth: — 16 Dec. 1904
Place/Date of Death: —
Place of Memorial: —
Town/County Connections: —
Remarks: (EGM)

Account of Deed: On 2nd May 1937, at Meerut, India, a sepoy of the Second Punjab Regiment ran amok, shot dead the Guard Commander and mortally wounded another sepoy of the Guard. Naik Barkat Singh, also of the Second Punjabis, although unarmed, grappled with the sepoy and held him until others came and overpowered him.

BARNETT

William
Rank/Title: Lance-Corporal (later Quartermaster Sergeant Instructor)
Unit/Force/Occupation: 1st Bn., The Royal Scots Fusiliers
Other Decorations: —
Date of Gazette: 27 Nov. 1936
Place/Date of Birth: — 1914
Place/Date of Death: Stone, Staffordshire — 10 Sep. 1972
Place of Memorial: —
Town/County Connections: Walton, Stone, Staffordshire
Remarks: (EGM); served in Second World War.

Account of Deed: For gallant and distinguished service in connection with the emergency operations in Palestine during the period 15th April to 14th September 1936 Lance-Corporal Barnett was awarded the Empire Gallantry Medal.

BARRACLOUGH

Arnold
Rank/Title: Sergeant (later Captain)
Unit/Force/Occupation: Assam-Bengal Railway Bn., Indian Auxiliary Force
Other Decorations: —
Date of Gazette: 25 Nov. 1930
Place/Date of Birth: Jhansi, India — 12 Jan. 1900
Place/Date of Death: Lancing, Sussex — 3 May 1974
Place of Memorial: —
Town/County Connections: —
Remarks: (EGM); served in First and Second World Wars.

Account of Deed: On the night of 18th/19th April 1930, at Chittagong, Bengal, armed raiders attacked the armouries and the telephone exchange with the object of seizing all available arms and ammunition, destroying communications and terrorising the population. Sergeant Barraclough of the Assam-Bengal Railway Battalion, who was an electrical engineer at the Pahartali Power House, took a Lewis gun and accompanied the Superintendent of Police to contact the raiders. Sergeant Barraclough brought the Lewis gun into action and engaged the raiders at close range. Although heavily fired on he went on firing his gun until the raiders dispersed and fled into the jungle.

BARRY, Mrs. Harriet Elizabeth — see **FRASER,** Harriet Elizabeth

BARWARI, Rajah of — see **BHUPENDRA NARAYAN SINGH**

BASTER

34

Norman
Rank/Title: Mr.
Unit/Force/Occupation: Colliery agent, South Kirkby Colliery, Yorkshire
Other Decorations: —
Date of Gazette: 17 Apr. 1936
Place/Date of Birth: — 11 Jan. 1892
Place/Date of Death: Lethbridge, Alberta, Canada — 11 Apr. 1987
Place of Memorial: —
Town/County Connections: South Kirkby, Yorkshire; Bournemouth, Dorset.
Remarks: (EM); served in Second World War (Lieutenant-Colonel, RAMC (TA)).

Account of Deed: On the evening of 22nd August 1935 two explosions occurred at South Kirkby Colliery in a district about 1¾ miles from the shaft. It was thought that these were due to a gob fire and it was decided to seal off a part of the district by erecting stoppings. At 3pm on 23rd August when this work was in progress there was a further explosion, severely injuring a number of men. Three of the others, who had rescue apparatus, at once started to look for and help the injured, ten of whom were carried out of the district alive, but only one of these eventually recovered. During the progress of these operations some of the rescuers were considerably affected by fumes. It was later found that one man was still missing and a search for him was renewed by Mr. Baster, the colliery agent, with the manager and four rescue men. The missing man, when found, was dead. A further explosion then occurred and all six members of the rescue party suffered burns and those nearer the shaft who were looking after the men first injured were also affected. Mr. Baster went back and did what was possible to reassure these men and later went in again to look for a member of the rescue party who had been injured, but he had no breathing apparatus and was eventually so much affected by fumes that he had to retire. The missing man was later brought safely to the surface. Mr. Baster showed outstanding courage during these operations, particularly during the second difficult and dangerous stage. (See also entries for BEAMAN, G.W. and POLLITT, J.)

BASTIAN

35

Gordon Love
Rank/Title: Mr.
Unit/Force/Occupation: Second Engineer Officer, Merchant Navy
Other Decorations: MBE, Lloyd's Medal for Bravery at Sea
Date of Gazette: 17 Aug. 1943
Place/Date of Birth: Barry, Glamorgan, Wales — 30 Mar. 1902
Place/Date of Death: Barrie, Ontario, Canada — 29 Oct. 1987
Place of Memorial: —
Town/County Connections: Barry, Glamorgan, Wales
Remarks: (AM)

Account of Deed: Mr. Bastian was on watch in the engine-room of his ship (SS *Bowman*) when it was torpedoed 500 miles off Brest on 30th March 1943, and sustained severe damage. He at once shut off the engines and then remembered that two firemen were on watch in the stokehold. The engine-room was in darkness and water was already pouring into it. Although there was grave risk of disastrous flooding in opening the watertight door between the stokehold and the engine-room, Mr. Bastian did not hesitate but groped his way to the door and opened it. The two firemen were swept into the engine-room with the inrush of water — one man had a broken arm and injured feet and the other was badly bruised and shaken. Mr. Bastian made efforts to hold them both but lost one, so he dragged the other to the escape ladder and helped him on deck. He then returned for the other and helped him to safety. The more seriously injured man had practically to be lifted up the ladder by Mr. Bastian, who was himself half choked by cordite fumes. He had taken a very great risk in opening the watertight door into the already flooded and darkened engine-room of the sinking ship.

BAXTER

William Frederick
Rank/Title: Mr.
Unit/Force/Occupation: Workman with the Service Department of the Standard Motor Co., Coventry
Other Decorations: —
Date of Gazette: 1 May 1942
Place/Date of Birth: — 22 Sep. 1907
Place/Date of Death: —
Place of Memorial: —
Town/County Connections: Filey, Yorkshire
Remarks: (EM)

Account of Deed: On 8th July 1941 an accident occurred in the Service Department of the Standard Motor Co. in which an employee of the firm was trapped by the arms between the rope and pulley at the end of a 130ft. long lattice work jib of a crane, so that he was in imminent danger of bleeding to death or falling a distance of 110 feet to the ground. Mr. Baxter, another employee of the firm, after obtaining a rope and some first-aid dressings, climbed to the top of the jib where he lashed the man more securely, applied dressings and a tourniquet to his injuries and stayed with him for an hour until a rescue was effected by the Fire Brigade.

BAYLEY

Clive Cyril Anthony
Rank/Title: Trooper (later Captain)
Unit/Force/Occupation: Surma Valley Light Horse, Indian Army
Other Decorations: BEM
Date of Gazette: 24 Jul. 1931
Place/Date of Birth: —
Place/Date of Death: — Jun. 1949
Place of Memorial: —
Town/County Connections: Hampshire
Remarks: (EGM); served in Second World War.

Account of Deed: On 22nd April 1930 raiders (who had previously attacked the armouries and the telephone exchange at Chittagong, Bengal) were located near Jijiriabahtali and a troop of the Surma Valley Light Horse, with 20 men of the Eastern Frontier Rifles, were immediately despatched to deal with them. The insurgents were found occupying a wooded hill and were at once engaged. Trooper Bayley, who was on the left of the attack, worked his way round through thick jungle and succeeded in killing three of the insurgents, including their leader, and wounding several others. He himself had his helmet shot off, but was not injured.

BEAMAN

George William
Rank/Title: Mr.
Unit/Force/Occupation: Miner, South Kirkby Colliery, Yorkshire
Other Decorations: —
Date of Gazette: 17 Apr. 1936
Place/Date of Birth: Sheffield, Yorkshire — 25 Jul. 1904
Place/Date of Death: Inglewood, Western Australia — 13 Jul. 1986
Place of Memorial: —
Town/County Connections: Barnsley, Yorkshire
Remarks: (EM)

Account of Deed: On the evening of 22nd August 1935 two explosions occurred at South Kirkby Colliery in a district about 1¾ miles from the shaft. It was thought that these were due to a gob fire and it was decided to seal off part of the district by erecting stoppings. At 3pm on 23rd August when this work was in progress there was a further explosion, severely injuring a number of men. Mr. Beaman and two others, who had rescue apparatus, at once went to look for and help the injured, and with the assistance of fresh arrivals on the scene, ten men were carried out of the district alive. One died almost immediately, eight within a few days, and one recovered. During these operations which involved repeated journeys to and from the face, some of the rescuers who were not equipped with special apparatus were considerably affected by fumes. They all displayed great courage and pertinacity and in particular Mr. Beaman rendered services of outstanding merit. (See also entries for BASTER, N. and POLLITT, J.)

BEATON

James Wallace
Rank/Title: Inspector (later Chief Superintendent)
Unit/Force/Occupation: Metropolitan Police (Royal Bodyguard)
Other Decorations: —
Date of Gazette: 27 Sep. 1974
Place/Date of Birth: St. Fergus, Aberdeenshire, Scotland — 17 Feb. 1943
Place/Date of Death: —
Place of Memorial: —
Town/County Connections: St. Fergus, Peterhead, Aberdeenshire, Scotland
Remarks: Director's Honor Award, US Secret Service

Account of Deed: At about 8pm on the 20th March 1974 HRH The Princess Anne and Captain Mark Phillips were returning to Buckingham Palace from an official engagement, accompanied by Princess Anne's personal police officer, Inspector Beaton, and her lady-in-waiting, when an attempt was made to kidnap the Princess. The kidnapper used two pistols at point blank range and hit the Inspector and three other men who had come to the assistance of the Princess. All those involved in foiling the kidnap attempt displayed outstanding courage and complete disregard for their own safety when they each faced this dangerous armed man who did not hesitate to use his weapons. It was entirely due to their actions as well as the calmness shown by Princess Anne and Captain Mark Phillips in circumstances of great peril, that the attack was unsuccessful.

BEATTIE

John
Rank/Title: Mr.
Unit/Force/Occupation: Miner, Trimdon Grange, Durham
Other Decorations: —
Date of Gazette: 3 May 1927
Place/Date of Birth: —
Place/Date of Death: — Mar. 1952
Place of Memorial: —
Town/County Connections: Durham, Co. Durham
Remarks: (EGM)

40

Account of Deed: On 19th November 1926 Mr. John Beattie and another man* although in grave personal danger from falling debris, gas and spontaneously generated heat, made persistent attempts to rescue a miner imprisoned in a narrow tunnel (*See also entry for CLARK, J.)

BECKETT

John Archibald
Rank/Title: Sergeant
Unit/Force/Occupation: Royal Air Force
Other Decorations: —
Date of Gazette: 16 Dec. 1947
Place/Date of Birth: ?Belfast, Ireland — 14 Mar. 1906
Place/Date of Death: Royal Air Force Station, Ein Shemer, Levant — 12 Apr. 1947
Place of Memorial: Khayat Beach War Cemetery, Israel
Town/County Connections: Bangor, Co. Down, Ireland
Remarks: —

41

Account of Deed: On the night of 28th March 1947, during the refuelling of a Lancaster aircraft of No. 38 Squadron, stationed at Ein Shemer Air Headquarters, Levant, a violent fire broke out suddenly in the pumping department of the refuelling vehicle, of which Sergeant Beckett was the driver. The flames enveloped Sergeant Beckett and set alight the front of the Lancaster's fuselage. Another airman beat out the flames on Sergeant Beckett but not before the latter had been severely burnt on the hands and face. There was grave danger that the main tank of the vehicle, containing over 2000 gallons of fuel, would explode, in which case it was practically certain that most, if not all, of the 20 or more aircraft in the park would have been destroyed. Despite his very serious injuries Sergeant Beckett jumped into the driver's seat of his blazing vehicle and drove it 400 yards outside the aircraft park where it could do no further damage. He then collapsed and died later of his injuries.

BELL

42

John Frederick
Rank/Title: Mr.
Unit/Force/Occupation: Underground Manager, Ariston Gold Mine, Prestea, Gold Coast (later Ghana)
Other Decorations: —
Date of Gazette: 20 Dec. 1930
Place/Date of Birth: —
Place/Date of Death: — pre-1965
Place of Memorial: —
Town/County Connections: Bridgend, Glamorgan, Wales
Remarks: (EGM)

Account of Deed: On 17th May 1930 Mr. John Frederick Bell showed great gallantry on the occasion of an accident in the Ariston Gold Mine at Prestea; he was instrumental in saving the lives of several natives who would otherwise have been gassed. The two men who afterwards went in search of him lost their lives by gas in the attempt, and Mr. Bell himself would probably have shared their fate had he not, when he became unconscious, fallen with his mouth close to a leak in a compressed-air pipe.

BENNER

43

Michael Paul
Rank/Title: Second Lieutenant
Unit/Force/Occupation: Corps of Royal Engineers
Other Decorations: —
Date of Gazette: 17 Jun. 1958
Place/Date of Birth: — 14 Apr. 1935
Place/Date of Death: Grossglockner, Austrian Alps — 1 Jul. 1957
Place of Memorial: Kals churchyard, Austria
Town/County Connections: Radlett, Hertfordshire
Remarks: —

Account of Deed: In the summer of 1957 Second Lieutenant Benner was in Austria, in command of a party of NCOs training to operate in mountainous country. On 1st July, after a week in the mountains, he led six of his men on a traverse on the 12,400ft. Grossglockner. The summit had been successfully reached at 6pm after a long ascent, made unexpectedly difficult by a storm. In preparation for the descent, not normally difficult, the party unroped and Lieutenant Benner led the way down a ridge. The storm and lateness of the hour made the steps, kicked in the snow, icy and slippery and the man behind the Lieutenant began to slide down a steep snow slope. His leader jumped out of his own secure foothold on to the open slope and caught the falling man, holding him with one hand and trying with the other to dig his ice-axe into the snow. This he failed to do and both men slid down the slope together until they disappeared to their death over the steep face of the mountain. In making this attempt to save the man in his charge, Lieutenant Benner took, as he well knew, a desperate risk — he could only have saved himself by releasing his grasp on the other's arm, but he did not do so. He held on to him to the last, struggling to get a grip in the frozen snow with his feet and axe.

BHIM SINGH YADAVA

44

Rank/Title: Sub-Inspector (later Superintendent)
Unit/Force/Occupation: Punjab Police
Other Decorations: —
Date of Gazette: 1 Jan. 1932
Place/Date of Birth: — 19 Dec. 1900
Place/Date of Death: — 17 Nov. 1983
Place of Memorial: —
Town/County Connections: —
Remarks: (EGM)

Account of Deed: Bhim Singh Yadava, who was a Sub-Inspector of Police, Punjab, displayed great courage and a total disregard of danger in capturing a native of the Jullundur District who had shot two people dead and was attacking another.

BHUPENDRA NARAYAN SINGH (Later Rajah of BARWARI)   45
Rank/Title: Shri
Unit/Force/Occupation: —
Other Decorations: —
Date of Gazette: 19 Jun. 1934
Place/Date of Birth: —
Place/Date of Death: — 25 Dec. 1961
Place of Memorial: —
Town/County Connections: —
Remarks: (EGM)

Account of Deed: On 8th May 1934, at Lebong Racecourse, Darjeeling, while the horses were being led in after the race for the Governor's Cup, an attempt was made by two Bengali youths to assassinate Sir John Anderson, the Governor of Bengal. Shri Bhupendra Narayan Singh, Zemindar Garh Barwari, Bhagalpur District, Bihar and Orissa, was in the race-stand outside the Governor's box. On hearing a shot from one of the assailants and seeing that the other was again taking aim, with his revolver resting on the rail separating the stand from the box, he immediately grappled with him, endeavouring to pull him back and divert his aim. While the two were struggling two shots were fired at his assailant by the Governor's personal guard and the Superintendent of Police respectively. Both shots took effect but failed to hit any vital part. Both Shri Bhupendra Narayan Singh and his assailant fell to the ground but the latter was not overpowered until at least one more shot had been fired at him at close quarters. (See also entry for GREEN, C.W. TANDY-)

BIGGS   46
Kenneth Alfred
Rank/Title: Major
Unit/Force/Occupation: Royal Army Ordnance Corps
Other Decorations: —
Date of Gazette: 11 Oct. 1946
Place/Date of Birth: — 26 Feb. 1911
Place/Date of Death: —
Place of Memorial: —
Town/County Connections: Totteridge, Hertfordshire; Ewhurst, Surrey; Stockland, Honiton, Devon
Remarks: —

Account of Deed: On 2nd January 1946, men from the RAOC, the Pioneer Corps and the RASC were completing the loading of a train with American and German ammunition in Savernake Forest, Wiltshire. In the same siding another British ammunition train was standing — there were 96 wagons in all. There was a sudden flash and explosion and two railway wagons and a 3-ton lorry literally disappeared, fire swept the yard and more wagons burst into flames. More explosions followed and a total of 27 railway wagons and two lorries had blown up — there was a great risk that fire would spread to all the remainder of the loaded wagons, causing more explosions and widespread damage. Eight men died in the original explosion and six more were badly hurt. Major Biggs was commanding the Sub-Depot and he and his Staff-Sergeant* together uncoupled a burning wagon and extinguished the flames. Although knocked over and shaken by one of the explosions, Major Biggs continued to direct his men in their frantic efforts to prevent the fire from spreading. They worked all through the night and succeeded in preventing any more wagons catching fire. Next day the remains of wagons, lorries, shells, mines, detonators, packages and telegraph poles could be seen strewn all over the countryside and there were two huge craters, but 69 of the wagons had been saved from exploding. (*See also entry for ROGERSON, S.G.)

BLACKBURN   47
Richard
Rank/Title: Private (later Sergeant with The Royal Warwickshire Regiment)
Unit/Force/Occupation: 1st Bn., The Cheshire Regiment
Other Decorations: —
Date of Gazette: 23 Jun. 1936
Place/Date of Birth: — 5 Dec. 1912
Place/Date of Death: —
Place of Memorial: —
Town/County Connections: Clubmoor, Liverpool
Remarks: (EGM)

Account of Deed: On 7th June 1935 during a forest fire at Kasauli, India, a party of troops was threatened by the flames and had to retire. The officer in charge of the party became separated from the others and was stumbling about in a dazed condition with his clothing alight. Private Blackburn, who had gone out to look for him, helped him to a place of safety and extinguished his burning clothes with his bare hands. But for Private Blackburn's courage and coolness the officer would undoubtedly have died.

BLACKBURN

48

Sydney
Rank/Title: Mr.
Unit/Force/Occupation: Shotfirer, Barnsley Main Colliery
Other Decorations: —
Date of Gazette: 21 Nov. 1947
Place/Date of Birth: — 15 Jul. 1908
Place/Date of Death: —
Place of Memorial: —
Town/County Connections: Barnsley, Yorkshire
Remarks: (EM)

Account of Deed: An explosion occurred at Barnsley Main Colliery just after mid-day on 7th May 1947. A chargeman filler and Sydney Blackburn, shotfirer, were at the end of the face away from the resulting flame; the chargeman filler was blown over by a gust of wind caused by the explosion but quickly recovered and with Mr. Blackburn, despite fumes and dust, assembled men who had scrambled from the face and led them to a place of safety. Returning they found a number of injured men to whom they gave assistance and then proceeded through fumes and clouds of dust in search of others. Both men, while taking every reasonable precaution, continued to disregard their own personal safety in their efforts to ensure that none of the victims were left unattended in the danger zone.

BLANEY

49

Michael Floud
Rank/Title: A/Captain
Unit/Force/Occupation: Corps of Royal Engineers
Other Decorations: —
Date of Gazette: 15 Apr. 1941
Place/Date of Birth: — 14 Nov. 1910
Place/Date of Death: Manor Park, Essex — 13 Dec. 1940
Place of Memorial: Newry Old Chapel Roman Catholic Cemetery, Co. Down, Ireland
Town/County Connections: Newry, Co. Down, Ireland
Remarks: —

Account of Deed: Very early in the morning of 18th September 1940 an unexploded bomb fell in the centre of Manor Way, a few yards from the junction with the East Ham and Barking By-Pass, dislocating traffic to the docks, the Royal Arsenal and other important industrial undertakings. Captain Blaney was called to the scene and removed the bomb, thus enabling many thousands of war-workers to resume their way to work. On 20th October an unexploded bomb fell in Park Avenue, East Ham. It had two very dangerous time fuses — one of the very few bombs so fitted — and so constituted a very real danger to Public Utility Services and, more important, to the Bomb Disposal Section in their efforts to remove it. Captain Blaney personally defused this bomb — it was his usual practice to work alone on these occasions. Again on 13th December 1940 he was called to remove the fuse from an unexploded bomb which had fallen in the premises abutting Romford Road, Manor Park several days previously and was causing serious dislocation of important traffic. As usual he crawled into the crater to tackle it himself, but the bomb exploded and he lost his life.

BLOGG

50

Henry George
Rank/Title: Coxswain
Unit/Force/Occupation: Royal National Lifeboat Institution
Other Decorations: BEM, RNLI Gold Medal (3 awards), RNLI Silver Medal (4 awards)
Date of Gazette: 30 Jun. 1924
Place/Date of Birth: Cromer, Norfolk — 6 Feb. 1876
Place/Date of Death: Cromer, Norfolk — 13 Jun. 1954
Place of Memorial: Stained glass window, Cromer Parish Church and tablet in bell-chamber; bust on pedestal on cliffs at Cromer
Town/County Connections: Cromer, Norfolk
Remarks: (EGM)

Account of Deed: On 9th January 1917 the SS *Fernebo* of Christianhaven was wrecked off Cromer, Norfolk, after being struck by a mine during a gale. The crew was rescued by the Cromer lifeboat which had only just returned from service to a Greek vessel and was immediately launched again. It was entirely due to the remarkable personality and great qualities of leadership of Coxswain Blogg which magnetised the tired men into re-launching, and when the boat was put to sea again, it was the consummate skill with which he launched her and the encouragement he gave his crew which brought their efforts to such a successful conclusion.

BOGDANOVICH

51

Theodore
Rank/Title: Mulazim
Unit/Force/Occupation: Trans-Jordan Frontier Force
Other Decorations: —
Date of Gazette: 30 Jun. 1939
Place/Date of Birth: —
Place/Date of Death: Cyprus — Apr. 1956
Place of Memorial: —
Town/County Connections: —
Remarks: (EGM); served in Second World War; after the war, worked as Security Officer of the Cyprus Mines Corporation; assassinated by EOKA terrorists.

Account of Deed: On 11th March 1939 Mulazim Bogdanovich, who had displayed outstanding qualities of leadership and loyalty on many occasions, was in charge of a mechanised troop despatched to the Zemal area to locate a band of armed men. He found them and pinned them in a wadi until the arrival of air and land reinforcements. Then, when his superior officer was killed, he took charge of the situation and gallantly led his men forward, driving the marauders on to the reinforcing troops.

BONAR

52

Eric WATT-
Rank/Title: Flight Sergeant (later Pilot Officer)
Unit/Force/Occupation: Royal Air Force Volunteer Reserve
Other Decorations: —
Date of Gazette: 5 Aug. 1932
Place/Date of Birth: — 22 Sep. 1899
Place/Date of Death: —
Place of Memorial: —
Town/County Connections: South Croydon, Surrey
Remarks: (EGM); Chief Pilot of Northern Air Transport Ltd.; served in Second World War.

Account of Deed: On 24th May 1932 at No. 5 Flying Training School, Sealand, RAF Barton, an aircraft had gone up on a training flight, the pupil being a leading aircraftman. The aircraft was seen to roll at a low altitude, to stall on the top of the roll, and then begin to spin to earth out of control. The airport fire engine was rushed to the blazing wreckage and whilst the fire extinguishers kept the flames in check, Flight Sergeant Bonar, wrapped in an asbestos blanket, plunged into the burning plane. The pupil was in the front cockpit and it was impossible to reach him. Flight Sergeant Bonar was, however, able to reach the pilot, release him from his parachute harness and drag him from the wreckage. He was rushed to hospital with very serious injuries from which he later died.

BOOKER

53

David Noel
Rank/Title: Mr.
Unit/Force/Occupation: Miner, Littleton Colliery, South Staffordshire
Other Decorations: —
Date of Gazette: 4 Feb. 1938
Place/Date of Birth: — 19 Oct. 1910
Place/Date of Death: Walsall, Staffordshire — 30 Mar. 1982
Place of Memorial: —
Town/County Connections: Walsall, Staffordshire
Remarks: (EM); brother of Mr. S. Booker, GC.

Account of Deed: On the afternoon of the 14th May 1937 three men were at work dismantling the plant at a conveyor face in a gate, at a distance of some 70 - 80 yards from the main level, in Littleton Colliery. Firedamp appeared to be spreading in the gate, since, at about 8pm, a fireman set off from the level to see what the men were doing up the gate and found that his lamp was extinguished at about 20 yards from the level. Between this time and about midnight, when full rescue apparatus became available and the bodies were recovered, efforts at rescue were made by a succession of men, some of whom themselves collapsed and thereby added to the task of later rescuers; of these one, the under-manager, himself lost his life, thus bringing the death roll to four. In these operations the brothers Booker were outstanding. Each of them forced his way up the gate on four or five separate occasions, and they were between them responsible for extricating four earlier rescuers who had succumbed to the gas; all these survived except the under-manager. On all of these occasions the brothers Booker displayed great courage reinforced by an almost equal measure of coolness and forethought. (See also entry for BOOKER, S.)

BOOKER

Samuel
Rank/Title: Mr.
Unit/Force/Occupation: Miner, Littleton Colliery, South Staffordshire
Other Decorations: —
Date of Gazette: 4 Feb. 1938
Place/Date of Birth: —
Place/Date of Death: — 1981
Place of Memorial: —
Town/County Connections: Walsall, Staffordshire
Remarks: (EM); brother of Mr. D.N. Booker, GC.

Account of Deed: On the afternoon of the 14th May 1937 three men were at work dismantling the plant at a conveyor face in a gate, at a distance of some 70 - 80 yards from the main level, in Littleton Colliery. Firedamp appeared to be spreading in the gate, since, at about 8pm, a fireman set off from the level to see what the men were doing up the gate and found that his lamp was extinguished at about 20 yards from the level. Between this time and about midnight, when full rescue apparatus became available and the bodies were recovered, efforts at rescue were made by a succession of men, some of whom themselves collapsed and thereby added to the task of later rescuers; of these one, the under-manager, himself lost his life, thus bringing the death roll to four. In these operations the brothers Booker were outstanding. Each of them forced his way up the gate on four or five separate occasions, and they were between them responsible for extricating four earlier rescuers who had succumbed to the gas; all these survived except the under-manager. On all of these occasions the brothers Booker displayed great courage reinforced by an almost equal measure of coolness and forethought. (See also entry for BOOKER, D.N.)

BRETT

Douglas Alexander
Rank/Title: Major (later Colonel)
Unit/Force/Occupation: 9th Jat Regiment, Indian Army
Other Decorations: MC
Date of Gazette: 8 May 1934
Place/Date of Birth: —
Place/Date of Death: Chichester, Sussex — 1 Dec. 1963
Place of Memorial: —
Town/County Connections: Chichester, Sussex
Remarks: (EGM)

Account of Deed: At about 5.30pm on 7th January 1934 cricket had just finished on the ground at Chittagong, India. Some 50 European players and spectators, including women and children, were in the tent chatting and having tea. An attack was suddenly made upon them by four Hindu terrorists armed with revolvers and bombs which might have caused serious casualties but for the fact that the first two bombs failed to explode, and Major Brett and another officer* though both unarmed, grappled with two of the assailants and held them down until help came. (*See also entry for DEEDES, R.)

BRIDGE

John
Rank/Title: T/Lieutenant (later Lieutenant-Commander)
Unit/Force/Occupation: Royal Naval Volunteer Reserve
Other Decorations: GM & Bar
Date of Gazette: 20 Jun. 1944
Place/Date of Birth: Culcheth, Warrington, Lancashire — 5 Feb. 1915
Place/Date of Death: —
Place of Memorial: —
Town/County Connections: Roker, Sunderland, Co. Durham
Remarks: Assistant Education Officer for Southport, 1947; Director of Education for Sunderland, 1963; honorary member of The Royal Society of St. George.

Account of Deed: In August 1943 Messina Harbour, Italy, needed to be cleared of depth charges. All the members of a bomb disposal party had been killed or wounded by six of these charges when Lieutenant Bridge took over the operation with the greatest enthusiasm, combined with skill and ingenuity. After a total of 28 dives they were all cleared, including two which were recovered with their previously unknown mechanisms intact. In addition, Lieutenant Bridge rendered safe or discredited a further 207 depth charges, above or below water, with all types of firing mechanisms. As a result of the efforts of this officer and his party Messina Harbour was declared open the day before the Allied assault on the Italian mainland, which proved to be of the utmost value during the follow-up.

BROADFOOT

57

David
Rank/Title: Mr.
Unit/Force/Occupation: Radio Officer, Merchant Navy
Other Decorations: —
Date of Gazette: 6 Oct. 1953
Place/Date of Birth: — 1899
Place/Date of Death: off Irish coast (MV *Princess Victoria*) — 31 Jan. 1953
Place of Memorial: —
Town/County Connections: Stranraer, Wigtownshire, Scotland
Remarks: —

Account of Deed: On 31st January 1953 the MV *Princess Victoria* left Stranraer for Larne carrying 127 passengers. After leaving Loch Ryan she encountered strong north-westerly gales and squalls of sleet and snow. A heavy sea struck the ship and burst open the stern doors and sea water flooded the space on the car deck, causing a list to starboard of about ten degrees. The Master tried to turn back to Loch Ryan but the weather conditions made that impossible and the ship developed a more severe list following the shifting of the cargo. When the *Princess Victoria* finally stopped in sight of the Irish coast, she was practically on her beam end and the order to abandon ship was given. Radio Officer Broadfoot, who had been sending messages all this time asking for help, remained in the W/T cabin receiving and sending calls although he must have realised that by so doing he would have no chance of surviving. His efforts had not been in vain and several vessels were standing by to pick up survivors when the *Princess Victoria* foundered.

BROOKE-SMITH, Francis Haffey — see SMITH, Francis Haffey BROOKE-

BROOKS

58

Arthur
Rank/Title: Private
Unit/Force/Occupation: 1st Bn., The Queen's Royal Regiment (West Surrey)
Other Decorations: —
Date of Gazette: 19 Nov. 1935
Place/Date of Birth: — 5 Jul. 1908
Place/Date of Death: — 1957
Place of Memorial: —
Town/County Connections: Bognor Regis, Sussex
Remarks: (EGM)

Account of Deed: At the time of the Quetta earthquake (31st May/1st June 1935) Private Arthur Brooks rescued a man who had been located some 18 feet below a very unsafe wall. A party of Military Police had dug down within five feet of the man but could not get any further. Private Brooks then pushed his way through the remainder of the wreckage with his bare hands, managed to reach the man, and removed him uninjured. Throughout the latter part of this rescue Private Brooks was in imminent danger of being buried himself.

BROWN

59

David
Rank/Title: Mr.
Unit/Force/Occupation: Overman, Burngrange Shale Mine, West Calder, Midlothian
Other Decorations: —
Date of Gazette: 13 Jan. 1948
Place/Date of Birth: — 7 May 1900
Place/Date of Death: — 1 Dec. 1977
Place of Memorial: —
Town/County Connections: Midlothian, Scotland
Remarks: (EM)

Account of Deed: An explosion occurred in the Burngrange Shale Mine, at about 8pm on the 10th January 1947 when a number of men were working underground. Firedamp was ignited by an open acetylene cap lamp and the initial explosion started fires which spread rapidly. David Brown, the overman, went down into the pit and with a fireman began to explore the narrow workings where the men were trapped. Increasing smoke made it impossible to progress far and they had to go back, but **Mr. Brown** made another attempt by himself. He managed to penetrate further this time, and shouted, but got no response to his calls. The atmospheric conditions were worsening all the time due to the spreading of the fires and Mr. Brown realised that there was no hope of undertaking further exploratory work without the use of rescue teams wearing self-contained breathing apparatus. The

National Fire Service, who were not meant to fight fires underground, nevertheless at once volunteered to supply a team for this duty. In addition Mr. Brown and another member of the Burngrange Mines Rescue Team, also using special breathing apparatus borrowed from the NFS, made two more attempts to rescue the trapped men, but without success. In the meantime there had been a fall of stone, sounds of strata movement were heard and another fire was discovered, which meant that no further attempts at rescue could be made. In fact the fire-fighting went on for four days before it became possible to bring out the bodies of the 15 men who had lost their lives in the explosion and resulting fires.

BROWN 60

John Weller
Rank/Title: Mr.
Unit/Force/Occupation: Workman
Other Decorations: —
Date of Gazette: 9 Jun. 1944 and 30 Jun. 1944
Place/Date of Birth: — 30 Sep. 1912
Place/Date of Death: Richmond, Yorkshire — 14 Dec. 1978
Place of Memorial: —
Town/County Connections: Richmond, Yorkshire
Remarks: (EM)

Account of Deed: When a violent explosion took place at an ammunition railhead at Catterick Bridge Station Mr. John Weller Brown was in a hut 40 yards away. The hut collapsed and he was blown a considerable distance. The explosion was followed immediately by extensive fires in the surrounding area, caused mainly by grenades and incendiary bombs scattered from adjoining trucks. Mr. Brown, though badly shaken, returned to the hut, which was already on fire. He was joined by another man, who, though injured himself, was able to assist him to extricate three other injured men from the ruins of the hut and to carry them to safety. They then assisted in the rescue of killed and injured from other burning and wrecked buildings. Mr. Brown continued the work until emergency parties had arrived and taken over the work of rescue and fire fighting. He knew that the area contained other loads of high explosives which might well have exploded and his behaviour showed great courage and initiative.

BROWN 61

Richard Leslie
Rank/Title: Second Lieutenant
Unit/Force/Occupation: The Royal Lancaster Regiment
Other Decorations: —
Date of Gazette: 4 Jan. 1918
Place/Date of Birth: Huddersfield, Yorkshire — 28 May 1898
Place/Date of Death: Annan, Dumfries-shire — 25 Sep. 1982
Place of Memorial: —
Town/County Connections: Annan, Dumfries-shire, Scotland; Huddersfield, Yorkshire
Remarks: (AM)

Account of Deed: In France on 27th March 1917 Lieutenant Brown was instructing a class in firing rifle grenades. Owing to a defective cartridge one of the grenades was lifted only about two inches, and then fell back into the cup. The safety catch had been released and the grenade was fusing. Lieutenant Brown at once ordered the men to clear and, running forward, picked up the rifle, seized it between his legs, grasped the grenade in his hands, and endeavoured to throw it away. While he was doing so it exploded, blowing off his right hand and inflicting other wounds. Had not Lieutenant Brown seized the grenade in his hand, thus sheltering the men, there can be little doubt that several of them would have been killed or severely injured.

BRYSON 62

Oliver Campbell
Rank/Title: Lieutenant (later Group Captain)
Unit/Force/Occupation: Royal Flying Corps (later Royal Air Force)
Other Decorations: MC, DFC and Bar
Date of Gazette: 11 Jan. 1918
Place/Date of Birth: — 18 Aug. 1896
Place/Date of Death: — 27 Mar. 1977
Place of Memorial: —
Town/County Connections: Guildford, Surrey
Remarks: (AM); wounded in yeomanry charge at Oggagia.

Account of Deed: On 15th March 1917 Lieutenant Bryson, with another officer as passenger, was piloting an aeroplane at Wye Aerodrome when, owing to a sideslip, the machine crashed to the ground and burst into flames. On disentangling himself from the burning wreckage Lieutenant Bryson at once went back into the flames, dragged the other man from the machine, and, notwithstanding his own injuries, which were undoubtedly aggravated by his gallant efforts to rescue his brother officer from the fire, tried to extinguish the fire on the other man's clothing.

BUCKLE 63
Henry
Rank/Title: Mate (later Commander)
Unit/Force/Occupation: Royal Navy
Other Decorations: OBE
Date of Gazette: 27 Apr. 1920
Place/Date of Birth: — 21 Aug. 1889
Place/Date of Death: Pimperne, Blandford Forum, Dorset — 22 Jan. 1975
Place of Memorial: —
Town/County Connections: Pimperne, Blandford Forum, Dorset
Remarks: (AM); served in Royal Navy until 1934 and from 1939-46; Whaling Inspector in South Atlantic 1934-39 and 1946-59.

Account of Deed: While HMS *Tiger* was undergoing repairs at Invergordon, on 27th August 1919, two dockyard fitters and an able seaman were overcome by noxious gas in the hold of the ship, and a stoker petty officer, accompanied by a sick berth attendant, made an unsuccessful attempt at rescue. Both he and his companion had put on respirators but found them useless. Mr. Buckle, the officer of the watch, then arrived on the scene, and in spite of the grave risk to life, which it was now evident would be incurred by further attempts at rescue, immediately went down and succeeded in passing a rope round one of the men. This man was rescued, but Mr. Buckle was considerably affected by the gas, and could do nothing further. The stoker petty officer succeeded in getting the other two men out, but they were found to be dead.

BURKE 64
James (or John Lewis Victor)
Rank/Title: Mr.
Unit/Force/Occupation: Fire Officer, Metro Vickers
Other Decorations: —
Date of Gazette: 3 Jun. 1925
Place/Date of Birth: Manchester — 1896
Place/Date of Death: Manchester — 1965
Place of Memorial: —
Town/County Connections: Manchester
Remarks: (EGM)

Account of Deed: Mr. Burke was awarded the Empire Gallantry Medal in recognition of his action in stopping runaway horses on two separate occasions, at great personal risk.

BURTON 65
Herbert Edgar
Rank/Title: Major
Unit/Force/Occupation: Honorary Superintendent, Tynemouth Motor Life-Boat
Other Decorations: OBE, RNLI Gold and Silver Medals
Date of Gazette: 30 Jun 1924
Place/Date of Birth: — 1864
Place/Date of Death: — 7 Dec. 1944
Place of Memorial: —
Town/County Connections: Chathill, Northumberland
Remarks: (EGM); Gold Cross of Honor (USA), served in RE in First World War.

Account of Deed: On 1st November 1914 Major Burton displayed great gallantry and very fine seamanship in bringing the Tynemouth motor life-boat 44 miles through a stormy night, unaided by coast lights, to Whitby and, after all other efforts had failed, rescued 50 people from the government hospital steamer *Rohilla*, which had been wrecked at Whitby two days earlier.

BUTSON

66

Arthur Richard Cecil
Rank/Title: Dr.
Unit/Force/Occupation: Member of Falkland Islands Dependencies Survey
Other Decorations: Polar Medal
Date of Gazette: 28 Sep. 1948
Place/Date of Birth: Hankow, China — 24 Oct. 1922
Place/Date of Death: —
Place of Memorial: —
Town/County Connections: —
Remarks: (AM); served with RAMC.

Account of Deed: On the evening of 26th July 1947 an American member of the Ronne Antarctic Research Expedition fell into a crevasse some 6 miles from Base. Two teams were sent to the rescue but the hazards of crossing a heavily crevassed glacier were much increased by darkness and it was not until 4 o'clock on the morning of 27th July that the crevasse into which the American had fallen was located. Dr. Butson immediately volunteered to be lowered into the crevasse where he found the man tightly wedged 106 feet down and suffering from shock and exhaustion. For nearly an hour Dr. Butson had to chip the ice away in an extremely confined space in order to free the American who was brought to the surface and placed inside a tent. Dr. Butson then rendered the necessary medical aid and at dawn a return to Base was made, carrying the injured man on one of the sledges.

BUTTON

67

William John
Rank/Title: Lance-Sergeant (later Sergeant)
Unit/Force/Occupation: No. 48 Bomb Disposal Section, Corps of Royal Engineers
Other Decorations: —
Date of Gazette: 17 Sep. 1940
Place/Date of Birth: Bath, Somerset — 1904
Place/Date of Death: Bath, Somerset — 10 Mar. 1969
Place of Memorial: —
Town/County Connections: Bath, Somerset
Remarks: (EGM)

Account of Deed: On the morning of 18th August 1940 Lance-Sergeant Button was ordered with his section to continue the work of excavating an unexploded bomb. Although he knew well that owing to the time already spent on excavation, the bomb was likely to explode at any moment, he continued working with his section with great coolness. The bomb eventually exploded, killing five sappers of the section and throwing Lance-Sergeant Button a considerable distance. Although shaken, he collected the rest of his section, ascertained that none of them was injured, notified the First Aid Detachment and then reported to his Section Officer.

BYWATER

68

Richard Arthur Samuel
Rank/Title: Mr.
Unit/Force/Occupation: Factory Development Officer, Ministry of Supply
Other Decorations: GM
Date of Gazette: 26 Sep. 1944
Place/Date of Birth: Birmingham — 3 Nov. 1913
Place/Date of Death: —
Place of Memorial: —
Town/County Connections: Liverpool, Lancashire
Remarks: Only civilian to date to win both the GC and GM.

Account of Deed: On 22nd February 1944 at one of the factory buildings belonging to the Ministry of Supply at Kirkby near Liverpool, 19 operatives, mostly women, were at work on the last stage of filling fuses; each operative had before her on a bench a tray of 25 fuses. The fuses were stacked on portable tables each holding 40 trays and there were over 12,000 fuses in the building at that time. At 8.30am that morning one fuse detonated, immediately involving the whole tray. The girl working on that tray was killed outright and the two standing behind her, though partially shielded by her body, were both injured, one fatally. The factory itself was badly damaged. The Superintendent was quickly on the spot with Mr. Bywater, and they realised that the damaged fuses might cause an explosion of fearful magnitude. The explosion had apparently been caused by a defective striker and it was obvious that the same defect might be present in some of the other fuses. Mr. Bywater therefore volunteered to remove all the fuses to a place of safety and he, with three other volunteers, worked for almost three days removing 12,724 fuses from the wrecked building — and a further 4,000 suspected of being defective. It was the inspiration of his leadership which enabled this dangerous assignment to be concluded successfully.

CAMPBELL

69

Alexander Fraser
Rank/Title: Second Lieutenant
Unit/Force/Occupation: Corps of Royal Engineers
Other Decorations: —
Date of Gazette: 22 Jan. 1941
Place/Date of Birth: — 2 May 1898
Place/Date of Death: Coventry, Warwickshire — 18 Oct. 1940
Place of Memorial: London Road Cemetery, Coventry
Town/County Connections: —
Remarks: —

Account of Deed: On 17th October 1940 Second Lieutenant Campbell was called upon to deal with an unexploded bomb which had fallen in the Triumph Engineering Company's works in Coventry. War production in two factories had ceased because of it, and a large number of people living nearby had had to be evacuated. Lieutenant Campbell found that the bomb was fitted with a delayed action fuse which it was impossible to remove, so he decided to transport it to a safe place. This was done by lorry, and he lay alongside the bomb so that he could hear if it started ticking and could warn the driver to stop and run for cover. Having taken it to a safe distance, he disposed of the bomb successfully, but was killed whilst dealing with another the next day. (See also entry for GIBSON, M.)

CAMPION

70

Michael Patrick
Rank/Title: Leading Aircraftman (later Warrant Officer)
Unit/Force/Occupation: 90 Bomber Squadron, Royal Air Force
Other Decorations: —
Date of Gazette: 5 Jul. 1940
Place/Date of Birth: — 8 May 1916
Place/Date of Death: The Azores — 4 Dec. 1943
Place of Memorial: The Runnymede Memorial, Surrey
Town/County Connections: London
Remarks: (EGM)

Account of Deed: Leading Aircraftman Campion, together with another airman*, displayed great courage when two Blenheim aircraft collided whilst taking off from Upwood, Huntingdonshire on 12th March 1940. At great risk to themselves they managed to rescue the unconscious pilot of one of the aircraft from the burning wreckage. Shortly afterwards the tanks exploded and the whole aircraft was rapidly burnt out. Unfortunately the pilot died later. (*See also entry for FROST, E.R.C.)

CANNON

71

Horace James
Rank/Title: Flight Sergeant
Unit/Force/Occupation: 24th Wing, Aeroplane Repair Section and 50 Training Squadron, Royal Flying Corps (later Royal Air Force)
Other Decorations: —
Date of Gazette: 26 Apr. 1918
Place/Date of Birth: — 26 Jul. 1895
Place/Date of Death: Bradford, Yorkshire — 21 Sep. 1975
Place of Memorial: —
Town/County Connections: Bradford, Yorkshire
Remarks: (AM)

Account of Deed: On 21st January 1918, while flying in England, a pilot when attempting to land lost control of his machine, which crashed to the ground from a height of about 150 feet, and burst into flames. Flight Sergeant Cannon and another Flight Sergeant went to the rescue of the pilot at great personal risk, as one tank of petrol blew up and another was on fire; moreover, the machine was equipped with a belt of live cartridges, which they dragged out of the flames. They managed to extricate the pilot, who was strapped to the burning plane, but he died shortly afterwards from his injuries and burns.

CHALMERS

72

Jack
Rank/Title: Mr.
Unit/Force/Occupation: —
Other Decorations: —
Date of Gazette: 7 Jul. 1922
Place/Date of Birth: Wellington, New Zealand — 11 Mar. 1894
Place/Date of Death: — 29 Mar. 1982
Place of Memorial: —
Town/County Connections: —
Remarks: (AM); served in First World War; won Australian Surf Life-saving Belt Championship 1922.

Account of Deed: On 4th February 1922 a man was swimming just outside the breakers at Coogee Beach, Sydney, New South Wales when he was attacked by a shark which bit deeply into his left forearm. He managed to free himself but was attacked again by the shark, this time on his right arm, and again broke the grip and got away. Observing what had happened Mr. Jack Chalmers had a line tied round his waist and immediately dashed across the rocks to the rescue. Although he slipped and fell, and was momentarily stunned when his head came into contact with a rock, he quickly recovered, plunged into the sea and swam out to the injured man who was floating helplessly. Mr. Chalmers caught hold of him round the body and held him until they were both hauled to safety. The injured man unfortunately succumbed to his injuries shortly after reaching hospital. That the danger was considerable was clear from the fact that a number of sharks were seen swimming around the spot where the rescue occurred immediately after the bather was taken ashore. Mr. Chalmers undoubtedly realised this and showed great gallantry in going to the bather's rescue.

CHALMERS

73

Robert Mills
Rank/Title: Petty Officer
Unit/Force/Occupation: Royal Navy
Other Decorations: —
Date of Gazette: 18 Jun. 1926
Place/Date of Birth: Chatham, Kent — 1 Jun. 1894
Place/Date of Death: — 7 Sep. 1974
Place of Memorial: —
Town/County Connections: Edinburgh, Scotland
Remarks: (EGM); served in Second World War.

Account of Deed: Petty Officer Chalmers was awarded the Empire Gallantry Medal in recognition of his services on 23rd June 1925 during the disturbances in China.

CHANT

74

Frederick
Rank/Title: Private
Unit/Force/Occupation: 2nd Bn., The Dorsetshire Regiment
Other Decorations: —
Date of Gazette: 2 Jun. 1923
Place/Date of Birth: Sherborne, Dorset — 1900
Place/Date of Death: — 9 Mar. 1968
Place of Memorial: —
Town/County Connections: Poyntington, Sherborne, Dorset; Lymington, Hampshire
Remarks: (EGM)

Account of Deed: Private Chant showed great coolness and disregard of danger during the military operations in Malabar, India in 1921/22. On one occasion he had been using his Lewis gun at a range of about 20 yards against the enemy who were occupying a house and firing at him at close range. His gun failed, but he calmly got up and fetched a rifle and bayonet and maintained his fire on the target he had originally been given with coolness and deliberation. He and Private Troake* subsequently showed great courage in clearing the gardens and jungle round the house occupied by the rebels. (*See also entry for TROAKE, F.H.)

CHARLTON

75

John Daniel
Rank/Title: Mr.
Unit/Force/Occupation: Deputy, Hylton Colliery, Durham
Other Decorations: —
Date of Gazette: 10 Feb. 1948
Place/Date of Birth: — 24 Dec. 1894
Place/Date of Death: Sunderland, Co. Durham — 25 Feb. 1976
Place of Memorial: —
Town/County Connections: Sunderland, Co. Durham
Remarks: (EM)

Account of Deed: On 30th March 1947 a repairer employed at Hylton Colliery, Durham was overcome by gas in an old disused road. Deputy Charlton was informed that the man was missing and at once conducted a search, testing for gas with his flame safety lamp. He had gone only a few yards when he found gas present, at the same time noticing ahead a light from an electric lamp. Accompanied by another man he went towards the light but owing to gas had to return. With the help of several other men he next endeavoured to clear the air, but the measures taken were not sufficiently effective and they could not get nearer than 12 yards from the man. Despite the conditions Mr. Charlton and another man then crawled on their knees and at times on their stomachs, to the man who was then alive but unconscious. Whilst dragging him out, Mr. Charlton and his fellow rescuer were each slightly overcome by the gas and had to have a short rest, but the rescue was at last completed, although the rescued man never recovered consciousness.

CHARLTON

76

Wilson Hodgson
Rank/Title: A/Flight Lieutenant (later Squadron Leader)
Unit/Force/Occupation: Royal Air Force
Other Decorations: —
Date of Gazette: 21 Jan. 1941
Place/Date of Birth: — 9 Apr. 1907
Place/Date of Death: Roehampton, Surrey — 12 May 1953
Place of Memorial: —
Town/County Connections: Petts Wood, Orpington, Kent
Remarks: He was in a Japanese Prisoner of War Camp 1942-45; commanded Bomb Disposal 5134 Squadron 1946-48; Group Armament Officer 1948-50.

Account of Deed: During September and October 1940 at the height of the Blitz, Flight Lieutenant Charlton was employed on Special Duty for bomb disposal and dealt with over 200 unexploded bombs, with undaunted and unfailing coolness. The manner in which he carried out his extremely dangerous duties called for courage of quite an exceptional order.

CHARRINGTON

77

Harold Francis
Rank/Title: Mr.
Unit/Force/Occupation: Assistant Civil Engineer, Air Ministry Works Department
Other Decorations: —
Date of Gazette: 8 Mar. 1940
Place/Date of Birth: — 7 Oct. 1910
Place/Date of Death: Stoke Poges, Buckinghamshire — 7 Jul. 1976
Place of Memorial: —
Town/County Connections: Stoke Poges and Amersham, Buckinghamshire
Remarks: (EGM)

Account of Deed: On 3rd February 1939 Mr. Charrington was travelling by air with another Civil Servant from Jerusalem to Haifa in Palestine. Air conditions were bad and when the plane got into an uncontrollable spin the pilot gave the order for the two passengers to bale out. When Mr. Charrington's companion tried to climb out over the side of the cockpit the pressure held him down so he tried to get out backwards, and then head first, but he still could not get away. Mr. Charrington, who had been in the rear cockpit, stayed to help him get out and then, with great difficulty, left the machine himself and met the ground almost immediately his parachute had opened. The route followed by the aircraft lay over mountains which rise to 3,000ft. and thick cloud obscured all sight of the ground, so in delaying his jump until he had helped his fellow passenger out, Mr. Charrington showed courage of a very high order. The pilot was killed.

CHILD

Frederick William Henry Maurice
Rank/Title: Mr.
Unit/Force/Occupation: Hairdresser
Other Decorations: —
Date of Gazette: 5 May 1939
Place/Date of Birth: — 2 Jan. 1897
Place/Date of Death: Chiswick, Middlesex — 20 Nov. 1975
Place of Memorial: Mortlake Crematorium, Surrey
Town/County Connections: Chiswick, Middlesex
Remarks: (EGM); served in both World Wars.

Account of Deed: On 29th March 1939, in the early hours of the morning, Mr. Child was walking across Hammersmith Bridge when he noticed a small leather suit-case on the structure of the bridge. On examining the case he saw that it was smoking, so he climbed through the structure on to the side of the bridge and threw the case into the water. The explosion which followed sent up a 60ft. high column of water and this was followed by a second explosion. Many windows in the vicinity were shattered and it took three months to repair the bridge, but no one was hurt owing to Mr. Child's courage and presence of mind.

CHURCHILL, Odette Marie Céline — see **SANSOM,** Odette Marie Céline

CLARK

Joseph
Rank/Title: Mr.
Unit/Force/Occupation: Miner, Trimdon Grange, Durham
Other Decorations: —
Date of Gazette: 3 May 1927
Place/Date of Birth: — ?1885
Place/Date of Death: — 1 Mar. 1965
Place of Memorial: —
Town/County Connections: Trimdon Grange, Co. Durham
Remarks: (EGM)

Account of Deed: On 19th November 1926 Joseph Clark and another man*, although in grave personal danger from falling debris, gas and spontaneously generated heat, made persistent attempts to rescue a miner imprisoned in a narrow tunnel. (*See also entry for BEATTIE, J.)

CLARKE

Azariah
Rank/Title: Mr.
Unit/Force/Occupation: Rescue Brigade, Holditch Colliery, N. Staffordshire
Other Decorations: BEM
Date of Gazette: 5 Aug. 1938
Place/Date of Birth: —
Place/Date of Death: Newcastle-under-Lyme, Staffordshire — 17 Feb. 1975
Place of Memorial: —
Town/County Connections: Newcastle-under-Lyme, Staffordshire
Remarks: (EM); served in First World War.

Account of Deed: On 2nd July 1937 at about 5.45am a fire started in the holing of the Four Feet Seam at Holditch Colliery. The fire spread rapidly but of the 55 men in the area at the time all except two were able to escape. An unsuccessful search was made for the missing men and at 6.50am an explosion occurred and one of the search party was found to be missing. Men from the Colliery Rescue Brigade led by Mr. Clarke made an unsuccessful search for the man and afterwards looked for the two men who were originally missing. The atmosphere was foul with gas and smoke and they had to wear breathing apparatus. While they were searching a severe explosion occurred resulting in the deaths of 27 men, most of whom had been sent down for the purpose of erecting stoppings to seal off the fire. This explosion was followed at intervals by two more of lesser intensity, but the Rescue Team carried on with their search. They eventually found a number of badly injured men and dead bodies, and these were successfully evacuated. By 3.25pm it was thought that all men known to be alive had been rescued, but to make quite certain Mr. Clarke led a party down the mine again at 6pm for a last search which lasted until 8.30pm The courage, initiative, endurance and qualities of leadership displayed by Mr. Clarke throughout these lengthy operations were outstanding.

CLARKE 81
Donald Owen
Rank/Title: Mr.
Unit/Force/Occupation: Apprentice, Merchant Navy
Other Decorations: Liverpool Shipowners' Silver Medal & Brave Conduct Badge
Date of Gazette: 20 Jul. 1943
Place/Date of Birth: Chester-le-Street, Co. Durham — 1923
Place/Date of Death: off Trinidad — 9 Aug. 1942
Place of Memorial: Tower Hill Memorial, London; bed in Royal Victoria Infirmary, Newcastle-upon-Tyne endowed by the owners of MV *San Emiliano*
Town/County Connections: Chester-le-Street, Co. Durham
Remarks: —

Account of Deed: In August 1942 the tanker *San Emiliano* was two days out of Trinidad with a cargo of petrol when she was struck by two torpedoes and immediately swept by flames. Apprentice Clarke was trapped in his cabin but fought his way out on deck and boarded the only lifeboat which was left intact. It was full of burnt and wounded men and he himself was severely burnt on his face, hands and legs. When the painter was cast off, the boat started to drift back on to the flaming tanker and it was evident that it would require a tremendous effort to pull it out of danger. Most of the occupants of the lifeboat, however, were so badly injured that they were unable to man an oar. Despite his own fearful injuries Apprentice Clarke took an oar and pulled heartily for two hours without a groan or murmur of complaint, and only when the boat was well clear did he collapse and then his burnt hands had to be cut away from the oar. As he lay dying in the bottom of the boat he sang cheerful songs to keep up the spirits of his injured shipmates.

CLEALL 82
Walter Charles
Rank/Title: Mr.
Unit/Force/Occupation: —
Other Decorations: Silver Medal of Society for Protection of Life from Fire
Date of Gazette: 30 Dec. 1919
Place/Date of Birth: — 25 Aug. 1896
Place/Date of Death: Cardiff — 27 Apr. 1983
Place of Memorial: —
Town/County Connections: Cardiff, Wales
Remarks: (AM); was on demobilisation leave when he won his AM, having served with the Army Service Corps.

Account of Deed: On 11th August 1919 when a fire broke out at the top of the Royal Hotel, Cardiff, one of the maids was seen gesticulating for help from the sixth floor. Mr. Cleall, who was in the crowd below, at once entered the building without a smoke helmet and eventually succeeded in getting into a room from which he could see the girl. From the window of that room he climbed along a narrow parapet, and reached the window where the girl was. Above the ledge which afforded him foothold was a stone balcony for a part of the intervening space, but a very dangerous corner had to be negotiated, with a sheer drop to the street of fully 100ft. The risk of falling was very great, but he succeeded in carrying the girl back along the parapet, and into the room from which he started. A portion of the roof collapsed as the girl was assisted from the room.

CLEMENTS 83
John
Rank/Title: Mr.
Unit/Force/Occupation: Schoolmaster
Other Decorations: —
Date of Gazette: 7 Dec. 1976
Place/Date of Birth: Codicote, Hertfordshire — 25 Aug. 1953
Place/Date of Death: Sappada, North Italy — 12 Apr. 1976
Place of Memorial: Memorial plaque at Sherrardswood School
Town/County Connections: Welwyn Garden City, Hertfordshire
Remarks: —

Account of Deed: At about 4am on 12th April 1976 smoke was noticed in a hotel at a ski resort in Northern Italy where there was a party of 6 adults and 37 children from Sherrardswood School, Welwyn Garden City. Mr. Clements was one of those who quickly raised the alarm and ordered the children to go downstairs, and a number of them were led to safety through dense smoke by other members of the staff. Meanwhile Mr. Clements had climbed down from a third floor balcony on the west side of the building to a second floor balcony, thence to the first floor where he organised the children into groups and helped them to escape down a rope he had improvised from knotted sheets. When all the children had been evacuated, Mr. Clements went back into the building, which by now was burning fiercely. He was seen on at least two occasions going back into the hotel after carrying or dragging people out, and he ignored repeated attempts to stop him. He was finally overcome by fumes and died in the fire, having shown no regard for his own safety but carried on with his efforts to save those still trapped in the burning building.

CLOSE 84
Gerald Charles Neil
Rank/Title: Pilot Officer (later Squadron Leader)
Unit/Force/Occupation: Royal Air Force
Other Decorations: —
Date of Gazette: 21 Dec. 1937
Place/Date of Birth: — 2 Feb. 1914
Place/Date of Death: France — 9 May 1941
Place of Memorial: Boulogne Eastern Cemetery, France
Town/County Connections: London
Remarks: (EGM)

Account of Deed: During the operations in Waziristan on the NW Frontier of India, an aircraft laden with bombs, crashed and burst into flames on the Miranshah aerodrome. Pilot Officer Close, who was duty pilot on the aerodrome, hastened to the scene of the accident and, in spite of the explosion of a bomb and some small-arms ammunition, made persistent attempts to extinguish the flames and to rescue the crew until ordered by a superior officer to withdraw.

COBHAM 85
Anthony John
Rank/Title: Midshipman (later Commander)
Unit/Force/Occupation: Royal Navy
Other Decorations: MBE
Date of Gazette: 1 Jan. 1930
Place/Date of Birth: — 10 Oct. 1909
Place/Date of Death: —
Place of Memorial: —
Town/County Connections: Porchester, Hampshire
Remarks: (EGM); served in Second World War.

Account of Deed: On 26th July 1929 HMS *Devonshire* was carrying out full calibre firing with all eight guns (twin turrets) together. At the first salvo there was a heavy explosion which blew off the roof of one of the turrets. Midshipman Cobham immediately took stretcher parties aft and ordered one crew to follow him and the other to rig hoses. When he reached the turret some very badly burnt men with their clothes still on fire were falling out of the hatch in the rear. He and an able seaman* did what they could for them and then went into the gunhouse, where there was still a lot of cordite burning fiercely, and pulled out more bodies, after which they turned on the hoses and helped to cool things down. Though they did not realise it at the time they had both inhaled a large quantity of cordite fumes which had a most unpleasant delayed action effect. (*See also entry for NIVEN, G.P.)

COCCIOLETTI, André Gilberto — see **KEMPSTER,** André Gilbert

COPPERWHEAT 86

Dennis Arthur
Rank/Title: Lieutenant (later Lieutenant-Commander)
Unit/Force/Occupation: Royal Navy
Other Decorations: —
Date of Gazette: 17 Nov. 1942
Place/Date of Birth: — 23 May 1914
Place/Date of Death: —
Place of Memorial: —
Town/County Connections: Streatham, London; Kettering, Northamptonshire
Remarks: —

Account of Deed: On 22nd March 1942 when the convoys to Malta were being devastated by enemy air attack one merchantman, which was loaded with ammunition, lay inside Grand Harbour, Valetta and was blazing furiously. As it was in imminent danger of exploding and doing grave damage to the harbour, Lieutenant Copperwheat of the cruiser *Penelope* was sent with a small party of ratings to scuttle the ship — a most dangerous assignment with fires and ammunition exploding all around them. Lieutenant Copperwheat sent his working party to take shelter and stayed by himself to fire the charges, which lifted him bodily and nearly caused his death.

COWLEY 87

John Guise (later Sir John)
Rank/Title: Lieutenant (later Lieutenant General)
Unit/Force/Occupation: 16th Army Troops Coy., Q.V.O., Madras Sappers and Miners, Corps of Royal Engineers
Other Decorations: KBE, CB
Date of Gazette: 19 Nov. 1935
Place/Date of Birth: Dorchester, Dorset — 20 Aug. 1905
Place/Date of Death: —
Place of Memorial: —
Town/County Connections: Boldre, Lymington, Hampshire
Remarks: (AM); Knight Commander, Order of Orange Nassau (Netherlands); Fellow, Royal Society of Arts; served in Second World War; Chief of Staff, HQ Eastern Command 1953-56; Vice Quartermaster General 1956-57; Controller of Munitions, Ministry of Supply 1957-60; Master-General of the Ordnance, War Office 1960-62; Colonel Commandant, Royal Pioneer Corps 1961-67; Colonel Commandant, Royal Engineers 1961-70; Chairman, Albert Medal Association 1966-72.

Account of Deed: At the time of the Quetta earthquake (31st May/1st June 1935), Lieutenant Cowley and his party were the first to start relief work at the Civil Hospital where the walls of all the wards had collapsed, bringing down the roofs intact on the inmates on whom the debris of the walls had already fallen. At first the men were too few in number to tear off the roofs, so they raised them up for short periods whilst Lieutenant Cowley crawled under them and dragged out survivors from their beds. These people were pre-earthquake hospital patients and most were quite helpless. Lieutenant Cowley lifted many men in his arms regardless of the warning that they were suffering from all manner of diseases. Had it not been for the work of this officer and the excellent example shown by him to his men, the numbers saved would have been greatly reduced.

CRADOCK 88

Frederick John
Rank/Title: Mr.
Unit/Force/Occupation: Boilerman
Other Decorations: —
Date of Gazette: 10 Sep. 1943
Place/Date of Birth: Acton, London — 1886
Place/Date of Death: Glemsford, Suffolk — 4 May 1943
Place of Memorial: —
Town/County Connections: Glemsford, Suffolk; London
Remarks: Served in First World War.

Account of Deed: In May 1943 an explosion occurred in a boiler-house at Glemsford, Suffolk. Mr. Cradock, who was in charge at the time, could quite easily have jumped to safety, but he tried to get down into the well to haul out his workmate. In doing this he was severely scalded and overcome by the escaping steam. Despite his terrible injuries, he could still have escaped with his own life, but was determined to make a second attempt to rescue the man, and in doing so he met his death.

CRAIG 89
Bert
Rank/Title: Mr.
Unit/Force/Occupation: Miner, Nixon's Navigation Colliery, Mountain Ash, Glamorgan
Other Decorations: —
Date of Gazette: 1 Jun. 1923
Place/Date of Birth: — 11 Mar. 1899
Place/Date of Death: — 14 Dec. 1978
Place of Memorial: —
Town/County Connections: Mountain Ash, Glamorgan, Wales
Remarks: (EM); served in First World War.

Account of Deed: On 14th November 1922 a workman at Nixon's Navigation Colliery was completely buried by a heavy fall of stones and rubbish. An attempt at rescue was made but had to be abandoned because of further falls of stones. Mr. Craig, on hearing what had happened, immediately ran to the assistance of the injured man. He had to work by himself until the falls ceased, when the men who had originally made a rescue attempt came to his aid. The injured workman was at last extricated and within two minutes of the rescue another very large fall took place. Mr. Craig was working under conditions of very great danger and his conduct was even more gallant in view of the fact that he suffered from the result of a severe bullet wound in the head and any blow might have been fatal.

CROSBY 90
Bertram Frederick
Rank/Title: Mr.
Unit/Force/Occupation: Workman (aged 16), Film Waste Products Ltd., Regent's Park, London
Other Decorations: —
Date of Gazette: 15 May 1928
Place/Date of Birth: — 6 Jul. 1912
Place/Date of Death: Seaford, Sussex — 30 Jan. 1972
Place of Memorial: —
Town/County Connections: Hampstead, London; Kingston-upon-Thames, Surrey; Seaford, Sussex
Remarks: (EM)

Account of Deed: On 9th September 1927 a serious fire broke out at the premises of the Film Waste Products Ltd. A quantity of cinematograph film which was being manipulated in a drying machine ignited and the fire immediately spread to other film on adjacent benches. Bertie Crosby, who was then only 16 years old, was passing through the drying room when the fire broke out. He ran to a door leading into a yard but turned back when he heard a scream from near the drying machine. He couldn't see anyone but when he and the foreman re-entered the room together Crosby saw a girl fall against one of the work tables. He ran to her and half pulled and half carried her towards the door. Outside the door they both fell; Crosby was stupefied by the heat and fumes and did not recover until he found himself outside with his clothes alight. He managed to extinguish the flames and was subsequently taken to hospital. He could easily have escaped from the building without injury, but on two separate occasions re-entered the room where the fire started in an endeavour to save life.

CROSSLEY 91
Edwin
Rank/Title: Mr.
Unit/Force/Occupation: Yard foreman, Admiralty Dockyard, Chatham
Other Decorations: —
Date of Gazette: 25 Feb. 1936
Place/Date of Birth: — 9 Nov. 1884
Place/Date of Death: Gillingham, Kent — 14 Feb. 1976
Place of Memorial: —
Town/County Connections: Gillingham, Kent
Remarks: (EGM)

Account of Deed: Mr. Crossley was on duty in the Admiralty Dockyard at Chatham in October 1935 when two workmen who had descended into a compartment to recover tools were overcome by gas. When Mr. Crossley heard this he seized a tackle which stood rigged above the hatch and went down into the compartment with two skilled labourers. The rescuers were successful in securing one of the two gassed workmen to the tackle and hoisting him through the hatchway into the open air, but after making fast the rope to the second man, were overcome by the gas. He was eventually hauled to safety by others on the deck above.

DANCKWERTS 92

Peter Victor
Rank/Title: Sub-Lieutenant
Unit/Force/Occupation: Royal Naval Volunteer Reserve
Other Decorations: MBE
Date of Gazette: 20 Dec. 1940
Place/Date of Birth: Southsea, Hampshire — 14 Oct. 1916
Place/Date of Death: Cambridge — 25 Oct. 1984
Place of Memorial: —
Town/County Connections: Cambridge, Cambridgeshire
Remarks: Fellow of the Royal Society; Fellow, Fellowship of Engineering; Emeritus Shell Professor of Chemical Engineering, Cambridge Univ.; Emeritus Fellow of Pembroke College, Cambridge; Demonstrator and Lecturer, Dept. of Chemical Engineering, Cambridge 1948-54; Deputy Director of Research & Development, Industrial Group, UK Atomic Energy Authority 1954-56; Professor of Chemical Engineering Science, Imperial College of Science & Technology 1956-59; Shell Professor of Chemical Engineering, Cambridge 1959-77; Fellow of Pembroke College, Cambridge 1959-77.

Account of Deed: In the latter part of 1940 at the height of the Blitz, Sub-Lieutenant Danckwerts, who had been less than six weeks in the Service, set out without orders and with incomplete equipment to deal with mines endangering his district. He had never before touched a mine, except under instruction, but he worked almost without rest for 48 hours and dealt successfully with 16 enemy mines. On one occasion he and a chief petty officer found two mines hanging from a parachute with their noses on a warehouse floor. Their footsteps started up the clock in one of them — they retreated — the clock stopped. So they went on undaunted and dealt with the mine, knowing well that its clock was highly sensitive and could only have a few seconds left to run. However, Sub-Lieutenant Danckwerts managed to withdraw the fuse and then he dealt with the fuse in the other mine.

DARKER 93

Richard Edward
Rank/Title: Mr.
Unit/Force/Occupation: Miner, Bentley Colliery, Yorkshire
Other Decorations: —
Date of Gazette: 30 Sep. 1932
Place/Date of Birth: — 27 May 1910
Place/Date of Death: Doncaster, Yorkshire — 15 Jan. 1988
Place of Memorial: —
Town/County Connections: Bentley, Doncaster, Yorkshire
Remarks: (EM)

Account of Deed: On 20th November 1931 in the afternoon, a violent explosion of firedamp, followed by fires, occurred in the North East District of the Bentley Colliery. Of some 47 men working at or near the coal face, 45 were either killed or died later. A number of miners rendered heroic assistance at the work of rescue, among them Mr. Darker, who displayed great gallantry and perseverance in extricating the injured and conveying them to a place of safety. They had to work in an atmosphere which was hot and vitiated and there was always risk of further explosion. One such explosion actually occurred at 10.30pm injuring members of one of the rescue parties, and this was followed by yet another. (See also entries for ALLPORT, E., SOULSBY, O., SYKES, F., TEMPERLEY, S.J. and YATES, P.W.)

DAVIES 94

Frederick
Rank/Title: Mr.
Unit/Force/Occupation: Fireman, National Fire Service
Other Decorations: —
Date of Gazette: 5 Feb. 1946
Place/Date of Birth: Shepherds Bush, London — 1913
Place/Date of Death: Harlesden, London — 22 Aug. 1945
Place of Memorial: —
Town/County Connections: Harrow, Middlesex
Remarks: —

Account of Deed: In August 1945, two children were trapped in a front room on the second floor of a burning building at Harlesden, London. Although the fire was so fierce that it was not considered possible for anyone to go inside, Fireman Davies ran up the escape ladder, entered the room and handed one child out of the window. He refused orders to come down and went back to find the other child, who was probably dead when he brought her down. When he reached the foot of the ladder he was a human torch, and later died of his injuries.

DAVIES

Robert
Rank/Title: T/Lieutenant
Unit/Force/Occupation: Corps of Royal Engineers
Other Decorations: —
Date of Gazette: 30 Sep. 1940
Place/Date of Birth: Cornwall — 3 Oct. 1900
Place/Date of Death: Kogarah, Sydney, New South Wales, Australia — 27 Sep. 1975
Place of Memorial: —
Town/County Connections: —
Remarks: —

Account of Deed: On 12th September 1940 Lieutenant Davies was detailed, with a party of sappers, to recover a bomb which had fallen in the close vicinity of St. Paul's Cathedral. It was a night of heavy raids on London and it was not at first realised exactly where the bomb was. It was one of the sappers* who discovered it deep down under the pavement in front of the Cathedral, and managed to remove it. Everyone in the party knew that it might explode at any minute and, in order to shield his men from further danger, Lieutenant Davies himself drove the vehicle in which the bomb was removed and personally carried out its disposal. (*See also entry for WYLIE, G.C.)

DAVIS

Thomas Neil
Rank/Title: Leading Seaman (later Lieutenant-Commander)
Unit/Force/Occupation: Royal Naval Reserve
Other Decorations: —
Date of Gazette: 23 Mar. 1918
Place/Date of Birth: — 18 May 1895
Place/Date of Death: Rhos Tryfan, Caernarvon, Wales — 8 Oct. 1978
Place of Memorial: —
Town/County Connections: Bethel, Caernarvon, Wales
Remarks: (AM); served in Second World War.

Account of Deed: On 6th December 1917 the French steamer *Mont Blanc*, with a cargo of high explosives, and the Norwegian steamer *Imo*, were in collision in Halifax Harbour. Fire broke out on the *Mont Blanc* immediately and the flames rose to a height of over 100 feet. A few minutes later a tremendous explosion took place and the tug *Musquash* was seen to be on fire forward. As the tug had a gun and ammunition on board there was danger of a further explosion. The captain of HMS *Highflyer* hailed a private tug which was brought alongside the ship. Leading Seaman Davis and an able seaman from *Highflyer* immediately volunteered, and having been transferred by the tug to the burning *Musquash*, which had by this time broken adrift, they secured a line from her stern, and she was towed into midstream. The line then parted and the two seaman passed another line from the *Musquash* to the pumping-lighter *Lee*, which had now arrived. They then both went forward to the burning part, and succeeded in getting to the ammunition, which was by this time badly scorched, pulled it away from the flames and threw it overboard. They broke open the door of the galley, which was on fire inside, to enable the *Lee* to play her hoses into it, and then broke open the doors of the cabin. By their efforts they made it possible to subdue the fire and save further damage and loss of life. At any moment whilst they were on board the *Musquash* the ammunition might have exploded.

DAY

Harry Melville Arbuthnot
Rank/Title: A/Lieutenant
Unit/Force/Occupation: Royal Marine Light Infantry
Other Decorations: OBE, DSO
Date of Gazette: 7 Jan. 1919
Place/Date of Birth: Sarawalk, South East Asia — 3 Aug. 1898
Place/Date of Death: Malta — 2 Dec. 1977
Place of Memorial: —
Town/County Connections: London; Brenchley, Kent
Remarks: (AM); later served in Royal Air Force (Group Captain); prisoner of war from October 1939 to 1944 — organised escape attempts including mass break-out from Stalag Luft III in March 1944. Only man to be awarded DSO for services whilst a prisoner of war.

Account of Deed: On 9th November 1918 HMS *Britannia* was torpedoed by an enemy submarine. The explosion was followed by another more violent explosion of ammunition, and fires were started, resulting in the spread of smoke and fumes. Shortly after the explosion Lieutenant Day went down to the wardroom to search for wounded. He heard groaning forward of the wardroom, but found that the heavy wooden door leading forward had jammed and was immovable. He burst open the trap hatch to the wardroom pantry, climbed through it and discovered the Engineer Lieutenant and a wardroom steward alive and conscious, but unable to move. Fearing that he would hurt them if he tried to drag them through the trap hatch single-handed, he climbed back into the wardroom and up to the quarter-deck to get help. He returned to the wardroom with two stokers and between them they carried the two dying men up to the deck. During the whole of this operation Lieutenant Day's life was in danger — the ship was listing, there was a fire close to the 12-lb magazine and the cordite fumes were very strong. Despite this danger he inspected all scuttles and dead-lights in the wardroom (and cabins before it) and made sure that all were properly closed before leaving.

DEEDES
98

Richard
Rank/Title: Captain (later Major)
Unit/Force/Occupation: The King's Shropshire Light Infantry
Other Decorations: —
Date of Gazette: 8 May 1934
Place/Date of Birth: — 7 Jan. 1896
Place/Date of Death: Shrewsbury, Shropshire — 28 Aug. 1975
Place of Memorial: —
Town/County Connections: Shrewsbury, Shropshire
Remarks: (EGM); served in First and Second World Wars.

Account of Deed: At about 5.30pm on 7th January 1934 cricket had just finished on the ground at Chittagong, India. Some 50 European players and spectators, including women and children, were in the tent chatting and having tea. An attack was suddenly made upon them by four Hindu terrorists armed with revolvers and bombs which might have caused serious casualties but for the fact that the first two bombs failed to explode and Captain Deedes and another officer* though both unarmed, grappled with two of the assailants and held them down until help came. (*See also entry for BRETT, D.A.)

DIN MATA — see MATA DIN

DINWOODIE
99

Hubert
Rank/Title: Squadron Leader (later Wing Commander)
Unit/Force/Occupation: 5150 Bomb Disposal Squadron, Royal Air Force Volunteer Reserve
Other Decorations: OBE, MC
Date of Gazette: 4 Feb. 1947
Place/Date of Birth: — 24 Mar. 1896
Place/Date of Death: Ringwood, Hampshire — 28 Aug. 1968
Place of Memorial: Cremated, Bournemouth Crematorium
Town/County Connections: Ringwood, Hampshire
Remarks: —

Account of Deed: On 20th August 1945 German high explosive bombs were being loaded into barges at Lubeck for disposal at sea. Two train loads of bombs weighing approximately 1,100 tons were drawn up at the quayside. Whilst loading was in progress a bomb with a 'tel' fuse was accidentally dropped a few feet by the German loading party. The bomb, which was one of a batch of 12 of a similar sort being handled at the time, exploded, killing 6 people and injuring 12. There was no obvious cause for the detonation of what should have been a harmless bomb, but if the other 11 of the same type exploded there could have been a serious disaster to the port of Lubeck. Squadron Leader Dinwoodie was sent at once to Lubeck with two assistants to deal with the matter and they proceeded to disarm the other 11 bombs in an atmosphere of great tension. No one knew what had caused the first one to explode, nor was it possible to be sure that what had caused the explosion of one would not cause the explosion of the rest. Squadron Leader Dinwoodie displayed courage and coolness in a situation of great potential danger.

DITTO RAM
100

Rank/Title: Sowar
Unit/Force/Occupation: Central India Horse, (21st King George V's Own Horse), Indian Armoured Corps
Other Decorations: —
Date of Gazette: 13 Dec. 1945
Place/Date of Birth: —
Place/Date of Death: Italy — 24 July 1944
Place of Memorial: The Cassino Memorial, Italy
Town/County Connections: —
Remarks: —

Account of Deed: On 23rd July 1944 in Italy, a night patrol found themselves in the middle of a minefield. Sowar Ditto Ram had his left leg blown off below the knee, but on hearing calls for help from another sowar, crawled forward through the minefield to help him. On reaching his comrade he found that his thigh had been shattered, and disregarding his own injuries he applied a field dressing to the wound before losing consciousness and dying a few minutes later. Sowar Ditto Ram was a very young soldier with only two years' service who set the finest example of self-sacrifice in putting another's life before his own. (See also entry for YOUNG, St.J.G)

DIXON

101

John
Rank/Title: Mr.
Unit/Force/Occupation: Electrician
Other Decorations: Bronze medal of the Society for the Protection of Life from Fire, Order of Industrial Heroism
Date of Gazette: 23 Feb. 1940
Place/Date of Birth: Bradford, Yorkshire — 23 Jun. 1913
Place/Date of Death: — 13 Apr. 1984
Place of Memorial: —
Town/County Connections: Bradford, Yorkshire; Lincoln and Grantham, Lincolnshire; Blackburn, Lancashire
Remarks: (EM); also awarded The Carnegie Hero Fund Trust Certificate.

Account of Deed: On 16th February 1939 an accident occurred during the casting of a mould at the foundry of Robey & Co. Ltd., Lincoln, which resulted in two large overhead electric cranes and the foundry roof being set on fire. Mr. Dixon, an electrician, was on the crane gantry to watch the electrical equipment and was able to escape from immediate danger, but the driver of one of the cranes, who managed to climb out of the cabin, collapsed on the top of the crane with his clothing ablaze. Mr. Dixon saw this and promptly went back to the rescue, although the fire was then at its height and there was some risk of an electric shock. He extinguished the flames from the crane driver's clothing and carried him from his own crane across the crane in the next bay, out on to the roof gutter, along and then across the roof and down a 31ft. ladder to the ground. Mr. Dixon then collapsed — he was badly burned about the arms and upper part of the body. His courageous action almost certainly saved the crane driver's life.

DOLPHIN

102

Albert George
Rank/Title: Mr.
Unit/Force/Occupation: Hospital porter, South Eastern Hospital, New Cross, London
Other Decorations: —
Date of Gazette: 17 Jan. 1941
Place/Date of Birth: — 1896
Place/Date of Death: New Cross, London — 7 Sep. 1940
Place of Memorial: —
Town/County Connections: ?Bromley, Kent; ?New Cross, London
Remarks: —

Account of Deed: On the night of 7th September 1940, a high explosive bomb fell on the kitchens of the South Eastern Hospital, New Cross, killing four nurses and injuring the night sister and some patients in the adjoining ward. Another nurse was pinioned by a block of masonry which had fallen across her legs. Mr. Dolphin and some fellow workers were trying to free her when the wall of the room began to crack. The other workers jumped clear before the wall fell, but Mr. Dolphin flung himself down across the nurse's body to protect her and in so doing took the full weight of the falling masonry. He was killed, but the nurse, though severely injured, was subsequently extricated, alive.

DONOGHUE

103

Raymond Tasman
Rank/Title: Mr.
Unit/Force/Occupation: Tram conductor, Hobart, Tasmania
Other Decorations: —
Date of Gazette: 11 Oct. 1960
Place/Date of Birth: Hobart, Tasmania — 10 Dec. 1920
Place/Date of Death: Hobart, Tasmania — 29 Apr. 1960
Place of Memorial: —
Town/County Connections: —
Remarks: —

Account of Deed: On 29th April 1960 in Hobart, Tasmania, during a peak traffic period, a tramcar bound for the northern suburb of Springfield collided with a motor vehicle near Warwick Street. The driver's cab was wrecked, the driver injured and the tram started to run backwards rapidly gaining speed on a steep hill. Mr. Donoghue, the tram conductor, could easily have saved his life, either by leaving the tram or by passing into the rear of the compartment to which he had moved the passengers, but realising the danger in the dense traffic, he deliberately scorned the way to safety so that he might, by continuous ringing of the alarm bell, warn other traffic, while attempting to stop the vehicle with the emergency handbrake. At the bottom of the hill the runaway tram collided with a stationary tram and Mr. Donoghue, who was still at his post at the moment of impact, was killed. By sacrificing his life he saved the lives of a number of other people.

DOUGLAS

104

Robert Ewing
Rank/Title: Leading Aircraftman (later Flying Officer)
Unit/Force/Occupation: Royal Air Force
Other Decorations: —
Date of Gazette: 27 Mar. 1931
Place/Date of Birth: — 7 Apr. 1906
Place/Date of Death: — 10 Aug. 1959
Place of Memorial: —
Town/County Connections: Banbury, Oxfordshire
Remarks: (EGM); served in Second World War.

Account of Deed: On 13th June 1930 at Kohat on the North West Frontier of India an aeroplane, on patrol with a crew of two and a load of live bombs, stalled shortly after take-off, crashed and burst into flames. LAC Douglas was the first to arrive at the scene of the crash and found the air gunner lying two yards from the wreckage, his clothes burning fiercely. LAC Douglas put out the flames with an extinguisher, disentangled part of the gun equipment from the injured man and with the help of another airman, dragged him clear of the aeroplane and got him into an ambulance. He then turned his attention to the pilot who was still inside the burning plane, being fully aware that the aircraft contained live bombs which were likely to explode at any second. He had approached to within 12 yards of the wreckage when the first one went off.

DOWLAND

105

John Noel
Rank/Title: Flight Lieutenant (later Wing Commander)
Unit/Force/Occupation: Royal Air Force Station, Manby, Lincolnshire
Other Decorations: —
Date of Gazette: 7 Jan 1941
Place/Date of Birth: — 6 Nov. 1914
Place/Date of Death: Malta — 13 Jan. 1942
Place of Memorial: Capuccini Naval Cemetery, Malta, GC
Town/County Connections: Wokingham, Surrey
Remarks: This was the first action for which the George Cross was awarded.

Account of Deed: On 11th February 1940 the steamship *Kildare*, a grain carrier, was hit by two bombs. One exploded in the grain, which shifted, causing the vessel to list heavily; the other lodged in the after deck cabin but did not explode. The ship limped into Immingham Dock, North Lincolnshire and Flight Lieutenant Dowland went with Civilian Armament Instructor Harrison* and another civilian instructor to deal with the situation. On entering the cabin they found that the crew had eased their task somewhat by placing mattresses under the bomb to stop it rolling about, and the fuses were uppermost. They then carried out the procedure laid down by Mr. Harrison for dealing with fuses — by applying a voltmeter they wore down the electric charge and removed the locking and location rings which rendered the bomb harmless. The bomb was then lowered over the side of the ship into an RAF vehicle and taken away for examination. (*See also entry for HARRISON, L.H.)

d'SOUZA

106

Baptista Joseph
Rank/Title: Shri
Unit/Force/Occupation: Excise Constable, Sholapur District, Bombay, India
Other Decorations: —
Date of Gazette: 3 Jun. 1931
Place/Date of Birth: ?Belgawm, Mysore State, India —
Place/Date of Death: Mysore — 26 Dec. 1980
Place of Memorial: —
Town/County Connections: —
Remarks: (EGM)

Account of Deed: Shri d'Souza, Excise Constable, was orderly to the Excise Sub-Inspector during the riots in May 1930 when they were both surrounded by the mob, severely beaten and stoned. The constable, although ordered by the sub-inspector to seek safety, refused to leave and remained to protect him. When the sub-inspector was knocked unconscious Shri d'Souza stood over him blowing his whistle until police help arrived. His devotion to duty in the face of great danger undoubtedly saved the sub-inspector's life.

DUFFIN
107

Charles Godfrey
Rank/Title: Mr.
Unit/Force/Occupation: Senior Shipwright Diver, HM Dockyard, Portsmouth
Other Decorations: —
Date of Gazette: 1 Feb. 1937
Place/Date of Birth: —
Place/Date of Death: — 16 Sep. 1957
Place of Memorial: —
Town/County Connections: Portsmouth, Hampshire
Remarks: (EGM)

Account of Deed: In August 1936 a diver was engaged under water at HM Dockyard, Portsmouth, in examining the launching gear below HMS *Aurora*. Signals of distress were received and when a stand-by diver went down he found the man jammed between the top of a dagger plank connecting the several launching-poppets and the bottom of the ship. Senior Shipwright Diver Duffin was sent for as an additional diver. He found the first man firmly wedged, with his head, arms and breast weights hanging over the inboard side of the inside dagger planks, his trunk and legs between the inner and outer planks. Mr. Duffin squeezed himself between the two planks while the stand-by diver released the two 10-inch screws joining the end of the plank. By this means the portion of plank imprisoning the trapped man was removed. Mr. Duffin then took hold of the man and forced him down between his own body and the poppets towards the stand-by diver, who dragged him down and then took him up to the surface.

DUNCAN
108

Charles Alfred
Rank/Title: Private
Unit/Force/Occupation: Parachute Regiment
Other Decorations: —
Date of Gazette: 9 Nov. 1943
Place/Date of Birth: Bexhill-on-Sea, Sussex — 13 Apr. 1908
Place/Date of Death: Near M'Saken, North Africa — 10 Jul. 1943
Place of Memorial: Enfidaville War Cemetery, Tunisia
Town/County Connections: Bexhill-on-Sea, Sussex
Remarks: —

Account of Deed: On 10th July 1943, Private Duncan was serving at M'Saken in North Africa when a live grenade fell amongst a group of his comrades. Realising that it was on the point of exploding, he threw himself over it and gave his life to save theirs.

DUPPA-MILLER, John Bryan Peter — see **MILLER,** John Bryan Peter Duppa-

DURRANI
109

Mahmood Khan
Rank/Title: Captain (later Lieutenant Colonel)
Unit/Force/Occupation: 1st Bahawalpur Infantry, Indian State Forces
Other Decorations: —
Date of Gazette: 23 May 1946
Place/Date of Birth: — 1 Jul. 1914
Place/Date of Death: —
Place of Memorial: —
Town/County Connections: —
Remarks: —

Account of Deed: During the withdrawal in Malaya in 1942 Captain Durrani was cut off with a small party and succeeded in remaining free in hiding for three months, when he was betrayed to the Indian Nationalist Army and was sent to a Japanese Prisoner of War Camp. He refused to become a member of the Japanese-sponsored Indian Nationalist Army and took active steps to thwart Japanese efforts to infiltrate members of that organisation into India. In fact he conceived the idea of founding a school to send Muslim agents into India to oppose the ideas the Japanese were trying to put across. To start with his efforts were successful, but in May 1944 the Japanese arrested him and he was subjected to every form of torture in an effort to find out his accomplices in the scheme. As this produced no result he was handed over to the Indian Nationalist Army where he was again tortured and even condemned to death, but he still refused to give any information. The end of the war brought his liberation, but his health was affected for many years.

EASTMAN 110

William Marsden
Rank/Title: Lieutenant (later Brigadier)
Unit/Force/Occupation: Royal Army Ordnance Corps
Other Decorations: —
Date of Gazette: 24 Dec. 1940
Place/Date of Birth: — 26 Oct. 1911
Place/Date of Death: Malta, GC — 8 Apr. 1980
Place of Memorial: —
Town/County Connections: —
Remarks: Commandant, RAOC Training Centre, Blackdown, Hampshire until 1966.

Account of Deed: Lieutenant Eastman was posted to Malta in March 1940 only a few months before Italy entered the war. At this time no expert Royal Engineer Bomb Disposal units had been formed and the job of attending to unexploded bombs and mines dropped on the island (with the exception of those dropped in the dockyard area and on the airfields, which were dealt with by the Royal Navy and the Royal Air Force) fell to the Royal Army Ordnance Corps. Between mid-June and mid-November 1940, when bomb disposal was taken over by the Royal Engineers, Lieutenant Eastman and Captain Jephson-Jones*, with incredible courage, dealt with some 275 unexploded bombs, and remained alive. (*See also entry for JONES, R.L. JEPHSON-)

EASTON 111

Jack Maynard Cholmondeley
Rank/Title: T/Sub-Lieutenant (later Lieutenant)
Unit/Force/Occupation: Royal Naval Volunteer Reserve
Other Decorations: —
Date of Gazette: 23 Jan. 1941
Place/Date of Birth: — 28 May 1906
Place/Date of Death: —
Place of Memorial: —
Town/County Connections: London
Remarks: —

Account of Deed: On 17th October 1940 Sub-Lieutenant Easton was called to deal with an unexploded bomb in Hoxton in the East End of London. The whole area had been evacuated and he and an able seaman* set off down the empty street with its slate-littered pavement to the house where the mine had crashed through the roof and was hanging suspended through a hole in the ceiling, its nose within six inches of the floor. Sub-Lieutenant Easton told the rating to stay in the passage outside the room and pass him whatever tools he needed, but they had only been working for about a minute when the bomb slipped, there was a sound of falling brickwork as the chimney pot overhead collapsed and twelve seconds later the bomb exploded. Sub-Lieutenant Easton shouted to the rating to run for safety and then ran himself, reaching a surface air-raid shelter just as the explosion occurred. When he recovered consciousness he was buried deep beneath bricks and mortar and his back was broken. He was dug out eventually and spent a year in plaster before continuing his service in command of a minesweeper. The rating was killed by the blast of the mine which destroyed six complete streets. (*See also entry for SOUTHWELL, B.)

EDWARDS 112

Arthur Frederick
Rank/Title: A/Bombardier
Unit/Force/Occupation: Royal Field Artillery
Other Decorations: —
Date of Gazette: 22 Jan. 1918
Place/Date of Birth: — 28 May 1895
Place/Date of Death: Henley-on-Thames, Oxfordshire — 28 May 1984
Place of Memorial: —
Town/County Connections: Henley-on-Thames, Oxfordshire
Remarks: (EM)

Account of Deed: Bombardier Edwards was one of 5 military personnel who were awarded the Edward Medal on account of their gallant action on the occasion of an explosion which occurred at the powder mill, Faversham, Kent on 2nd April 1916, when 172 people were killed. Wartime security precluded the publication of a detailed citation. (See also entry for HARRIS, C.T.)

ELLINGWORTH

Reginald Vincent
Rank/Title:　Chief Petty Officer
Unit/Force/Occupation:　Royal Navy
Other Decorations:　—
Date of Gazette:　20 Dec. 1940
Place/Date of Birth:　Wolverhampton, Staffordshire — 28 Jan. 1898
Place/Date of Death:　Dagenham, Essex — 21 Sep. 1940
Place of Memorial:　Milton Cemetery, Portsmouth, Hampshire
Town/County Connections:　Hilsea, Portsmouth, Hampshire
Remarks:　—

Account of Deed:　Chief Petty Officer Ellingworth worked as assistant to Lieutenant Commander Ryan* in rendering safe magnetic mines. They worked on many assignments together, sharing the dangers involved. The principal hazard of these mines was the fact that the clock of the bomb fuse was normally timed to explode the mine about 22 seconds after its fall. If it failed to do so, it could be re-started by the slightest movement, even a footfall. The amount of the clock already run off could not be known, and once it was re-started the time for escape could not be more than a few seconds. At Dagenham, Essex, the two men tackled such a mine hanging by a parachute in a warehouse, and were both killed by its explosion. Chief Petty Officer Ellingworth had previously been commended by HMS *Vernon* for his work on mines. (*See also entry for RYAN, R.J.H.)

ELLIS

Bernard George
Rank/Title:　Lieutenant
Unit/Force/Occupation:　The Buffs (East Kent Regiment)
Other Decorations:　—
Date of Gazette:　18 Jul. 1919
Place/Date of Birth:　Surbiton, Surrey — 21 Nov. 1890
Place/Date of Death:　Letchworth, Hertfordshire — 1 Jul. 1979
Place of Memorial:　—
Town/County Connections:　Purley, Surrey; Letchworth, Hertfordshire
Remarks:　(AM)

Account of Deed:　On 21st August 1918 Lieutenant Ellis was with a party at Shahaban, in Mesopotamia, under instruction in the firing of rifle grenades. A volley was fired, but one of the grenades, owing to a defective cartridge, did not leave the rifle, but fell back into the barrel with the fuse burning. The firer lost his head and dropped the rifle and grenade in the trench, but Lieutenant Ellis, who was separated from the man by four other men in a narrow trench, at once forced his way past them and seized the rifle. Failing to extract the grenade, he dropped the rifle and placed his steel helmet over the grenade, which at once exploded, severely injuring him. There can be no doubt that his prompt and courageous action greatly minimized the force of the explosion.

ELSTON

Ernest Matthew
Rank/Title:　Private
Unit/Force/Occupation:　1st Bn. The West Yorkshire Regiment
Other Decorations:　—
Date of Gazette:　19 Nov. 1935
Place/Date of Birth:　Kingston-upon-Hull, Yorkshire — 17 Dec. 1908
Place/Date of Death:　Kingston-upon-Hull, Yorkshire — 8 Aug. 1982
Place of Memorial:　—
Town/County Connections:　Kingston-upon-Hull, Yorkshire
Remarks:　(EGM); served in Second World War.

Account of Deed:　At the time of the earthquake at Quetta, India (31st May/1st June 1935) Private Elston worked with untiring energy at rescue work in the days immediately following the 'quake and in salvage operations afterwards. He was personally responsible for saving the lives of several Indians buried under the debris and worked at great risk for over four hours to rescue an Indian child entombed alive under a collapsed double-storey building. He had heard the child crying and in order to reach it he had to tunnel his way beneath some very unsafe wreckage. In doing so he came across the dead bodies of several other members of the family, but found the child still living and brought it up safely and unscathed.

EMANUEL

116

Errol John
Rank/Title: Mr.
Unit/Force/Occupation: District Commissioner, Papua
Other Decorations: —
Date of Gazette: 1 Feb. 1972
Place/Date of Birth: — 13 Dec. 1918
Place/Date of Death: Gazelle Peninsula, New Guinea — 19 Aug. 1971
Place of Memorial: —
Town/County Connections: —
Remarks: —

Account of Deed: Mr. Emanuel was posted to Rabaul, East New Britain, in July 1969 on special duties, with the object of bringing mutual understanding and peace to deeply hostile indigenous groups, and restoring in the Gazelle Peninsula a system of local government. He was appointed District Commissioner for the East New Britain District in March 1971, continuing to give priority to the special task for which he was originally posted to the area. He visited villages at all times of day and night, almost always alone, deliberately leaving the cover of police protection, in order to talk to leaders of all factions to gain their confidence and trust. He moved among dissidents trying to pacify them and was frequently able to avert bloodshed and loss of life on both sides. He knew that he was risking his life every time he went alone into crowds such as these, but he chose to expose himself to danger rather than risk the lives of his fellow officers and the police. On 19th August 1971 he undertook the role of peaceful negotiator during a confrontation with a group of hostile people. Despite recent threats to his life and the fact that some of the Tolai people were in war paint, he left the protection of the police at the invitation of one of the group of dissidents and went alone down a bush track to try to quell the disturbance and prevent bloodshed. He was then attacked and killed.

ERRINGTON

117

Harry
Rank/Title: Mr.
Unit/Force/Occupation: Fireman, Auxiliary Fire Service
Other Decorations: —
Date of Gazette: 8 Aug. 1941
Place/Date of Birth: Westminster, London — 20 Aug. 1910
Place/Date of Death: —
Place of Memorial: —
Town/County Connections: London
Remarks: Treasurer, VC & GC Association, 1981-.

Account of Deed: On 17th September 1940 in London, Fireman Errington was in a basement used as a private air-raid shelter for Auxiliary Fire Service personnel to rest in, beneath a large three-storey garage. Just before midnight there was a direct hit on the building and all the floors caved in, killing about 20 people, including six firemen. Fireman Errington recovered consciousness to find a fierce fire sweeping the basement. He was running for the exit when he heard cries of pain and went back to find one of his comrades lying face down with his legs pinned under fallen debris. Although the heat was intense and his hands were burned, Mr. Errington got him out and helped him up the narrow back staircase which was partially choked with burning debris. On the way he saw another fireman lying unconscious, trapped by a large radiator, so, having got the first man safely out, he returned for the second and carried him up to safety too. They were all three taken to hospital and although badly burned, they recovered after two or three months and were able to return to duty.

EVANS

118

David Hywel
Rank/Title: Sub-Lieutenant (later Instructor-Commander)
Unit/Force/Occupation: Royal Naval Volunteer Reserve
Other Decorations: —
Date of Gazette: 31 Jan. 1919
Place/Date of Birth: — 28 May 1898
Place/Date of Death: Near Ripon, Yorkshire — 8 Dec. 1985
Place of Memorial: —
Town/County Connections: Galphay, Ripon, Yorkshire
Remarks: (AM); served in HMS *Trident* at Zeebrugge in 1918; served in Second World War; Secretary of the Albert Medal Association 1966-72. Member of VC & GC Association Executive Committee.

Account of Deed: On 16th September 1918 a serious explosion occurred amidships in HMS *Glatton* whilst lying in Dover Harbour. Fire broke out, the oil fuel burning furiously and spreading fore and aft. The foremost magazines were flooded, but it was not possible to get to the after magazine flooding positions. The explosion and fire cut off the after part of the ship causing a great many casualties, and the ship was in danger of blowing up at any moment. Sub-Lieutenant Evans, with another officer, a petty officer and an able seaman were in boats which were rescuing men who had been blown or had jumped overboard. They boarded HMS *Glatton*, entered the superstructure which was full of dense smoke and succeeded in rescuing seven or eight badly injured men from the messdeck, in addition to 15 whom they found and brought out from inside the superstructure. They continued in their rescue work until all hope of saving any more men was passed, and they were ordered to abandon ship. She was then sunk by torpedo as the fire was spreading and it was not possible to flood the after magazines.

FAIRCLOUGH
John
Rank/Title: Gunner
Unit/Force/Occupation: Royal Regiment of Artillery
Other Decorations: —
Date of Gazette: 8 May 1928
Place/Date of Birth: St. Helen's, Lancashire — 29 Oct. 1900
Place/Date of Death: St. Helen's, Lancashire — 12 Oct. 1984
Place of Memorial: —
Town/County Connections: St. Helen's, Lancashire
Remarks: (AM)

119

Account of Deed: On the night of 27th April 1927 a serious fire broke out in a petrol godown in Ambala. Three Indian boys had gone down to the godown in a lorry to get petrol and the naked light in the lantern they carried ignited the petrol vapour with which, in the hot weather, the building was filled and almost immediately the whole building was ablaze. On the outbreak of the fire the lorry driver departed and the boys were trapped in the burning building without help. Gunner Fairclough, who was walking nearby, at once went to their aid. In spite of the intense heat he went in three times to rescue the three boys, being severely burned in the process.

FAIRFAX
Frederick William
Rank/Title: Detective Constable (later Detective Sergeant)
Unit/Force/Occupation: Metropolitan Police Force
Other Decorations: —
Date of Gazette: 6 Jan. 1953
Place/Date of Birth: Westminster, London — 17 Jun. 1917
Place/Date of Death: —
Place of Memorial: —
Town/County Connections: Sherborne, Dorset
Remarks: —

120

Account of Deed: On the evening of 2nd November 1952 two armed youths were seen to climb over the side gate of a warehouse at Tamworth Road, Croydon and to reach the flat roof of the building about 22 feet above. The alarm was given and Detective Constable Fairfax, together with other police officers, went to the premises in a police van. One of the youths fired at the detective constable and wounded him in the right shoulder, but he did not give up the chase. Several more shots were fired at the police officers as they tried to corner the two men on the roof, and one of them was shot dead. Despite his wound Detective Constable Fairfax continued to lead the chase until both men were captured, and repeatedly risked death in so doing.

FARR
John Henry
Rank/Title: Mr.
Unit/Force/Occupation: Foundryman
Other Decorations: —
Date of Gazette: 26 Jul. 1940
Place/Date of Birth: Tonypandy, South Wales — 27 Apr. 1911
Place/Date of Death: — 24 Jan. 1973
Place of Memorial: —
Town/County Connections: Slough, Buckinghamshire
Remarks: (EGM)

121

Account of Deed: In the summer of 1940 an explosion occurred at a factory in Slough. In spite of the grave danger due to molten metal and the risk of electrocution from the loose high tension cables, Mr. Farr, a foundryman at the factory, removed a colleague from the danger zone. With his brother he then returned to the factory and between them, working in complete darkness, they cleared two large furnaces each containing 1,000 lbs. of molten aluminium.

FARROW
Kenneth

Rank/Title: Police Constable (later Sergeant)
Unit/Force/Occupation: Cardiff City Police Force
Other Decorations: —
Date of Gazette: 15 Oct. 1948
Place/Date of Birth: — 29 May 1924
Place/Date of Death: —
Place of Memorial: —
Town/County Connections: Llandaff, Glamorgan, Wales
Remarks: (AM); awarded Carnegie Trust Fund Certificate; served in the Second World War as Sergeant Air Gunner in the RAF.

122

Account of Deed: On 21st June 1948 Constable Farrow was on patrol duty in Pembroke Terrace, Cardiff when he was told that a child had fallen into the Feeder — an aqueduct which supplies water from the river Taff to Cardiff, running under concrete slabs, but uncovered where the child fell in. Constable Farrow at once ran to the place, tore off his clothes and dived into the Feeder and swam underneath a long concrete covering for a distance of about 180 yards in search of the child. The speed of the current was about 6 miles an hour and whereas headroom at the end of the concrete covering was 2ft. 6ins. it decreased to only 6 ins. The water was black with a considerable amount of mud or silt at the bottom and it was not possible to stand up with head above water level. Although the child's body was not recovered until later, Constable Farrow, not a strong swimmer, exhausted himself in the search in appalling conditions and was, in fact, underneath the concrete slabs for about 15 minutes in pitch darkness.

FASSON
Francis Anthony Blair

Rank/Title: Lieutenant
Unit/Force/Occupation: Royal Navy
Other Decorations: —
Date of Gazette: 14 Sep. 1943
Place/Date of Birth: — 17 Jul. 1913
Place/Date of Death: Mediterranean (U-boat incident) — 30 Oct. 1942
Place of Memorial: Portsmouth Naval Memorial, Hampshire
Town/County Connections: Jedburgh, Roxburghshire, Scotland
Remarks: —

123

Account of Deed: On 30th October 1942 a German submarine was sunk by the Twelfth Destroyer Flotilla in the Mediterranean. The U-boat had been sighted on the surface by a British aircraft and after a lengthy search by the Destroyer Flotilla her approximate position was ascertained, depth charges were dropped and she was forced to the surface when she was immediately holed by gun fire from the destroyers. The crippled submarine at once surrendered and her crew was taken off. It was, however, important that the U-boat's papers and documents should be recovered so HMS *Petard* came alongside and Lieutenant Fasson, who had given valuable assistance in tracking down the submarine, boarded her, taking with him Able Seaman Grazier*. They were both fully aware that in the darkness, with the water rising rapidly in the sinking submarine, time was not on their side. They went on handing over instruments and papers until the submarine suddenly sank like a stone, taking them both to their death. (*See also entry for GRAZIER, C.)

FATTAH
Rashid Abdul

Rank/Title: Rais
Unit/Force/Occupation: Transjordan Frontier Force
Other Decorations: —
Date of Gazette: 12 Jul. 1938
Place/Date of Birth: Dunnaba, Tulkarm, Jordan — 1901
Place/Date of Death: — 21 Aug. 1975
Place of Memorial: —
Town/County Connections: —
Remarks: (EGM); served in First and Second World Wars.

124

Account of Deed: This officer, by exceptionally cool leadership, captured a village on 1st March 1938. Again on 4th March, by outstanding leadership, he seized a hill commanding another village. He had shown great gallantry on previous occasions when leading troops against armed bands.

FEETHAM 125

Christopher
Rank/Title: Mr.
Unit/Force/Occupation: Fireman, SS *Hornsey*
Other Decorations: —
Date of Gazette: 18 Mar. 1919
Place/Date of Birth: — 25 Dec. 1890
Place/Date of Death: Battersea, London — 2 Oct. 1976
Place of Memorial: —
Town/County Connections: Battersea, London
Remarks: (AM); he was involved in rescue operations after the Messina earthquake in 1908; served in the First World War (Merchant Navy) and helped in the building and installation of the Mulberry Harbour in 1944.

Account of Deed: On 10th November 1918 while the SS *Hornsey* was lying at Sunderland a fire broke out in the mess-room and adjoining saloon. A quantity of ammunition was on board, and there was accordingly a great risk, if it exploded, of loss of life and property as the effects of the explosion would probably have spread to the quay. The whole of the ship's company behaved admirably in their efforts to get the fire under control but Mr. Feetham's heroism was the decisive factor in extinguishing it and saving lives. He volunteered to be let down into the cabin and, standing waist-high in water, he was able to direct his hose on to that part of the fire which would have exploded the ammunition in a very short time — as it was, some of the ammunition cases were already scorched.

FISHER 126

Bernard
Rank/Title: Mr.
Unit/Force/Occupation: Jib crane driver, Messrs. Steel, Peech & Tozer, Ltd., Sheffield
Other Decorations: —
Date of Gazette: 15 Aug. 1939
Place/Date of Birth: — 14 Dec. 1911
Place/Date of Death: —
Place of Memorial: —
Town/County Connections: Rotherham, Yorkshire
Remarks: (EM)

Account of Deed: In the early morning of 26th April 1939 a fire broke out in the cabin of an electrically driven gantry crane running at a height of about 55 feet above the ground level in the Templeborough Steel Melting Shop of Messrs. Steel, Peech & Tozer Ltd. of Sheffield. The driver shouted and then lost consciousness. Mr. Fisher, who was the driver of a travelling jib crane in the same department, heard the shout and saw the fire. He promptly climbed from his own box and ascended the ladder to the crane track. He crossed the 80 foot span of the gantry and went down into the cabin, which by that time was blazing. He then carried the unconscious man through a trap door and up a vertical ladder for a distance of approximately 12 feet.

FLEMING 127

William George
Rank/Title: Mr.
Unit/Force/Occupation: Coxswain, Royal National Lifeboat Institution
Other Decorations: RNLI Gold Medal
Date of Gazette: 30 Jun. 1924
Place/Date of Birth: — 1865
Place/Date of Death: — Oct. 1955
Place of Memorial: Memorial plaque at Gorleston Lifeboat Station
Town/County Connections: Gorleston-on-Sea, Norfolk
Remarks: (EGM)

Account of Deed: Coxswain Fleming endeavoured to save the crew of 24 of the SS *Hopelyn* on 21st October 1922. After nearly 24 hours of effort in the Gorleston Lifeboat he put off in the Lowestoft Lifeboat and assisted in saving the crew in circumstances of great peril.

FLETCHER

Donald
Rank/Title: Mr.
Unit/Force/Occupation: Miner, Cresswell Colliery, Derbyshire
Other Decorations: —
Date of Gazette: 26 Jan. 1926
Place/Date of Birth: — 17 Jan. 1902
Place/Date of Death: Derby, Derbyshire — 22 Aug. 1986
Place of Memorial: —
Town/County Connections: Derby, Derbyshire
Remarks: (EM)

Account of Deed: On 10th September 1925 a heavy fall of roof to a depth of 16 feet took place at the Cresswell Colliery, completely burying a miner. Some of the larger pieces of the roof became interlocked, giving him some protection from the full weight of the fall and so prevented him being crushed to death. It was found possible to free the man's head from the debris and then his shoulders, but his body and legs were held fast. The only way in which rescue could be accomplished was for someone to crawl under the debris and by working a passage alongside and over the man, release him very gradually, stone by stone. Mr. Fletcher at once volunteered for this task and was successful after two hours' continuous work. Throughout the operation Mr. Fletcher was exposed to the risk of being crushed to death either by a second fall or by a settling down of the first.

FLINTOFF

Harwood Henry
Rank/Title: Mr.
Unit/Force/Occupation: 13-year-old schoolboy
Other Decorations: —
Date of Gazette: 8 Dec. 1944
Place/Date of Birth: — 3 Sep. 1930
Place/Date of Death: —
Place of Memorial: —
Town/County Connections: Kirkbymoorside, Yorkshire
Remarks: (EM)

Account of Deed: On 23rd June 1944 at Farndale, Yorkshire, a farmer was driving a bull which turned on him, knocked him down, and knelt on his chest. Henry Flintoff, who was working for the farmer in a neighbouring field, immediately ran to his aid. After a struggle with the savage bull, in which the farmer was injured, Henry, though unarmed, caught hold of the animal and he and the farmer managed to grasp the ring in the bull's nose and to hold on to it until they both became exhausted. The bull then broke loose but was caught and led to its shed by a farm labourer who came to their help with a pitchfork.

FORD

Albert
Rank/Title: Sergeant
Unit/Force/Occupation: The Royal Welch Fusiliers
Other Decorations: —
Date of Gazette: 21 Aug. 1917
Place/Date of Birth: Stoke-on-Trent, Staffordshire — 31 Mar. 1894
Place/Date of Death: Stoke-on-Trent — Jul. 1976
Place of Memorial: —
Town/County Connections: Stoke-on-Trent, Staffordshire
Remarks: (AM)

Account of Deed: On 30th May 1916 while a class of men was under instruction in bombing at Gorre in France, a member of the class hit with his bomb the traverse in front of him, so that the smoking bomb fell into the trench. The man immediately ran away, knocking down Sergeant Ford, the instructor. The latter jumped up, pushed past the man and managed to pick up the bomb and throw it clear of the trench; it exploded immediately it left his hand.

FORD

131

Douglas
Rank/Title: Captain
Unit/Force/Occupation: The Royal Scots
Other Decorations: —
Date of Gazette: 18 Apr. 1946
Place/Date of Birth: Galashiels, Selkirkshire — 18 Sep. 1918
Place/Date of Death: Sham Shui Po Prison Camp, Hong Kong — 18 Dec. 1943
Place of Memorial: Stanley Military Cemetery, Hong Kong
Town/County Connections: Edinburgh, Scotland
Remarks: —

Account of Deed: Captain Ford was taken prisoner at Hong Kong in December 1941 and whilst in captivity managed, with a number of other prisoners, to gain contact with British agents. They were arranging a scheme for a general break-out when, on 10th July 1943, he, Colonal Newnham* and several others were arrested. Captain Ford was interrogated, starved, tortured and finally sentenced to death in an endeavour to make him talk, but he refused to implicate his fellow prisoners and was executed on 18th December 1943. (*See also entry for NEWNHAM, L.A.)

FOSTER

132

William George
Rank/Title: Lieutenant
Unit/Force/Occupation: 7th Wiltshire (Salisbury) Bn., Home Guard
Other Decorations: MC, DCM
Date of Gazette: 27 Nov. 1942
Place/Date of Birth: at sea — 12 Dec. 1881
Place/Date of Death: Clarendon Park, Near Salisbury, Wiltshire — 13 Sep. 1942
Place of Memorial: St. Mary's Churchyard, Alderbury, near Salisbury, Wiltshire; memorial plaque in church
Town/County Connections: Alderbury, Wiltshire
Remarks: —

Account of Deed: On 13th September 1942 at Ashley Hill, Clarendon Park, near Salisbury, Wiltshire, Lieutenant Foster was instructing a group of recruits in the art of grenade throwing from a slit trench. One of the men threw a live grenade which instead of going over the top, hit the parapet, hung there for a brief moment, before, to the horror of all there, it rolled back into the trench and lay at their feet. Lieutenant Foster, realising that the fuse had at most only a second left to burn, threw himself upon it and was killed instantly when it exploded.

FOX

133

Leslie Owen
Rank/Title: Mr.
Unit/Force/Occupation: Deputy Party Leader, London County Council Heavy Rescue Service
Other Decorations: —
Date of Gazette: 20 Feb. 1945
Place/Date of Birth: — 4 Dec. 1904
Place/Date of Death: Fareham, Hampshire — 26 Dec. 1982
Place of Memorial: —
Town/County Connections: Fulham, London; Fareham, Hampshire
Remarks: —

Account of Deed: On 20th February 1944 the Heavy Rescue Service was called to an incident in Fulham where some houses had been destroyed by high explosive and incendiary bombs. Cries were heard from under the debris and Mr. Fox immediately began to tunnel his way through the blazing ruins. He had to be continually sprayed with water to lessen the intolerable heat from the flames and after two hours' work he found the casualty, but a wall collapsed blocking the tunnel he had made and he had to start again. After a further two hours' tunnelling Mr. Fox reached the injured man, who was trapped by his feet, and freed his head so that a doctor could give him restoratives and he was eventually brought to safety.

FRASER (later BARRY)   **134**
Harriet Elizabeth
Rank/Title: Miss (later Mrs.)
Unit/Force/Occupation: Staff Nurse, Territorial Force Nursing Service
Other Decorations: —
Date of Gazette: 31 Jan. 1919
Place/Date of Birth: — 1889
Place/Date of Death: Guildford, Surrey — 17 Jun. 1980
Place of Memorial: —
Town/County Connections: Guildford, Surrey
Remarks: (AM)

Account of Deed: Early in the morning of the 1st October 1918 a serious fire broke out in No. 36 Casualty Clearing Station at Rousbrugge, in Belgium. At the time some of the patients were undergoing serious operations in the abdominal and general operating theatres, the walls of which were composed of wood. The first intimation of danger in the theatres was the extinction of the electric light accompanied by volumes of smoke, and almost immediately the wooden walls burst into flames. The two Sisters and Staff Nurse Fraser helped to carry the unconscious patients to safety and then returned to the burning wards to help the other patients. During this time ether bottles and nitrous oxide cylinders were continually exploding, filling the air with fumes and flying fragments of steel.

FRASER   **135**
John Alexander
Rank/Title: Mr.
Unit/Force/Occupation: Assistant Attorney General, Colonial Service, Hong Kong, serving with British Army Aid Group
Other Decorations: MC & Bar
Date of Gazette: 29 Oct. 1946
Place/Date of Birth: Edinburgh, Scotland — 1897
Place/Date of Death: Hong Kong — 29 Oct. 1943
Place of Memorial: Stanley Military Cemetery, Hong Kong
Town/County Connections: Edinburgh, Scotland
Remarks: Served in the First World War in The Royal Scots Fusiliers.

Account of Deed: When the Japanese invaded Hong Kong in December 1941 Mr. Fraser was interned in the Civil Internment Camp in Stanley. He immediately started to organise escape plans and a clandestine wireless service for his fellow prisoners. Eventually he was arrested and subjected to prolonged torture by the Japanese to make him disclose the names of those who were working with him. His fortitude was such that it was even commented upon by the Japanese guards. He steadfastly refused to utter one word and, unable to break his spirit, the Japanese executed him.

FROST   **136**
Ernest Ralph Clyde
Rank/Title: Aircraftman First Class
Unit/Force/Occupation: 90 Bomber Squadron, Royal Air Force
Other Decorations: —
Date of Gazette: 5 Jul. 1940
Place/Date of Birth: Three Rivers, Quebec, Canada — 22 Jul. 1917
Place/Date of Death: Sarnia, Ontario, Canada — 28 Jul. 1969
Place of Memorial: —
Town/County Connections: —
Remarks: (EGM); became Chief Pilot of The Great Lakes Airlines.

Account of Deed: Aircraftman First Class Frost, together with another airman*, displayed great courage when two Blenheim aircraft collided whilst taking off from Upwood, Huntingdonshire on 12th March 1940. At great risk to themselves they managed to rescue the unconscious pilot of one of the aircraft from the burning wreckage. Shortly afterwards the tanks exploded and the whole aircraft was rapidly burnt out. Unfortunately the pilot died later. (*See also entry for CAMPION, M.P.)

GHULAM MOHI-ud-DIN

137

Rank/Title: Sub-Inspector
Unit/Force/Occupation: Punjab Police
Other Decorations: —
Date of Gazette: 3 Jun.1931
Place/Date of Birth: —
Place/Date of Death: Punjab, India — 1972
Place of Memorial: —
Town/County Connections: —
Remarks: (EGM)

Account of Deed: From the beginning of the civil disobedience campaign in the Punjab in 1930 Sub-Inspector Ghulam Mohi-ud-Din, an officer with the highest reputation for energy, courage and strength of character, was called upon to deal with many dangerous situations. On several occasions, while behaving with commendable restraint, he had to take grave decisions and he was never deterred from taking them when they appeared necessary to maintain law and order.

GIBBONS

138

John Edward
Rank/Title: T/Lieutenant (later Commander)
Unit/Force/Occupation: Royal Naval Volunteer Reserve
Other Decorations: DSC
Date of Gazette: 11 Aug. 1942
Place/Date of Birth: Burnham, Buckinghamshire — 26 Apr. 1905
Place/Date of Death: Johannesburg, South Africa — 12 Nov. 1971
Place of Memorial: —
Town/County Connections: —
Remarks: (AM)

Account of Deed: When a motor launch was mined in the English Channel her commanding officer, Lieutenant Gibbons, was wounded in the head, and blown into the sea. He was rescued and went at once to save others. He saw a seaman some 100 yards away in the water and swam to him through burning fuel. His gallant action helped to save the man's life.

GIBBS

139

Stanley Frederick
Rank/Title: Mr.
Unit/Force/Occupation: —
Other Decorations: —
Date of Gazette: 8 Feb. 1927
Place/Date of Birth: Sydney, New South Wales, Australia — 2 Jan. 1909
Place/Date of Death: —
Place of Memorial: —
Town/County Connections: —
Remarks: (AM)

Account of Deed: On 3rd January 1927 at Port Hacking, near Sydney, New South Wales, a youth was swimming near the shore when he was attacked by a large shark. Mr. Gibbs, who was standing on the nose of a launch ready to give help if necessary, saw the attacking shark. He dived from the launch and fought the shark with his hands and feet and eventually succeeded in getting the victim, who was very badly injured, away from the jaws of the shark and into a rowing boat.

GIBSON

140

Michael
Rank/Title: Sergeant
Unit/Force/Occupation: No. 9 Coy., Corps of Royal Engineers
Other Decorations: —
Date of Gazette: 22 Jan. 1941
Place/Date of Birth: — 1906
Place/Date of Death: Coventry, Warwickshire — 18 Oct. 1940
Place of Memorial: London Road Cemetery, Coventry
Town/County Connections: Chopwell, Newcastle-upon-Tyne, Northumberland
Remarks: —

Account of Deed: Sergeant Gibson was awarded a posthumous George Cross in recognition of his most conspicuous gallantry in carrying out hazardous work during the Coventry Blitz on 18th October 1940. He was killed while trying to defuse a bomb, and Second Lieutenant Campbell*, with whom he was working, was killed at the same time. (*See also entry for CAMPBELL, A.F.)

GIDDEN

Ernest Oliver
Rank/Title: T/Lieutenant (later Lieutenant-Commander)
Unit/Force/Occupation: Royal Naval Volunteer Reserve
Other Decorations: OBE, GM
Date of Gazette: 9 Jun. 1942
Place/Date of Birth: — 15 Mar. 1910
Place/Date of Death: London — 20 Dec. 1961
Place of Memorial: Cremated Golders Green, London
Town/County Connections: Neath, Glamorgan, Wales; Hampstead, London
Remarks: —

Account of Deed: On 17th April 1941 an unexploded mine dropped on Hungerford Bridge, London. Some trains and many sleepers were on fire and the Charing Cross Hotel was burning in the background. The underground trains had to be stopped and many buildings evacuated, including the War Office. Lieutenant Gidden arrived at the bridge shortly after dawn and found the mine lying across a live electric wire, with the bomb fuse primer release mechanism face downwards. The bomb had first to be turned over before the fuse, which was of the highly sensitive clockwork variety and likely to be detonated by any movement, could be tackled. At last Lieutenant Gidden managed to turn it over, prised a lump of molten metal from the surface of the fuse and tried to insert a gag to stop the mechanism. The gag would not fit properly owing to the molten metal, and Lieutenant Gidden had to work at it with a hammer and chisel. This operation took six hours.

GILLETT

Ivor John
Rank/Title: Aircraftman First Class
Unit/Force/Occupation: Royal Air Force
Other Decorations: —
Date of Gazette: 3 Oct. 1950
Place/Date of Birth: — 16 Sep. 1928
Place/Date of Death: Seletar, Singapore — 26 Mar. 1950
Place of Memorial: —
Town/County Connections: Marlborough, Wiltshire; Cheltenham and Gloucester, Gloucestershire
Remarks: —

Account of Deed: On 26th March 1950 a Sunderland Flying Boat blew up at its moorings at Far East Flying Boat Wing, Seletar, Singapore. Aircraftman First Class Gillett was a member of the ground crew on board, and when the survivors from the explosion were flung into the water, a life belt was thrown to AC1 Gillett from a rescue launch which was quickly on the spot. He was suffering from blast and superficial injuries but, seeing a seriously injured corporal nearby in danger of drowning, gave him his life belt. He himself was drowned.

GIMBERT

Benjamin
Rank/Title: Mr.
Unit/Force/Occupation: Driver, London & North Eastern Railway
Other Decorations: LNER Silver Medal for courage and resource, Order of Industrial Heroism
Date of Gazette: 25 Jul. 1944
Place/Date of Birth: Ely, Cambridgeshire — 1903
Place/Date of Death: March, Cambridgeshire — 6 May 1976
Place of Memorial: Buried in churchyard of St. John the Evangelist, March; plaque formerly at Soham station now in Soham Village College; old people's bungalows named after him in March; Gimbert Cup given annually at Soham Village College; locomotive named after him
Town/County Connections: March, Cambridgeshire
Remarks: —

Account of Deed: In the early hours of 2nd June 1944 an ammunition train of 51 trucks, filled with unfused bombs destined for the American Air Force bases in East Anglia, was approaching Soham station in Cambridgeshire. Suddenly Mr. Gimbert, the engine driver, saw that the wagon next to the engine, containing forty 500lb. bombs, was on fire. He at once began to apply the steam brake very gradually, so as not to precipitate an explosion, and sounded two blasts on the engine whistle to give the fire warning to the guard and the signalman. When the train finally came to a halt just outside Soham station, the fireman* jumped down, ran back to the burning wagon and attacked the coupling with a hammer. Within a minute he had uncoupled the truck and raced back to the footplate. Mr. Gimbert then gently urged the engine into motion, slowly pulling the burning truck away from the rest of the train. As they approached the signal box, he leant out of the cab to shout to the signalman to stop the mail train which was almost due. At that moment the bombs in the blazing wagon exploded. A massive crater some 20 feet deep and 60 feet wide was blown in the middle of the railway track and all the buildings of Soham station were virtually obliterated. The station hotel was wrecked and 600 other buildings damaged. The fireman was killed and the signalman died of his injuries, but Mr. Gimbert, although blown sky-high, was not killed; thirty two pieces of metal were removed from his body during his stay in hospital. (*See also entry for NIGHTALL, J.W.)

GLEDHILL 144
Anthony John
Rank/Title: Police Constable (later Detective Sergeant)
Unit/Force/Occupation: Metropolitan Police Force
Other Decorations: —
Date of Gazette: 23 May 1967
Place/Date of Birth: Doncaster, Yorkshire — 10 Mar. 1938
Place/Date of Death: —
Place of Memorial: —
Town/County Connections: Deptford, London; Bromley, Kent
Remarks: —

Account of Deed: On 25th August 1966 Constable Gledhill and another police officer were on patrol in a police car in Deptford when they were sent after a car, containing five men, being driven recklessly against the one-way traffic. During a chase of five miles at speeds of up to 80 miles an hour, 15 shots were fired at the police car by the occupants of the bandit vehicle, who were using a sawn-off shot gun and a revolver. The escaping car crashed into a lorry and the five men abandoned it. A running fight ensued, in which the unarmed police officers bravely closed with the bandits, hung on to them and eventually overpowered one of the gunmen and held him until help arrived. Both Constable Gledhill and the other officer were injured and had to receive hospital treatment.

GOAD 145
Roger Philip
Rank/Title: Captain
Unit/Force/Occupation: Explosives Officer, Metropolitan Police
Other Decorations: BEM
Date of Gazette: 1 Oct. 1976
Place/Date of Birth: — 1935
Place/Date of Death: London — 29 Aug. 1975
Place of Memorial: —
Town/County Connections: Basingstoke, Hampshire
Remarks: —

Account of Deed: On 29th August 1975 a telephone call was made to the office of a national newspaper stating that a bomb had been left in a shop doorway. The police were informed and went to investigate. They found a plastic bag and on examining it found a pocket watch fixed to the top of the contents by adhesive tape. As it was almost certainly a bomb the street was taped off and occupants of surrounding buildings were warned to keep clear. Captain Goad arrived to deal with this device and, having been briefed by a senior police officer, approached the shop doorway alone. He was seen to bend over the bomb and was in the process of defusing it when it exploded, killing him instantly.

GOAD 146
William
Rank/Title: A/Leading Seaman (later Chief Petty Officer)
Unit/Force/Occupation: Royal Navy
Other Decorations: —
Date of Gazette: 26 Jan. 1943
Place/Date of Birth: — 10 May 1922
Place/Date of Death: —
Place of Memorial: Goad Avenue, Daget's Wood, Chatham, Kent named after him
Town/County Connections: Stretham, Ely, Cambridgeshire
Remarks: (AM); served in Korean waters before retiring in 1953.

Account of Deed: In 1942 while serving in HMS *Ashanti* Leading Seaman Goad went over his ship's side on a line, in water well below freezing point, and rescued an unconscious man. It was blowing a full gale and there was a very great risk that he would either be washed away by the breaking seas, or swept under the bilge keel of his ship, which was rolling heavily.

GOLANDAZ

147

Abdus Samid Abdul Wahid
Rank/Title: Mr.
Unit/Force/Occupation: Landlord, property owner and sand contractor
Other Decorations: —
Date of Gazette: 4 Jun. 1934
Place/Date of Birth: —
Place/Date of Death: — 1949
Place of Memorial: —
Town/County Connections: —
Remarks: (EGM)

Account of Deed: On 16th September 1933 the Tapti River in India had swollen to such proportions that one of the sluices in the Bombay city wall had been damaged and water was pouring in through it, threatening to flood the city. Mr. Golandaz owned a fleet of boats and trained boatmen which he placed at the disposal of the authorities whenever floods threatened. Frequently in the past he had risked his life in leading his men to works of rescue and on this occasion he volunteered to dive into the flooded river and, having found the nature and extent of the damage, blocked the sluice with sand-bags at considerable risk to his own life. In 1930 he had rescued boys of the Government High School and the family of the Excise Inspector whose bungalows had been completely cut off by floods.

GOLDSWORTHY

148

Leon Verdi
Rank/Title: T/Lieutenant (later Lieutenant-Commander)
Unit/Force/Occupation: Royal Australian Naval Volunteer Reserve
Other Decorations: DSC, GM
Date of Gazette: 19 Sep. 1944
Place/Date of Birth: Broken Hill, New South Wales, Australia — 19 Jan. 1909
Place/Date of Death: —
Place of Memorial: —
Town/County Connections: —
Remarks: —

Account of Deed: Lieutenant Goldsworthy was an expert in mine disposal and was awarded the George Cross for skill and courage of a high order during a series of underwater mine recoveries extending from June 1943 to April 1944. These included four German ground mines, three magnetic mines and one acoustic mine. On one of these occasions (13th August 1943) he made safe a German ground mine off Sheerness. It was only the second time that such a weapon had been rendered safe under water, and it was regarded as a particularly hazardous assignment for the diver, who had no means of escape should the fuse operate. Again, on 10th April 1944, Lieutenant Goldsworthy dealt with an especially dangerous acoustic mine near Milford Haven, successfully extracting the fuse and primer and later removing the whole mine intact.

GOODMAN

149

George Herbert
Rank/Title: T/Lieutenant (later Lieutenant-Commander)
Unit/Force/Occupation: Royal Naval Volunteer Reserve
Other Decorations: MBE
Date of Gazette: 15 Sep. 1942
Place/Date of Birth: Bromsgrove, Worcestershire — 25 Nov. 1900
Place/Date of Death: Near Rotterdam, Netherlands — 31 May 1945
Place of Memorial: Westduin General Cemetery, The Hague, The Netherlands
Town/County Connections: Harborne, Birmingham
Remarks: —

Account of Deed: On 15th January 1942 Lieutenant Goodman rendered safe and stripped the only Italian self-destroying surface torpedo which had been recovered on the North African coast, by removing three detonating pistols and separating the strikers from the detonators and primers. A similar weapon had killed the Torpedo Officer of HMS *Medway* and other members of his party only a few days before. On 24th December 1941 Lieutenant Goodman had also rendered safe and stripped the first 'Sammy' mine recovered in the eastern Mediterranean.

GOSSE

150

George
Rank/Title: Lieutenant (later Lieutenant-Commander)
Unit/Force/Occupation: Royal Australian Naval Volunteer Reserve
Other Decorations: —
Date of Gazette: 30 Apr. 1946
Place/Date of Birth: Harvey, Western Australia — 16 Feb. 1912
Place/Date of Death: — 31 Dec. 1965
Place of Memorial: —
Town/County Connections: —
Remarks: Appointed Lieutenant-Commander (Special Branch) of the Citizen Naval Forces (RANR), 1955.

Account of Deed: On 8th May 1945, divers searching Ubersee Hafen Bremen reported the presence of a mine which appeared to be of an entirely new type. Lieutenant Gosse immediately dived and verified that it was a GD pressure type which was commonly known as 'Oyster'. As it was necessary to recover the mine intact, it was decided to attempt first to render it safe under water. The following day therefore, Lieutenant Gosse succeeded in removing the primer which was followed by a loud metallic crash — if he had attempted to remove the fuse mechanism first in the ordinary way, or if any attempt had been made to raise the mine without first making it safe, it would have exploded. The mine was eventually lifted on to the quayside where it was thoroughly examined. During the subsequent ten days Lieutenant Gosse rendered safe two similar mines which were lying in close proximity to shipping and in each case the detonator fired immediately the primer had been removed and before the mine reached the surface. The form of operation conducted by Lieutenant Gosse called for an exceptionally high standard of personal courage and a very high degree of skill.

GOUGH

151

John Ingram
Rank/Title: Mr.
Unit/Force/Occupation: Miner, Bretby Colliery, Burton-on-Trent, Staffordshire
Other Decorations: —
Date of Gazette: 17 Jun. 1930
Place/Date of Birth: Swadlincote, Derbyshire — 14 Apr. 1898
Place/Date of Death: — 23 Mar. 1977
Place of Memorial: —
Town/County Connections: Bretby, Burton-on-Trent, Staffordshire
Remarks: (EM)

Account of Deed: On 11th September 1929 two men were trapped at the Bretby Colliery when about 10 tons of roof fell and buried them. While a team of rescuers worked to release one of the trapped men, Mr. Gough, with others, at great personal risk removed the fallen coal from the second man's head and shoulders and managed to place some covering timber over his body, which undoubtedly saved his life when a second large fall occurred. During these operations the rescuers were several times compelled to take shelter from the falling material and it was only after two hours of exceedingly dangerous work that they succeeded in rescuing one man alive and recovering the body of the other.

GRAVELEY

152

Reginald Cubitt
Rank/Title: Flying Officer (later Squadron Leader)
Unit/Force/Occupation: 88 Squadron, Royal Air Force
Other Decorations: —
Date of Gazette: 11 Nov. 1939
Place/Date of Birth: Leyton, London — Mar. 1914
Place/Date of Death: — 16 Sep. 1961
Place of Memorial: —
Town/County Connections: Birmingham
Remarks: (EGM)

Account of Deed: In September 1939 the aircraft in which Flying Officer Graveley was the pilot, crashed in flames. With total disregard for his own safety and though badly burned, he pulled his wounded observer from the wreckage and then returned to rescue the air gunner. Unfortunately he found that the man was dead, and was unable to lift his body from the cockpit.

GRAVELL

153

Karl Mander
Rank/Title: Leading Aircraftman
Unit/Force/Occupation: Royal Canadian Air Force
Other Decorations: —
Date of Gazette: 11 Jun. 1942
Place/Date of Birth: Norrköping, Sweden — 27 Sep. 1922
Place/Date of Death: Calgary, Alberta, Canada — 10 Nov. 1941
Place of Memorial: Mountain View Cemetery, Vancouver, Canada
Town/County Connections: —
Remarks: —

Account of Deed: Leading Aircraftman Gravell was under training at the Canadian Wireless School in Calgary in November 1941, when his training aircraft crashed and burst into flames. He managed to extricate himself from the wreckage and get clear, but in spite of the intense shock he had suffered, the loss of one eye and severe burns all over his body, his only thought was for the safety of his pilot. He tried to get back into the aircraft to pull him out, but a mass of flames engulfed him and forced him back. He subsequently died of his burns.

GRAY

154

Hector Bertram
Rank/Title: Flight Lieutenant
Unit/Force/Occupation: Royal Air Force
Other Decorations: AFM
Date of Gazette: 19 Apr. 1946
Place/Date of Birth: Gillingham, Kent — 6 Jun. 1911
Place/Date of Death: Sham Shui Po Prison Camp, Hong Kong — 18 Dec. 1943
Place of Memorial: Stanley Military Cemetery, Hong Kong
Town/County Connections: West Hampstead and Kilburn, London; Felixstowe, Suffolk
Remarks: —

Account of Deed: Flight Lieutenant Gray was taken prisoner in Hong Kong in December 1941 and while in captivity he did all he could to sustain the morale of his fellow prisoners. He smuggled much-needed drugs into the camp and distributed them to those who were seriously ill, and he also ran a news service on information he received from people outside the camp. He was tortured continually over a period of nearly six months to make him divulge the names of his informants, but he disclosed nothing, and was finally executed by the Japanese.

GRAY

155

Roderick Borden
Rank/Title: Flying Officer
Unit/Force/Occupation: Royal Canadian Air Force
Other Decorations: —
Date of Gazette: 13 Mar. 1945
Place/Date of Birth: Sault Ste. Marie, Ontario, Canada — 2 Oct. 1917
Place/Date of Death: Atlantic Ocean — 27 Aug. 1944
Place of Memorial: The Runnymede Memorial, Surrey
Town/County Connections: —
Remarks: —

Account of Deed: In August 1944, a Wellington bomber was shot down in the Atlantic by a German U-boat. Flying Officer Gray, the navigator, and three other members of the crew extricated themselves from the aircraft and despite a very severe wound in the leg, Flying Officer Gray managed to inflate his own dinghy and help his Captain, who had also been wounded, into it. Shortly afterwards cries were heard from another member of the crew, who had a broken arm. Flying Officer Gray helped him into the dinghy too, but knowing that it could hold no more people, and although in intense pain, he refused to get into it himself. He held on to the side for some hours, but eventually lost consciousness and died.

GRAZIER

156

Colin
Rank/Title: Able Seaman
Unit/Force/Occupation: Royal Navy
Other Decorations: —
Date of Gazette: 14 Sep. 1943
Place/Date of Birth: Two Gates, Tamworth, Staffordshire — 7 May 1920
Place/Date of Death: Mediterranean (U-boat incident) — 30 Oct. 1942
Place of Memorial: Portsmouth Naval Memorial, Hampshire
Town/County Connections: Two Gates, Tamworth, Staffordshire
Remarks: —

Account of Deed: On 30th October 1942 a German submarine was sunk by the Twelfth Destroyer Flotilla in the Mediterranean. The U-boat had been sighted on the surface by a British aircraft and after a lengthy search by the Destroyer Flotilla her approximate position was ascertained, depth charges were dropped and she was forced to the surface when she was immediately holed by gun fire from the destroyers. The crippled submarine at once surrendered and her crew taken off. It was, however, important that the U-boat's papers and documents should be recovered, so HMS *Petard* came alongside and Lieutenant Fasson*, who had given valuable assistance in tracking down the submarine, boarded her, taking with him Able Seaman Grazier. They were both fully aware that in the darkness, with the water rising rapidly in the sinking submarine, time was not on their side. They went on handing over instruments and papers until the submarine suddenly sank like a stone, taking them both to their death. (*See also entry for FASSON, F.A.B.)

GREEN

157

Charles William TANDY—
Rank/Title: Mr. (later Lieutenant Colonel)
Unit/Force/Occupation: Superintendent Engineer, Bengal Public Works Department
Other Decorations: —
Date of Gazette: 19 Jun. 1934
Place/Date of Birth: Denmead, Hampshire — 21 May 1887
Place/Date of Death: Denmead, Hampshire — 26 Sep. 1978
Place of Memorial: —
Town/County Connections: Denmead, Hampshire; Gerrards Cross, Buckinghamshire
Remarks: (EGM); served in First and Second World Wars.

Account of Deed: On 8th May 1934 at Lebong Racecourse, Darjeeling, while the horses were being led in after the race for the Governor's Cup, an attempt was made by two Bengali youths to assassinate Sir John Anderson, the Governor of Bengal. Sir John was standing in his box facing the course; Mr. Tandy-Green was on the judge's stand; he was steward and starter at the race-meeting. Hearing a shot he looked round and saw a man pointing a pistol at the Governor. He rushed at him and brought him down and they rolled together to the bottom of the steps where Mr. Tandy-Green pinned the assailant to the ground and held him until others came to his assistance.(See also entry for BHUPENDRA NARAYAN SINGH)

GREGSON

158

John Sedgwick
Rank/Title: Mr.
Unit/Force/Occupation: Apprentice, Merchant Navy
Other Decorations: Lloyd's War Medal for Bravery at Sea
Date of Gazette: 2 Feb. 1943
Place/Date of Birth: Bombay, India — 4 Jan. 1924
Place/Date of Death: —
Place of Memorial: —
Town/County Connections: —
Remarks: (AM); went to New Zealand in 1952, pilot with Bay of Plenty Harbour Board, then returned to sea-going duties as navigating officer with Union Steamship Co. of New Zealand Ltd.

Account of Deed: On 12th August 1941, near Malta the MV *Deucalian* was set on fire by the explosion of a torpedo during an attack by enemy aircraft. The flames spread rapidly and almost immediately orders were given to abandon ship. One of the ship's gunners, however, was pinned under a raft. Apprentice Gregson at once went to his assistance and, with help, freed him. The gunner was very badly injured and as it was impossible to get him into a boat or on to a raft he was dropped overboard. Apprentice Gregson dived into the sea after him, and, in the darkness, towed his helpless shipmate to a ship which picked them up, a distance of about 600 yards. But for Apprentice Gregson's gallant and determined action, undertaken with complete disregard for his personal safety, the injured man would have had little chance of survival.

GUERISSE, Albert Marie Edmond — see **O'LEARY,** Patrick Albert

HALLER
159

Fred
Rank/Title: Mr.
Unit/Force/Occupation: Deputy, Rossington Main Colliery, Yorkshire
Other Decorations: BEM
Date of Gazette: 20 Jan. 1939
Place/Date of Birth: Rossington, near Doncaster, Yorkshire — 29 Mar. 1892
Place/Date of Death: — 17 Sep. 1983
Place of Memorial: —
Town/County Connections: Doncaster, Yorkshire
Remarks: (EM); served in the First World War.

Account of Deed: On 8th October 1938 at about 1.30am a driver employed by contractors engaged in enlarging the road near an abandoned heading in Rossington Main Colliery was missed. The heading itself had been pronounced dangerous on account of gas, but it was assumed that the driver had entered the heading for some reason and got into difficulties, so Mr. Haller and another deputy went to his aid. A compressed air hose had been turned on, but was too short, by two yards. Mr. Haller sent for more hosepipe and, taking a singlet saturated with water, went to rescue the man who was some 40 yards beyond the fence shutting off the heading. He found the driver unconscious and with great effort succeeded in dragging him up to the fence. It was some hours before the man recovered complete consciousness.

HALLOWES, Odette Marie Céline — see **SANSOM,** Odette Marie Céline

HAND
160

William George
Rank/Title: Sergeant
Unit/Force/Occupation: 2nd Bn., The Dorset Regiment
Other Decorations: MM
Date of Gazette: 2 June 1923
Place/Date of Birth: Nunton, Wiltshire — 17 Oct. 1896
Place/Date of Death: Nottingham — 28 Oct. 1961
Place of Memorial: —
Town/County Connections: Salisbury, Wiltshire; Nottingham, Nottinghamshire
Remarks: (EGM); after discharge from the army, joined the War Department Constabulary and became an Inspector; served in Second World War.

Account of Deed: Sergeant Hand showed great courage on 24th September 1921 near Nilambur, Malabar, India, when the advanced guard of the column was ambushed. Whilst subjected to close fire at about 15 yards range, Sergeant Hand successfully bombed the enemy and by his coolness and initiative, with Private Miller*, materially assisted in clearing up the situation. (*See also entry for MILLER, T.F.)

HARDY
161

Benjamin Gower
Rank/Title: Private
Unit/Force/Occupation: 22nd Garrison Bn., Australian Military Forces
Other Decorations: —
Date of Gazette: 1 Sep. 1950
Place/Date of Birth: Marrickville, New South Wales, Australia — 28 Aug. 1898
Place/Date of Death: Prisoner of War Camp, Cowra, New South Wales — 5 Aug. 1944
Place of Memorial: Cowra War Cemetery, New South Wales, Australia
Town/County Connections: —
Remarks: —

Account of Deed: In the early hours of 5th August 1944 there was a break-out at No. 12 Japanese Prisoner of War Camp at Cowra, New South Wales. The mass of Japanese, armed with every sort of home-made improvised weapon, stormed out of their huts, which they set on fire. The garrison sprang into action and Privates Hardy and Jones* at once manned their Vickers machine guns, covering the eastern perimeter wire. The Japanese bore down on them, but the two Australians stood their ground and kept firing until they were bashed to death. Their gallant stand gained for the other defence posts just a few minutes of invaluable time and the Japanese, who had overrun their gun and were bringing it into action, were mown down by fire from another Vickers. The greater number of the surviving Japanese were pinned down in a large drain and surrendered at daylight and in the days that followed many who had escaped were rounded up or committed suicide. (*See also entry for JONES, R.)

HARRIS   162
Charles Thomas
Rank/Title: A/Sergeant
Unit/Force/Occupation: Corps of Royal Engineers
Other Decorations: —
Date of Gazette: 22 Jan. 1918
Place/Date of Birth: —
Place/Date of Death: Gillingham, Kent — 28 Jan. 1972
Place of Memorial: —
Town/County Connections: Gillingham, Kent
Remarks: (EM)

Account of Deed: Sergeant Harris was one of 5 military personnel who were awarded the Edward Medal on account of their gallant action on the occasion of an explosion which occurred at the powder mill, Faversham, Kent on 2nd April 1916 when 172 people were killed. Wartime security precluded the publication of a detailed citation. (See also entry for EDWARDS, A.F.)

HARRIS   163
Roy Thomas
Rank/Title: Mr.
Unit/Force/Occupation: ARP Engineers Service, Croydon
Other Decorations: —
Date of Gazette: 17 Dec. 1940
Place/Date of Birth: — 1 Aug. 1902
Place/Date of Death: Wolverhampton, Staffordshire — 18 Aug. 1973
Place of Memorial: —
Town/County Connections: Wolverhampton, Staffordshire
Remarks: Later joined the army (Royal Engineers) and attained the rank of Lieutenant Colonel.

Account of Deed: Mr. Harris was awarded the George Cross for dismantling unexploded bombs at Langdale Road School, Thornton Heath, Surrey on 18th September 1940. Massive air raids on London had begun a few days earlier and the problem of dealing with unexploded bombs was a new one. Mr. Harris was at the time Chief Combustion Officer to Croydon Corporation and a member of the ARP Engineers Service, and he showed conspicuous bravery in dealing with these exceptionally dangerous devices.

HARRISON,   164
Barbara Jane
Rank/Title: Miss
Unit/Force/Occupation: Stewardess, British Overseas Airways Corporation
Other Decorations: —
Date of Gazette: 8 Aug. 1969
Place/Date of Birth: Bradford, Yorkshire — 24 May 1945
Place/Date of Death: Heathrow Airport — 8 Apr. 1968
Place of Memorial: Fulford Cemetery, York; memorial fund for muscular dystrophy research
Town/County Connections: Bradford and Osbaldwick, Yorkshire
Remarks: —

Account of Deed: On 8th April 1968, soon after take-off from Heathrow Airport, No. 2 engine of a BOAC Boeing 707 caught fire and fell from the aircraft, leaving a fierce fire burning at No. 2 engine position. About two and a half minutes later the aircraft made an emergency landing at the airport and the fire on the port wing intensified. Miss Harrison was a stewardess in the aircraft and one of her duties in an emergency was to help the steward at the aft station in opening up the escape route for the passengers at the rear of the aircraft. When they landed, Miss Harrison and the steward opened the rear galley door and inflated the chute which unfortunately became twisted on the way down so that the steward had to climb down to straighten it before it could be used. Once out of the aircraft he was unable to return; hence Miss Harrison was left alone to help the passengers out of the air-craft. She encouraged some to jump from the machine and pushed out others. With flames and explosions all around her, escape from the tail of the machine became impossible and she directed her passengers to another exit while she remained at her post. She was finally overcome while trying to save an elderly cripple who was seated in one of the last rows and whose body was found close to that of the stewardess.

HARRISON, 165
George Willet
Rank/Title: Able Seaman
Unit/Force/Occupation: Royal Navy
Other Decorations: —
Date of Gazette: 1 Jan. 1931
Place/Date of Birth: — ? 1884/85
Place/Date of Death: — 4 Jun. 1959
Place of Memorial: —
Town/County Connections: Southsea, Hampshire
Remarks: (EGM)

Account of Deed: On 15th February 1930 a bad accident occurred in HMS *Hood* at Portsmouth dockyard. Workmen were engaged in opening up the starboard after-bilge compartments for inspection when a shipwright who had entered a compartment through the man-hole, was overcome by gas and collapsed. As soon as the alarm was given a rescue party entered the bulge but were unable to locate the shipwright owing to the gas and absence of effective lighting. Nevertheless Able Seaman Harrison made his way through successive compartments and, at great personal risk, eventually rescued the shipwright, who unfortunately died later.

HARRISON, 166
Leonard Henry
Rank/Title: Mr.
Unit/Force/Occupation: Civilian Armament Instructor (Grade 1), Air Ministry, RAF Station, Manby, Lincolnshire.
Other Decorations: —
Date of Gazette: 3 Jan. 1941
Place/Date of Birth: Devonport, Devon — 6 Jun. 1906
Place/Date of Death: Bexleyheath, Kent — 15 Jul. 1989
Place of Memorial: —
Town/County Connections: Bexleyheath, Kent
Remarks: First action for which the GC was awarded. Re-joined the Royal Air Force in 1941 (having previously served for 12 years — 1922-34) and attained the rank of Wing Commander; retired from RAF in 1949 but remained at Air Ministry until 1970. Later Honorary Treasurer VC & GC Association.

Account of Deed: On 11th February 1940 the steamship *Kildare*, a grain carrier, was hit by two bombs. One exploded in the grain which shifted, causing the vessel to list heavily; the other lodged in the after deck cabin but did not explode. The ship limped into Immingham Dock, North Lincolnshire and Civilian Armament Instructor Harrison, with Flight Lieutenant Dowland* and another civilian instructor, as his assistants, went to deal with the situation. On entering the cabin they found that the crew had eased their task somewhat by placing mattresses under the bomb to stop it rolling about, and the fuses were uppermost. Mr. Harrison then carried out the procedure which he, as an instructor, had laid down for dealing with fuses, and when this operation had been successfully completed, the bomb was lowered over the side of the ship on to a waiting RAF lorry and taken away for examination. A month later he was called to Grimsby where he dealt successfully with an enemy missile which had fallen on the deck of a small fishing boat in the Humber. (*See also entry for DOWLAND, J.N.)

HARWOOD 167
Harrie Stephen
Rank/Title: Air Mechanic 1st Class (later Flight Lieutenant)
Unit/Force/Occupation: Royal Flying Corps
Other Decorations: —
Date of Gazette: 19 May 1916
Place/Date of Birth: — 10 Jul 1884
Place/Date of Death: Didcot, Oxfordshire — 13 Nov. 1975
Place of Memorial: —
Town/County Connections: Didcot, Oxfordshire
Remarks: (AM); served in Royal Air Force 1939-48.

Account of Deed: On 3rd January 1916 at about 3pm a fire broke out inside a large bomb store belonging to the Royal Flying Corps, which contained nearly 2,000 high explosive bombs, some of which had very large charges, and a number of incendiary bombs which were burning freely. An officer at once took all necessary precautions, and then, assisted by an air mechanic, poured water into the shed through a hole made by the flames. The key of the store was fetched and then these two men, together with a corporal and Air Mechanic Harwood, went into the building and succeeded in putting out the flames. The wooden cases containing the bombs were burnt, and some of them were charred to a cinder.

HAVERCROFT 168
Percy Roberts
Rank/Title: Mr.
Unit/Force/Occupation: Miner, Waleswood Colliery, Sheffield, Yorkshire
Other Decorations:
Date of Gazette: 22 Jun. 1917
Place/Date of Birth: — 1884
Place/Date of Death: Sheffield, Yorkshire — 15 Jul. 1976
Place of Memorial: —
Town/County Connections: Sheffield, Yorkshire
Remarks: (EM)

Account of Deed: On 27th August 1915 a descending cage containing ten men collided about half-way down one of the shafts of the Waleswood Colliery with an empty ascending cage. The impact was violent, severely injuring all the men and breaking the winding ropes. Both cages were wedged in the shaft, so neither of them fell to the bottom though there was danger that they might do so at any moment. A hoppit manned by Mr. Havercroft and two other men was sent down to rescue the imprisoned men who were carried from the damaged car along a girder to the hoppit, which made five descents altogether. During the whole of the two hours of the rescue Mr. Havercroft and his two companions were exposed to great danger either from the hoppit being upset by the winding ropes swinging in the shaft or from the damaged cage breaking loose and falling down the shaft.

HAWKINS 169
Eynon
Rank/Title: Able Seaman (later Leading Seaman)
Unit/Force/Occupation: Royal Navy
Other Decorations: Lloyd's War Medal for Bravery at Sea
Date of Gazette: 29 Jun. 1943
Place/Date of Birth: — 27 Jun. 1920
Place/Date of Death: —
Place of Memorial: —
Town/County Connections: Llanharan, Glamorgan, South Wales
Remarks: (AM)

Account of Deed: Able Seaman Hawkins was serving in a merchant vessel which was hit by three torpedoes and immediately began to burn furiously. Many of the crew jumped overboard and Able Seaman Hawkins, with the greatest coolness and courage, organised a party of survivors in the water and kept them away from the fire until they were later picked up by one of HM ships. Twice he swam to the assistance of other survivors who were in difficulties, himself receiving burns in the face as he pulled them to safety.

HAY (later the Marquess of TWEEDDALE) 170
David George Montagu
Rank/Title: Cadet (later Lieutenant)
Unit/Force/Occupation: Royal Naval Reserve
Other Decorations: Lloyd's War Medal for Bravery at Sea; Royal Life Saving Medal
Date of Gazette: 8 Jul. 1941
Place/Date of Birth: Gifford, East Lothian, Scotland — 25 Oct. 1921
Place/Date of Death: Islay, Scotland — 23 Jan. 1979
Place of Memorial: —
Town/County Connections: Isle of Mull, Scotland
Remarks: (AM); first sitting Member of either House of Parliament to hold the GC.

Account of Deed: Cadet Hay was serving in a Merchantman, SS *Eurylochus*, which was sunk by an enemy raider. She was heavily shelled and machine-gunned, and many of her crew were killed. Two boats were got away, but the others were shot to pieces. Those of the crew who were left on board launched two rafts, and just before the ship went down they jumped in and swam for them. Cadet Hay reached a raft, but, although sharks were swimming all round him, he dived in again and rescued the Radio Officer. As he swam back to the raft his clothing was torn by a shark.

HEMEIDA

El Amin Effendi
Rank/Title: Yuzbashi (later Bimbashi)
Unit/Force/Occupation: Sudan Defence Force
Other Decorations: —
Date of Gazette: 23 Jun 1936
Place/Date of Birth: —
Place/Date of Death: — 25 May 1973
Place of Memorial: —
Town/County Connections: —
Remarks: (EGM); served in Second World War.

Account of Deed: On 4th January 1936 Yuzbashi El Amin Effendi Hemeida was in charge of a section of a working party making explosive charges in the barracks at Omdurman. It was the duty of this particular section to place the gun-cotton and primers in containers. A charge which was being assembled accidentally exploded, killing one NCO and injuring a native officer and eight NCOs. The building was extensively damaged and fire broke out in several places. El Amin was badly shaken and dazed by the explosion, but nevertheless he went to help the injured and then took steps to extinguish the fires and removed the unexploded charges to a safe place.

HEMING

Albert Edward
Rank/Title: Mr.
Unit/Force/Occupation: Section Leader, Civil Defence Rescue Service, Bermondsey
Other Decorations: —
Date of Gazette: 17 Jul. 1945
Place/Date of Birth: Ireland — 13 Jun. 1910
Place/Date of Death: Forest Hill, London — 3 Jan. 1987
Place of Memorial: —
Town/County Connections: Peckham and Dulwich, London
Remarks: —

Account of Deed: On 2nd March 1945, as a result of enemy action, several people were trapped in the wreckage of the Roman Catholic Church and adjacent buildings in Parkers Row, Bermondsey. When Mr. Heming arrived with his rescue section he found the whole area completely devastated. He was told that there were some priests and two women somewhere in the ruins, and there could be no possibility of their still being alive, but as he searched amongst the debris, he heard a call for help coming from the direction of the crypt of the church. Despite the fact that the Regional Commissioner had decided that conditions were too dangerous for any attempt at rescue to be made, Mr. Heming dug his way into the ruins of the church towards the sound of the voice he had heard, and although there was the added danger of coal gas which was escaping from a damaged pipe nearby, he went on burrowing head downwards into the ruins, until he found one of the priests who had been buried. He was badly injured and firmly trapped by fallen timbers, but Mr. Heming was eventually able to drag him to safety.

HENDERSON

George Campbell
Rank/Title: Mr.
Unit/Force/Occupation: Sub-Officer, Gibraltar Dockyard Fire Service
Other Decorations: —
Date of Gazette: 20 Nov. 1951
Place/Date of Birth: Scotland — 15 Jan. 1910
Place/Date of Death: Gibraltar — 27 Apr. 1951
Place of Memorial: North Front Cemetery, Gibraltar
Town/County Connections: —
Remarks: —

Account of Deed: On 27th April 1951 a lighter, loaded with ammunition and explosives, caught fire in the harbour at Gibraltar alongside the Naval Armament Vessel *Bedenham*. Sub-Officer Henderson was in charge of the first fire appliance sent to fight the fire, and in spite of the great heat and in face of almost certain death he climbed aboard *Bedenham*, which had by this time been abandoned, and continued to fight the fire with his hose until the whole cargo detonated and blew up in one shattering explosion.

HENDERSON

Herbert Reuben

174

Rank/Title: Mr.
Unit/Force/Occupation: Employee, Film Treatment Works, London
Other Decorations: —
Date of Gazette: 3 May 1927
Place/Date of Birth: — 17 Sep. 1902
Place/Date of Death: Bearsted, Maidstone, Kent — 1983
Place of Memorial: —
Town/County Connections: Larkfield, Maidstone, Kent
Remarks: (EGM)

Account of Deed: On 18th March 1927 a dangerous fire started at a film treatment works in London. Although seriously burnt himself, Mr. Henderson, an employee of the firm, succeeded in carrying to a place of safety a blazing cinematograph film and in removing other films which were in danger of igniting and causing a major explosion.

HENDRY

James

175

Rank/Title: Corporal
Unit/Force/Occupation: No. 1 Tunnelling Coy., Corps of Royal Canadian Engineers.
Other Decorations: —
Date of Gazette: 2 Apr. 1943
Place/Date of Birth: Falkirk, Scotland — 20 Dec. 1911
Place/Date of Death: Loch Laggan, Inverness-shire, Scotland — 13 Jun. 1941
Place of Memorial: Brookwood Military Cemetery, Surrey
Town/County Connections: —
Remarks: —

Account of Deed: In the summer of 1941 a company of Canadian Engineers was constructing a tunnel at Loch Laggan in Scotland. On 13th June at about 1600 hours Corporal Hendry came out of the tunnel to find the powder house on fire. Shouting the alarm he ran to warn the compressor men and the steel sharpeners in the workshop and then went to try to put out the fire. Although he could have got clear himself, others nearby were also in danger and if the magazine blew up the resulting damage would put a stop to the work for some time. He was an experienced miner and knew the chance he took. There was an explosion in which Corporal Hendry died. One other man was killed and a number were hurt, but others had been able to take cover because of the timely warning.

HENSHAW

George

176

Rank/Title: Lance-Corporal
Unit/Force/Occupation: 1st Bn., The Queen's Royal Regiment (West Surrey)
Other Decorations: —
Date of Gazette: 19 Nov. 1935
Place/Date of Birth: — 19 May 1910
Place/Date of Death: — 14 Feb. 1972
Place of Memorial: —
Town/County Connections: Eastbourne, Sussex
Remarks: (EGM)

Account of Deed: At the time of the earthquake at Quetta, India (31 May/1 June 1935) the 1st Bn. The Queen's Royal Regiment, who were returning from manoeuvres and had been marching all night, were directed to the city and allotted an area in which to carry out rescue operations. Lance-Corporal Henshaw was set to work in the ruins of Quetta Grammar School and was prominent in the rescue work which took place in a particularly dangerous building. An Indian child was heard crying below some very unsafe debris, and Lance-Corporal Henshaw dug under the wreckage and carried the child out alive.

HESLOP 177

George Christopher
Rank/Title: Mr.
Unit/Force/Occupation: Manager, Loftus Ironstone Mine, Yorkshire
Other Decorations: MC, Carnegie Medal
Date of Gazette: 26 May 1936
Place/Date of Birth: — 25 Dec. 1885
Place/Date of Death: Saltburn-by-the-Sea, Yorkshire — Dec. 1978
Place of Memorial: —
Town/County Connections: Saltburn-by-the-Sea, Yorkshire
Remarks: (EM); served with The Durham Light Infantry, reaching the rank of Captain in First World War.

Account of Deed: At about 8.30am on 17th December 1935 a fall of roof occurred at the Loftus Ironstone Mine and two workmen were buried in the debris. When Mr. Heslop arrived at about 9am no one had ventured to go to the rescue of the two men as falls were still occurring and there was considerable roof movement. He however immediately crawled into a cavity until he reached the first man who was pinned down by a baulk across his legs. Mr. Heslop cleared stones from the man's face and gave instructions to other rescuers to pile a road through the fall to protect the trapped man from further falls. He then crawled further under the fall and found the other man who was pinned by one of his feet. It took Mr. Heslop four hours, working in a very small cavity, to release him. He then returned to the first man and supervised the cutting of the runner baulk by which he was pinned and the man was finally released after being trapped for eight hours. Shortly afterwards there was a heavy fall and the whole of the piling which had been erected to assist the release collapsed.

HISCOCK 178

William Ewart
Rank/Title: A/Lieutenant-Commander
Unit/Force/Occupation: Royal Navy
Other Decorations: DSC
Date of Gazette: 16 Jun. 1942
Place/Date of Birth: — 13 Jan. 1886
Place/Date of Death: Malta — 15 Feb. 1942
Place of Memorial: Capuccini Naval Cemetery, Malta, GC
Town/County Connections: Glasgow, Scotland
Remarks: Joined the Royal Navy 1900; retired 1934; recalled 1939 and sent to St. Angelo, Malta to take charge of sea mines disposal.

Account of Deed: In September 1941 a Torpedo Machine (a device in which the Italians specialised) was dropped in 15 feet of water in St. George's Bay, Malta, and Lieutenant-Commander Hiscock was given the task of disarming it. The operation of salvage was one of considerable danger as, quite apart from the possibility of booby traps, no information was available as to the firing mechanism of the explosive head and its behaviour when parted from the body was a matter of complete uncertainty. While Lieutenant-Commander Hiscock and his assistant were working on the bomb, the clock mechanism started and it was only their cool determination and skill which brought the operation to a successful conclusion.

HODGE 179

Alexander Mitchell
Rank/Title: Sub-Lieutenant (later Captain)
Unit/Force/Occupation: Royal Naval Volunteer Reserve
Other Decorations: VRD
Date of Gazette: 2 Aug. 1940
Place/Date of Birth: Blairgowrie, Perthshire, Scotland — 23 Jun. 1916
Place/Date of Death: —
Place of Memorial: —
Town/County Connections: Barnton, Midlothian, Scotland
Remarks: (EGM); CO, Forth Division, RNVR 1953-57; Chairman, Edinburgh District Sea Cadet Committee 1959-63; Chairman, Lady Haig's Poppy Factory 1961-67; Member of Council, Earl Haig's Fund (Scotland) 1963-67; DL, Edinburgh.

Account of Deed: In April 1940 the aircraft carrier HMS *Eagle* was badly damaged by an explosion in the bomb-room. The room was in darkness and full of heat and fumes. Sub-Lieutenant Hodge left the main deck, went into the bomb-room and was able to rescue several badly injured men. He found one man crushed under two very heavy bombs which he could not move, but with help managed to drag the wounded man clear and sent him up on deck. Although there was obvious danger of further explosion Sub-Lieutenant Hodge did not leave the bomb-room until he was satisfied that no one was left alive below.

HOLLOWDAY 180
Vivian
Rank/Title: Aircraftman (later Corporal)
Unit/Force/Occupation: Royal Air Force
Other Decorations: —
Date of Gazette: 21 Jan. 1941
Place/Date of Birth: Barton-on-Humber, Lincolnshire — 16 Oct. 1916
Place/Date of Death: Bedford — 15 Apr. 1977
Place of Memorial: Cremated at Bedford
Town/County Connections: Bedford, Bedfordshire
Remarks: Member of the VC & GC Association Committee 1958-77; member of the Legion of Frontiersmen; Committee member of the Royal Society of St. George.

Account of Deed: On two occasions, in July and August 1940 at Cranfield, Bedfordshire, Aircraftman Hollowday tried to rescue airmen from crashed aircraft which had burst into flames. On the second occasion, in spite of the danger of exploding ammunition, he managed to extricate two of the three airmen, but unfortunately all three were dead.

HORSFIELD 181
Kenneth
Rank/Title: Corporal
Unit/Force/Occupation: The Manchester Regiment, attd. Special Air Service
Other Decorations: —
Date of Gazette: 23 Mar. 1945
Place/Date of Birth: —
Place/Date of Death: Brindisi, Italy — 18 Aug. 1944
Place of Memorial: Bari War Cemetery, Italy
Town/County Connections: Hyde, Cheshire
Remarks: —

Account of Deed: Corporal Horsfield was employed in the demolition area at Bari, Italy when, on 18th August 1944, an ammunition explosion occurred. He made the most gallant attempts to save a man who was trapped in the rubble and continued his efforts until a second explosion caused severe injuries from which he subsequently died.

HOWARTH 182
Albert
Rank/Title: Ordinary Seaman
Unit/Force/Occupation: Royal Navy
Other Decorations: —
Date of Gazette: 2 Sep. 1941
Place/Date of Birth: Nelson, Lancashire — 10 May 1917
Place/Date of Death: Burnley, Lancashire — 13 Jun. 1976
Place of Memorial: —
Town/County Connections: Burnley and Nelson, Lancashire
Remarks: (AM)

Account of Deed: Ordinary Seaman Howarth was one of a boat's crew from HMS *Foresight* sent to board a burning and abandoned merchantman. The merchantman blew up as they drew near her, throwing the boat's crew into the water. Ordinary Seaman Howarth saw near him a stoker who was badly shaken, so he held him up for ten minutes until a lifebelt was thrown to him. This he put round the stoker, and before being hauled on board his ship, made sure that his shipmate was safe. When he himself reached the deck, after nearly half an hour in the water, it was seen that his right foot had been blown off.

HUDSON

183

Murray Ken
Rank/Title: Sergeant
Unit/Force/Occupation: Royal New Zealand Infantry Regiment
Other Decorations: —
Date of Gazette: 26 Sep. 1974
Place/Date of Birth: Opotiki, New Zealand — 24 Feb. 1938
Place/Date of Death: Waiouru Military Camp, New Zealand — 13 Feb. 1974
Place of Memorial: —
Town/County Connections: —
Remarks: The first GC awarded to a New Zealander by birth and the first given for an incident in New Zealand. Had previously served in Malaya, Borneo and Vietnam.

Account of Deed: On 13th February 1974, while supervising a live grenade practice, Sergeant Hudson suddenly became aware that the NCO in his grenade throwing bay had accidentally, and perhaps unknowingly, armed the grenade he was about to throw. Sergeant Hudson immediately ordered the man to throw the grenade, but there was no reaction. The Sergeant was then seen to grasp the NCO's throwing hand in both his and attempt to throw the grenade over the front parapet of the throwing bay. He was within inches of success when the grenade exploded, killing both men. As an experienced soldier, Sergeant Hudson would have realised immediately that once the grenade became armed, there was less than four seconds to detonation, but while he must have been aware of the great risk involved, he took no action to safeguard himself.

HUGHES

184

Joseph
Rank/Title: Driver
Unit/Force/Occupation: Royal Army Service Corps
Other Decorations: —
Date of Gazette: 26 Jun. 1947
Place/Date of Birth: Glasgow — 1927
Place/Date of Death: Lyemun Barracks, Hong Kong — 23 Mar. 1946
Place of Memorial: Colonial Cemetery, Happy Valley, Hong Kong
Town/County Connections: Glasgow, Scotland
Remarks: —

Account of Deed: On 21st March 1946 Driver Hughes was driving a three-ton lorry carrying explosives into the magazine at Lyemun Barracks, Hong Kong when it started to smoulder and caught fire. Instead of running for safety he did everything possible to put out the fire. He used the extinguisher, dragged the blazing camouflage net on to the ground and shouted to warn everyone to keep away. He was, of course, killed when the whole three tons of ammunition exploded, but he had delayed the explosion and given time for everyone to take cover. Had it not been for his action, the casualties might have been very heavy.

HULME

185

Thomas
Rank/Title: Mr.
Unit/Force/Occupation: Manager, Parsonage Colliery, Leigh, Lancashire
Other Decorations: Bronze Medallion of Carnegie Hero Fund Trust
Date of Gazette: 16 May 1941
Place/Date of Birth: Leigh, Lancashire — 23 Oct. 1903
Place/Date of Death: St. Helen's, Lancashire — 27 Oct. 1988
Place of Memorial: —
Town/County Connections: St. Helen's, Lancashire
Remarks: (EM)

Account of Deed: On 23rd January 1941 a fall of a roof took place above the coal face in a pit at the Parsonage Colliery and two hewers were trapped. One of them was quickly released, but the other could not get away and as the fall was continuing, he was in an extremely dangerous position. The only access to this man was along the conveyor belt over which the roof had squeezed down to two feet, and Mr. Hulme crawled along this belt, a distance of about seven feet, and succeeded in building three hardwood chocks round the trapped man to prevent the roof closing down on him. This operation took about one and a half hours, with the ever-present risk of the total collapse of the roof, which was visibly and audibly moving the whole time. Fortunately at the end of this time the trapped miner was able to crawl out practically unhurt.

HUMEIDA, El Amin Effendi — see **HEMEIDA,** El Amin Effendi

HUMPHREYS

186

Patrick Noel
Rank/Title: Lieutenant (later Lieutenant-Commander)
Unit/Force/Occupation: Royal Navy
Other Decorations: —
Date of Gazette: 12 Nov. 1937
Place/Date of Birth: — 6 Feb. 1913
Place/Date of Death: West Malling, Kent — 26 Nov. 1943
Place of Memorial: Maidstone Cemetery, Kent
Town/County Connections: West Malling, Kent
Remarks: (EGM)

Account of Deed: Lieutenant Humphreys was awarded the Empire Gallantry Medal for courageous and distinguished services when HMS *Hunter* was mined off Almeria on the coast of Spain on 13th May 1937.

HUTCHINSON

187

John
Rank/Title: Mr.
Unit/Force/Occupation: Overman, Louisa Old Section, Louisa Colliery, Durham
Other Decorations: —
Date of Gazette: 20 Jul. 1948
Place/Date of Birth: — 25 Jul. 1907
Place/Date of Death: Stanley, Co. Durham — 9 Jun. 1975
Place of Memorial: —
Town/County Connections: Stanley, Co. Durham
Remarks: (EM)

Account of Deed: Shortly before midnight on 22nd August 1947 a serious explosion of firedamp and coal dust occurred in the Louisa Colliery. Three deputies*, who with their intimate knowledge of the geography of the mine could have made their way to safety, went at once to the scene of the disaster, where they were soon joined by Mr. Hutchinson who came down from the surface. Twenty-four men, all of whom were either injured or incapacitated by carbon-monoxide poisoning, were in the district at the time; 19 of them died and but for the prompt and continuous heroic work performed by the three deputies and Mr. Hutchinson there is little doubt that not one would have survived. The atmosphere was so thick that the beams of the cap lamps could penetrate only a foot or so, which meant that the rescuers could do nothing to guard against danger from falls of ground, a very real danger after an explosion, and the road in places was almost completely blocked by tubs derailed by blast. (*See also entries for ROBINSON, H., SHANLEY, J. and YOUNGER, W.)

HUTCHISON

188

Albert James
Rank/Title: Sergeant
Unit/Force/Occupation: Highland Light Infantry
Other Decorations: —
Date of Gazette: 4 Jan. 1918
Place/Date of Birth: Gibraltar — 11 Sep. 1891
Place/Date of Death: Kilcreggan, Dunbartonshire — 4 Jan. 1988
Place of Memorial: —
Town/County Connections: Kilcreggan, Helensburgh, Dunbartonshire
Remarks: (AM)

Account of Deed: At the Curragh Camp, Ireland, on 2nd April 1917, during bombing practice, a live grenade hit the parapet of the trench and fell back at the feet of the man who had thrown it. The man was too terrified to move, and obstructed the efforts of Sergeant Hutchison to pick up the bomb. After the fuse had been burning for three seconds, Sergeant Hutchison managed to push the man away, pick up the bomb and throw it over the parapet, where it immediately exploded.

HYDERABAD, The Begum of — see **ASHRAF-UN-NISA**

HYSLOP 189
Alexander Henry MAXWELL-
Rank/Title: Lieutenant-Commander (later Captain)
Unit/Force/Occupation: Royal Navy
Other Decorations: —
Date of Gazette: 11 Nov. 1929
Place/Date of Birth: — 25 May 1895
Place/Date of Death: Par, Cornwall — 28 Aug. 1978
Place of Memorial: —
Town/County Connections: Par, Cornwall
Remarks: (AM); served in Second World War; ADC to King George VI 1944-45.

Account of Deed: HMS *Devonshire* was carrying out full calibre firing on 26th July 1929 when at the first salvo there was a heavy explosion which blew off the roof of one of the turrets. Lieutenant-Commander Maxwell-Hyslop was in the fore control when the explosion occurred and immediately went to the turrret and climbed inside. Having made a general examination he descended the gun well through most dangerous conditions of fumes and smoke and remained there until the emergency was over, directing arrangements for the safety of the magazine and supervising the evacuation of the wounded. He was fully aware of the danger to himself from the results of cordite fumes and the grave risk of further explosions.

IDRIS 190
Taha
Rank/Title: Shawish
Unit/Force/Occupation: Blue Nile Province Police
Other Decorations: —
Date of Gazette: 2 Mar. 1934
Place/Date of Birth: — 1 Jan. 1900
Place/Date of Death: —
Place of Memorial: —
Town/County Connections: —
Remarks: (EGM)

Account of Deed: In September 1933 Shawish Taha Idris showed conspicuous gallantry and devotion to duty in arresting an armed policeman. This native non-commissioned officer, who was in charge of a police guard, temporarily lost his self-control and, after loading his rifle with nine rounds of ammunition, ran amok. The guard, not knowing how to deal with the situation, sent word to Shawish Taha Idris who at once came to their assistance. He was unable to approach without being seen and the NCO waited until his target got within a few paces and then shot at him, but the cartridge did not explode. Shawish Taha Idris then ran forward and disarmed him.

INAYAT-KHAN 191
Noor (wrongly gazetted as 'Nora')
Rank/Title: Assistant Section-Officer
Unit/Force/Occupation: Women's Auxiliary Air Force, seconded to Women's Transport Service (FANY)
Other Decorations: —
Date of Gazette: 5 Apr. 1949
Place/Date of Birth: Moscow, Russia — 1 Jan. 1914
Place/Date of Death: Dachau Concentration Camp, Germany — 13 Sep. 1944
Place of Memorial: The Runnymede Memorial, Surrey
Town/County Connections: London
Remarks: —

Account of Deed: Assistant Section-Officer Inayat Kahn was the first woman operator to be infiltrated into enemy-occupied France (on 16th June 1943). During the weeks immediately following her arrival, the Gestapo made mass arrests in the Paris Resistance Groups to which she had been detailed, but although given the opportunity to return to England, she refused to abandon what had become the principal and most dangerous post in France. She was a wireless operator and did not wish to leave her French comrades without communications and she hoped also to rebuild her group. The Gestapo did their utmost to catch her and so break the last remaining link with London. After three and a half months she was betrayed, taken to Gestapo Headquarters in the Avenue Foch and asked to co-operate. She refused to give them information of any kind and was imprisoned in the Gestapo HQ, remaining there for several weeks, and making two unsuccessful attempts to escape during that time. She was asked to sign a declaration that she would make no further attempts but refused, so was sent to Germany for 'safe custody' — the first agent to be sent to Germany. She was imprisoned at Karlsruhe in November 1943 and later at Pforsheim, where her cell was apart from the main prison as she was considered a particularly dangerous and unco-operative prisoner. She still refused to give any information either as to her work or her colleagues and on 12th September 1944 she was taken to Dachau and shot.

INWOOD
192

George Walter
Rank/Title: Section-Commander
Unit/Force/Occupation: 30th Warwickshire (Birmingham) Bn., Home Guard
Other Decorations: —
Date of Gazette: 27 May 1941
Place/Date of Birth: — 14 Sep. 1906
Place/Date of Death: Birmingham — 16 Oct. 1940
Place of Memorial: Yardley Cemetery, Birmingham
Town/County Connections: Birmingham
Remarks: —

Account of Deed: On the night of 15/16th October 1940 the Luftwaffe carried out a heavy attack on the city of Birmingham. Section-Commander Inwood took his section to help in the rescue work and found that a number of people were trapped in a cellar below a house which had been hit by a bomb. The cellar was full of gas and all its occupants were unconscious. Mr. Inwood was lowered into the cellar by a rope and managed to get two men out alive, and although he was obviously suffering from the gas himself, he insisted on going down again, but collapsed and died.

ISLAM-ud-DIN
193

Rank/Title: Lance-Naik
Unit/Force/Occupation: 6/9th Jat Regiment, Indian Army
Other Decorations: —
Date of Gazette: 5 Oct. 1945
Place/Date of Birth: —
Place/Date of Death: Pyawbwe, Central Burma — 12 Apr. 1945
Place of Memorial: The Rangoon Memorial, Burma
Town/County Connections: —
Remarks: —

Account of Deed: On 12th April 1945 Lance-Naik Islam-ud-Din won a posthumous award of the George Cross when he threw himself on a live grenade to save the lives of his comrades. He had previously shown high qualities of leadership and courage in action on 24th March 1945 near Khanda, north of Meiktila.

JAK TAHA — see TAHA, El Jak Effendi

JAMESON
194

Thomas
Rank/Title: Mr.
Unit/Force/Occupation: Agent, Bold Colliery, St. Helens, Merseyside
Other Decorations: —
Date of Gazette: 8 Oct. 1940
Place/Date of Birth: — 14 Feb. 1898
Place/Date of Death: Buckley, Flint, Wales — 29 Mar. 1980
Place of Memorial: —
Town/County Connections: Buckley, Flint, Wales; Bold, St. Helens, Lancashire
Remarks: (EM)

Account of Deed: On 14th February 1940 at about 8.45pm a serious fall of roof occurred in the main loading level of the Bold Colliery, completely burying five men. Rescue work was immediately begun and in a little over an hour one of the men was rescued. He was able to tell Mr. Jameson, who had arrived and taken charge, the position of the other four men. Mr. Jameson and a night shift foreman*, whose father was one of the men buried, worked with their hands, removing stones and dirt, and sawed through a conveyor chain and a rail. After prolonged efforts one of the men was rescued by 2am next morning and a third man was released an hour later. The other two men could be seen but appeared to be dead. The rescue had to be carried out in a very confined space and in conditions of extreme difficulty and danger, owing to the risk of further falls as the debris which covered the buried men was removed. (*See also entry for SCHOFIELD, C.M.)

JAMIESON

195

William
Rank/Title: Mr.
Unit/Force/Occupation: European Shift Superintendent, Ariston Gold Mine, Prestea, Gold Coast (now Ghana)
Other Decorations: —
Date of Gazette: 23 Jun. 1936
Place/Date of Birth: —
Place/Date of Death: Muirfield, Perth, Scotland — 28 Sep. 1965
Place of Memorial: New Cemetery, Wanlockhead, Lanarkshire
Town/County Connections: Burghmuir, Perth, Scotland
Remarks: (EGM)

Account of Deed: Sometime early in 1936 at the Ariston Gold Mine Mr. Jamieson was being lowered underground in the service cage when he found one of the native workmen lying unconscious on the shaft station. He appeared to have been gassed, as did four more workmen whom Mr. Jamieson and a companion found when they went to investigate the cause of the trouble. They removed the men to the shaft station and Mr. Jamieson then went alone to the working face of the drift, where he found six more men lying gassed and in a serious condition. He managed to drag them back from the fumes and was eventually overcome himself and had to be helped out of the mine.

JEPHSON-JONES, Robert Llewellyn — see **JONES,** Robert Llewellyn JEPHSON-

JOHNSTON

196

James
Rank/Title: Mr.
Unit/Force/Occupation: Senior European Overseer, Mohpani Colliery of the G.I.P. Railway, India
Other Decorations: —
Date of Gazette: 19 Mar. 1926
Place/Date of Birth: — 12 Dec. 1881
Place/Date of Death: Salisbury, Wiltshire — 7 Sep. 1974
Place of Memorial: —
Town/County Connections: Salisbury, Wiltshire
Remarks: (EM)

Account of Deed: On 7th January 1925 a very heavy fall of roof took place in the Mohpani Colliery, killing one miner instantaneously and completely burying another. On a report of the accident reaching the under-manager of the mine, he went with Mr. Johnston and a native timber-drawer, and crawling through the fall of stone and earth, they eventually got the man out. Within 20 minutes of the rescue 20 tons of rock fell on the very spot where the injured man had been lying.

JOLLY

197

Richard Frank
Rank/Title: Commander
Unit/Force/Occupation: Royal Navy
Other Decorations: —
Date of Gazette: 23 Dec. 1939
Place/Date of Birth: — 28 Aug. 1896
Place/Date of Death: Queensferry, Firth of Forth, Scotland — 16 Oct. 1939
Place of Memorial: St. Peter's Churchyard, Boughton Monchelsea, Kent
Town/County Connections: Boughton Monchelsea, Kent; Bucknall, Shropshire
Remarks: (EGM); served in First World War.

Account of Deed: HMS *Mohawk* was patrolling off the East Coast soon after the outbreak of the Second World War when she was attacked by an enemy aircraft and suffered a large number of casualties. Commander Jolly, who was on the bridge, was severely wounded in the stomach but refused to leave the bridge or allow himself to be attended to. He continued to direct *Mohawk* for the 35-mile passage up the Firth of Forth which lasted one hour and twenty minutes. He was too weak for his orders to be heard but they were repeated by his wounded Navigating Officer. Having brought his ship into port, Commander Jolly rang off the main engines and immediately collapsed, and died some five hours after landing.

JONES

Benjamin Littler
Rank/Title: Mr.
Unit/Force/Occupation: Quarryman, Llysfaen Quarry, Caernarvon
Other Decorations: —
Date of Gazette: 9 Sep. 1938
Place/Date of Birth: — 13 Jul. 1918
Place/Date of Death: Colwyn Bay, Denbighshire, Wales — 5 Aug. 1975
Place of Memorial: —
Town/County Connections: Colwyn Bay, Denbighshire, Wales
Remarks: (EM); served in Second World War

Account of Deed: Blasting was about to take place at the Llysfaen Quarry on the morning of 21st May 1938. All the men, with the exception of Mr. Jones and two others whose duty it was to light the fuses, had been withdrawn from the danger zone. The first six fuses had been lighted when the third man trod on a stone which tipped up and trapped his foot so that he could not move. The shots were timed to go off in 80 seconds, and the man was in imminent danger of being killed. Mr. Jones and the other quarryman tried to release their trapped companion and, failing to do so, all three men pulled out the lighted fuses. In doing so they ran considerable risk; had any one of the detonators exploded, it would certainly have had serious or even fatal results.

JONES

Ralph
Rank/Title: Private
Unit/Force/Occupation: 22nd Garrison Bn., Australian Military Forces
Other Decorations: —
Date of Gazette: 1 Sep. 1950
Place/Date of Birth: Gorleston, near Great Yarmouth, Norfolk — 26 Sep. 1900
Place/Date of Death: Prisoner of War Camp, Cowra, New South Wales — 5 Aug. 1944
Place of Memorial: Cowra War Cemetery, New South Wales, Australia
Town/County Connections: Great Yarmouth, Norfolk
Remarks: Served in the Rifle Brigade after the First World War.

Account of Deed: The Japanese prisoners at No.12 Prisoner of War Camp near Cowra, New South Wales, planned a mass break-out for the night of 4th/5th August 1944. At 2am, armed with every sort of home-made improvised weapon, they stormed out of their huts, which they set on fire. The garrison sprang into action and Privates Jones and Hardy* at once manned their Vickers machine guns, covering the eastern perimeter wire. The Japanese bore down on them, but the two Australians stood their ground and kept firing until they were bashed to death. They had, however, gained for the other defence posts just a few minutes of invaluable time and the Japanese, who had overrun their gun and were bringing it into action, were mown down by fire from another Vickers. Most of the surviving prisoners were pinned down in a large drain and surrendered at daylight, and in the days that followed many who had escaped were rounded up or committed suicide. (*See also entry for HARDY, B.G.)

JONES

Robert Llewellyn JEPHSON-
Rank/Title: Captain (later Brigadier)
Unit/Force/Occupation: Royal Army Ordnance Corps
Other Decorations: —
Date of Gazette: 24 Dec. 1940
Place/Date of Birth: — 7 Apr. 1905
Place/Date of Death: Ferndown, Dorset — 27 Oct. 1985
Place of Memorial: —
Town/County Connections: Ferndown, Dorset
Remarks: Deputy Director of Ordnance Services, Scottish Command 1954-57; Commandant, Central Ordnance Depot, Branston 1957-60.

Account of Deed: Captain Jephson-Jones was living in Malta at the outbreak of war. When Malta became a prime target for the German and Italian air forces in June 1940 there were no expert Royal Engineer Bomb Disposal units and the task of attending to unexploded bombs and mines dropped on the island (with the exception of those dropped in the dockyard area and on airfields, which were dealt with by the Royal Navy and the Royal Air Force) fell to the Royal Army Ordnance Corps. Between mid-June and mid-November, when bomb disposal was taken over by the Royal Engineers, Captain Jephson-Jones and Lieutenant Eastman*, with incredible courage, dealt with some 275 unexploded bombs, and remained alive. (*See also entry for EASTMAN, W.M.)

KAVANAUGH

201

Robert Murray
Rank/Title: Mr.
Unit/Force/Occupation: Dental Student
Other Decorations: —
Date of Gazette: 16 Oct. 1930
Place/Date of Birth: Wingham, New South Wales, Australia — 18 Dec. 1906
Place/Date of Death: New South Wales — 12 Nov. 1976
Place of Memorial: —
Town/County Connections: —
Remarks: (AM); served in RAAF in Second World War as a Dental Officer.

Account of Deed: On the evening of 12th January 1929 a boy of 14 was bathing at Bondi Beach, New South Wales, some 50 yards from the shore when he was attacked by a shark and was seriously injured on his right side and hip. Mr. Kavanaugh of Darlinghurst, New South Wales, who was bathing a few yards from the boy, without hesitation swam to his aid and had almost reached him when the shark made a second attack on the boy. Undeterred by the danger to himself, Mr. Kavanaugh caught hold of the injured lad and struggled with him towards the shore. He had gone a considerable distance when he was met by two other men and together they carried the boy to the beach where he was given medical attention before being taken to hospital, where he died the next morning.

KELLY

202

Cecil Francis
Rank/Title: Mr.
Unit/Force/Occupation: Assistant River Surveyor, Port Commissioners, Calcutta, India
Other Decorations: —
Date of Gazette: 1 Feb. 1937
Place/Date of Birth: India — 1900
Place/Date of Death: — 1948
Place of Memorial: —
Town/County Connections: —
Remarks: (EGM)

Account of Deed: On 6th May 1936 an Inspector* of the River Traffic Police, with Mr. Kelly as pilot, was in charge of two Port Police launches escorting a cargo of defective dynamite. This cargo was being taken for destruction up the Hoogly river in a barge towed by a launch. The barge proved quite unseaworthy and, after a journey of 15 miles, was sinking. The inspector and his assistants had no responsibility except for escorting the cargo, but in spite of this they tried at great personal risk to keep the barge afloat by bailing from 7am until midnight, when they finally had to give up and beach the barge on the bank near a large jute mill. The beaching took 5½ hours and as it was found impossible to remove the 2½ tons at the bottom owing to its dangerous condition, it had to be re-floated, towed into deep water and sunk. Mr. Kelly supervised the handling of the barge throughout and his skilful assistance ensured the successful accomplishment of the operation. (*See also entry for ADAMSON, G.J.)

KELLY

203

Thomas Raymond
Rank/Title: Able Seaman
Unit/Force/Occupation: Merchant Navy
Other Decorations: —
Date of Gazette: 10 Feb. 1948
Place/Date of Birth: Newry, Co. Down, Ireland — 1928
Place/Date of Death: Bay of Biscay — 18 Mar. 1947
Place of Memorial: —
Town/County Connections: Newry, Co. Down, Ireland
Remarks: —

Account of Deed: On 18th March 1947, the SS *Famagusta* of London, while on a voyage to Cyprus, encountered very severe weather conditions in the Bay of Biscay and developed a list to port. The weather worsened, the list increased and the vessel pounded and began to ship water. In response to an SOS message the SS *Empire Plover* went to her assistance and stood by. The *Famagusta* launched a lifeboat which pulled towards the *Empire Plover* but the boat capsized and threw its ten occupants into the water. The *Empire Plover* quickly manoeuvred into position and lowered ropes, ladders and scrambling nets, and three of her crew stripped and entered the water. Able Seaman Kelly from the *Empire Plover* swam off with a line to the crew of the lifeboat who were struggling in the raging sea. He first brought to safety an officer who had been badly injured, and then swam out again and returned with a second member of the crew. Although very exhausted, for a third time he left the ship and went to help a woman some 50 yards away. He succeeded in reaching her, but both were struck by a heavy wave and were never seen again.

KEMPSTER (formerly COCCIOLETTI)   **204**
André Gilbert (formerly André Gilberto)
Rank/Title: T/Major
Unit/Force/Occupation: Duke of Wellington's Regiment, Royal Armoured Corps
Other Decorations: —
Date of Gazette: 9 Nov. 1943
Place/Date of Birth: Westminster, London — 26 Oct. 1916
Place/Date of Death: Philippeville, Algeria — 21 Aug. 1943
Place of Memorial: Bone War Cemetery, Algeria; name on Roll of Honour in Big Classical, Cheltenham College and memorial tablet in the Dining Hall.
Town/County Connections: Pulborough, Sussex
Remarks: —

Account of Deed: Captain Kempster was conducting grenade throwing practice at Philippeville on the Algerian coast. There were two other men with him in the pit when a grenade he threw rolled back into the pit. He tried to scoop it up and failed, whereupon he threw himself on it, it exploded and he was killed. The other two men with him were, however, saved.

KENNEDY   **205**
James
Rank/Title: Mr.
Unit/Force/Occupation: Security Officer, British Rail Engineering Ltd., Glasgow
Other Decorations: Glasgow Corporation Bravery Medal
Date of Gazette: 15 Aug. 1975
Place/Date of Birth: Carmunnock, Glasgow, Scotland — 1930
Place/Date of Death: Glasgow — 21 Dec. 1973
Place of Memorial: Locomotive named after him
Town/County Connections: Bearsden, Glasgow, Scotland
Remarks: —

Account of Deed: In the early hours of the morning of 21st December 1973 six armed men attacked Security Guards who were moving the British Rail Engineering Works' pay-roll from the Administrative Block to various pay-out points within the complex. During the attack two Security Guards were slightly wounded by shots from a sawn-off shot gun. The robbers then headed towards the main exit of the works. Mr. Kennedy, who was the Security Officer on duty at the main gate, heard the shots and, knowing that the raiders were armed, stood in the gateway in an attempt to prevent their escape. He tackled the first man and prevented him leaving the yard, but he was released by his companions who attacked Mr. Kennedy and stunned him by hitting him on the head with the barrels of their shot guns. (It was subsequently found that Mr. Kennedy had two deeply lacerated wounds on his skull). At this point the raiders climbed into a van which one of the gang had driven into position. Mr. Kennedy, having recovered consciousness and undeterred by his injuries, made another attempt to prevent the criminals' escape by running towards the front passenger door of the van, but he was killed by two shots fired by the man in the passenger seat. The seven men involved in this murder were later caught and sentenced.

KENT   **206**
Ernest William
Rank/Title: Mr.
Unit/Force/Occupation: Workman at Hackney Wick Stadium
Other Decorations: —
Date of Gazette: 20 Dec. 1938
Place/Date of Birth: — 2 Aug. 1914
Place/Date of Death: Basildon, Essex — 23 Aug. 1973
Place of Memorial: —
Town/County Connections: Basildon, Essex
Remarks: (EM)

Account of Deed: On the night of 25th October 1938 gangs of workmen were engaged in concrete piling work at the Hackney Wick Stadium. Metal cylinders, about 15 inches in diameter, were being sunk into the ground, the earth inside them then being removed. At about 2.30am a gang of three workmen encountered an obstruction at the bottom of one of these cylinders which had been sunk to a depth of 18 feet. The man in charge of this gang, being small, decided to have himself lowered down the cylinder, presumably with the idea of clearing the obstruction with his feet. He was therefore lowered into the shaft hanging with out-stretched arms on the hook of the winch rope. When he was about 12 feet down, however, he shouted for help but before he could be hauled up to the top he lost his grip on the hook and fell to the bottom. Messages for help were sent, but in the meantime Mr. Kent, who was also a small man, volunteered to be lowered head first down the cylinder in an attempt to pull the first man up by his hands. After he had been lowered some distance, however, he gave signs of distress and had to be hauled up in a state of semi-collapse. The Fire Brigade and police had now arrived and further attempts at rescue were made, with no success. Mr. Kent, who by this time had partially recovered, again volunteered to go down and this time he succeeded in grasping the unconscious man and had just sufficient strength to retain his grip until they were drawn up to the top of the shaft. He then collapsed, practi-cally unconscious, and was taken to hospital with the man he had rescued who was unfortunately found to be dead.

KEOGH
207

Michael Sullivan
Rank/Title: Chief Petty Officer (later Group Captain with Royal New Zealand Air Force)
Unit/Force/Occupation: Royal Naval Air Service
Other Decorations: OBE
Date of Gazette: 14 Jan. 1916
Place/Date of Birth: Co. Cork, Ireland — 15 May 1889
Place/Date of Death: Sheerness, Kent — 22 Jul. 1983
Place of Memorial: —
Town/County Connections: Sheerness, Kent
Remarks: (AM); served in RNZAF 1938-47; returned to UK 1966.

Account of Deed: On 19th August 1915 an aeroplane took off from the Island of Imbros Aerodrome and had reached a height of 150 feet when the engine stopped. The machine was upset by the powerful air currents from the cliffs and plunged to the ground where it burst into flames. Chief Petty Officer Keogh of HMS *Ark Royal* at once dashed to the wreckage and succeeded in dragging the fatally injured pilot nearly clear of the flames when he was himself overcome by the burns which he had received from the blazing petrol.

KHALIFA
208

Muhammad
Rank/Title: A/Shawish
Unit/Force/Occupation: Berber Province Police
Other Decorations: —
Date of Gazette: 29 Sep. 1925
Place/Date of Birth: —
Place/Date of Death: — 29 Jul. 1966
Place of Memorial: —
Town/County Connections: —
Remarks: (EGM)

Account of Deed: On 27th November 1924 at Wadi Adarowfie, Berber Province, Sudan, Shawish Muhammad Khalifa showed conspicuous gallantry and skill when in command of a patrol of three mounted police, in arresting a murderer and three canal thieves in the face of armed opposition and superior numbers.

KING
209

Richard Henry
Rank/Title: Mr.
Unit/Force/Occupation: Miner, Hedley Pit, Co. Durham
Other Decorations: —
Date of Gazette: 20 Oct. 1931
Place/Date of Birth: — 13 Jan. 1905
Place/Date of Death: — 25 Nov. 1983
Place of Memorial: —
Town/County Connections: Hedley, Co. Durham
Remarks: (EM)

Account of Deed: On 29th September 1930 a fall of roof occurred in the Hedley Pit, partially burying a hewer. It was found that a small passage remained open and Mr. King, together with the chargeman (who was his father and had been first on the scene) and another miner were able to reach the buried man and to build two chocks of timber to keep the passage open. This passage was seven yards long and about two feet square and the only practicable method of rescue was for three men to crawl along the passage-way and lie full length, two in the passage-way and one over the trapped man's body, and pass back, one at a time, the stones that were pinning him down. This dangerous and arduous work was carried on for nine hours by a team of miners and at last the man was released shaken but otherwise uninjured, despite the fact that he had been buried four more times by further falls. Shortly after the rescue had been successfully completed the whole of the tunnel collapsed.

KINNE
Derek Godfrey
Rank/Title: Fusilier
Unit/Force/Occupation: 1st Bn., The Royal Northumberland Fusiliers
Other Decorations: —
Date of Gazette: 13 Apr. 1954
Place/Date of Birth: — 11 Jan. 1930
Place/Date of Death: —
Place of Memorial: —
Town/County Connections: Leeds, Yorkshire
Remarks: —

210

Account of Deed: Fusilier Kinne was captured by the Chinese Communist forces on 25th April 1951. From that time he had only two objectives — firstly to escape and secondly to raise the morale of his fellow prisoners by his utter contempt for his captors and his disregard for the brutal treatment they meted out to their prisoners of war. Because he put his aims into practice (he escaped twice, but was recaptured, and was frequently interrogated but refused to give any information) he was kept in solitary confinement in no less than seven different places of imprisonment, under conditions of the most extreme degradation and increasing brutality. Every possible method, both physical and mental, was employed by his captors to break his spirit, a task which proved utterly beyond their powers. He was always determined to show that he would not be intimidated or cowed by brutal treatment at the hands of a barbarous enemy. His powers of resistance and his determination to oppose and fight the enemy to the maximum were beyond praise and his example was an inspiration to all ranks who came into contact with him. His last award of solitary confinement was on 2nd June 1953 when he was sentenced for defying Chinese orders and wearing a rosette in celebration of Coronation Day. He was eventually exchanged on 10th August 1953.

KIRPA RAM
Rank/Title: Naik
Unit/Force/Occupation: 8th Bn., 13th Frontier Force Rifles, Indian Army
Other Decorations: —
Date of Gazette: 15 Mar. 1946
Place/Date of Birth: —
Place/Date of Death: Thondebhavi, India — 12 Sep. 1945
Place of Memorial: The Rangoon Memorial, Burma
Town/County Connections: —
Remarks: —

211

Account of Deed: At Thondebhavi on 12th September 1945 Naik Kirpa Ram was commanding a section on a field firing exercise. He was lying close to a sepoy who was firing grenades from a discharge cup, the remainder of his section being in position beside him. The third grenade to be fired fell short and landed only about 8 yards from the section position. Naik Kirpa Ram saw that if it exploded many of his section would be killed or wounded. Without a moment's hesitation he leapt up and dashed forward shouting to his men to get back and take cover. He then picked up the grenade, but before he could throw it into a place where it could cause no damage, it exploded. The main force of the explosion was taken by Naik Kirpa Ram and he died from his injuries shortly afterwards. As a result of his action only two men of his section were slightly injured.

KNOWLTON
Richard John
Rank/Title: Ordinary Seaman
Unit/Force/Occupation: Royal Navy
Other Decorations: —
Date of Gazette: 12 Dec. 1917
Place/Date of Birth: — 11 May 1899
Place/Date of Death: Wolverhampton, Staffordshire — 24 Aug. 1981
Place of Memorial: —
Town/County Connections: Burlesdon, Southampton, Hampshire
Remarks: (AM)

212

Account of Deed: On 14th September 1917 on Hornsea Island a seaplane collided with a Poulsen mast and remained wedged in it; the pilot was unconscious and had been thrown out of his seat and on to one of the wings. Ordinary Seaman Knowlton, together with two other seamen, at once climbed up the mast for 100 feet, when one of them, making use of the boatswain's chair, was hoisted up by men at the foot of the mast to the place, over 300 feet from the ground, where the seaplane was fixed. He then climbed out on the plane and held the pilot until the arrival of Ordinary Seaman Knowlton and the other seaman*. A gantline was then secured round the pilot who was safely lowered to the ground. All three men were very well aware of the damaged and insecure condition of the mast — one of the supports was fractured — which was bent to an angle where the seaplane had become wedged, and the mast or seaplane might have collapsed at any time. (*See also entry under ABBOTT, G.F.P.)

LATUTIN   213

Simmon
Rank/Title: Captain
Unit/Force/Occupation: Somerset Light Infantry, seconded Somalia Gendarmerie
Other Decorations: —
Date of Gazette: 10 Sep. 1946
Place/Date of Birth: London — 25 Jul. 1916
Place/Date of Death: Mogadishu, Somalia — 30 Dec. 1944
Place of Memorial: Nairobi War Cemetery, Kenya; name on Roll of Honour at the Royal Academy of Music
Town/County Connections: London
Remarks: —

Account of Deed: On 29th December 1944 a fire occurred at the Training School store of the Somaliland Gendarmerie at Mogadishu. The fire started in the rocket store which became a white-hot inferno. Captain Latutin, together with another officer, the Company Sergeant Major and a boy were in the store selecting explosives and when the rockets started to explode Captain Latutin managed to drag out the other officer who was almost unconscious and badly burnt. Although he was now alight himself, he again rushed into the blazing store and rescued the Company Sergeant Major, but could not save the boy. Captain Latutin died of his injuries the next day.

LEE   214

Walter Holroyd
Rank/Title: Mr.
Unit/Force/Occupation: Workman, Wombwell Main Colliery, Yorkshire
Other Decorations: —
Date of Gazette: 10 May 1949
Place/Date of Birth: — 29 May 1919
Place/Date of Death: Wombwell, Barnsley, Yorkshire — 24 May 1984
Place of Memorial: —
Town/County Connections: Wombwell, Barnsley, Yorkshire
Remarks: (EM)

Account of Deed: A fall of roof occurred at about 4pm on 11th November 1947 at Wombwell Main Colliery, burying three men. The first man on the scene was a workman and his calls for help attracted a coal cutter team of three men. These four climbed over the fall in an attempt to reach the trapped men but a second fall occurred and although the cuttermen were just able to draw back in time, the first rescuer could not escape and was killed instantly. Shortly afterwards Mr. Lee arrived and it became clear from their cries that two of the men trapped by the original fall were still alive. Mr. Lee took the lead in making a way through the fall and after some two hours one of the men was rescued alive.

LEWIN   215

Raymond Mayhew
Rank/Title: Sergeant (later Pilot Officer)
Unit/Force/Occupation: 148 Squadron, Royal Air Force Volunteer Reserve
Other Decorations: —
Date of Gazette: 11 Mar. 1941
Place/Date of Birth: — 14 Jan. 1915
Place/Date of Death: Oakington, Cambridgeshire — 21 Nov. 1941
Place of Memorial: London Road Cemetery, Kettering, Northamptonshire; stained glass window at St. Edward's School, Oxford
Town/County Connections: Kettering, Northamptonshire
Remarks: —

Account of Deed: On 3rd November 1940 Sergeant Lewin was captain of an aircraft which took off from Malta on a night bombing mission. Shortly after take-off the aircraft began to lose height and crashed into a hillside where it burst into flames. Sergeant

Lewin extricated himself and saw three of his crew of four climbing out of the escape hatch. He then ran round the blazing wing in which full fuel tanks were burning, and crawled under it to rescue his injured second pilot. In spite of his own injuries — a cracked knee-cap and severe contusions on the face and legs — he dragged and carried the pilot some 40 yards from the aircraft to a hole in the ground, where he lay on him just as the bombs exploded.

LITTLE   216
Robert Stead
Rank/Title: Mr.
Unit/Force/Occupation: Fitter, Imperial Chemical Industries, Blackley, Manchester
Other Decorations: Carnegie Hero Medal
Date of Gazette: 5 May 1939
Place/Date of Birth: — 23 Jun. 1892
Place/Date of Death: Wallasey, Cheshire — 31 May 1976
Place of Memorial: —
Town/County Connections: Wallasey, Cheshire
Remarks: (EM)

Account of Deed: On 11th January 1939, a fitter engaged on repairs in a chemical reaction pan at the works of the British Dye-stuffs Corporation at Blackley, fell into the pan. Mr. Little, who was in charge of the shift, was called and while rescue apparatus was being brought, he descended into the pan at great risk to himself and carried his unconscious fellow-worker up the ladder. Unfortunately, however, another man who had started to go down the man-hole collapsed on the top of Mr. Little and the rescued man, knocking them both to the bottom where all three remained unconscious. The rescue party then arrived and brought them to the surface. Two of them were dead, but Mr. Little recovered.

LLOYD   217
William
Rank/Title: Mr.
Unit/Force/Occupation: Sub-foreman, Quibell Brothers Ltd., Newark-on-Trent
Other Decorations: —
Date of Gazette: 9 Dec. 1927
Place/Date of Birth: — 1906
Place/Date of Death: Newark, Nottinghamshire — 16 Jun. 1978
Place of Memorial: —
Town/County Connections: Newark, Nottinghamshire
Remarks: (EM); served in Home Guard during the Second World War.

Account of Deed: On the night of 3rd October 1927 a man was engaged in attending a grease extracting plant used for extracting grease from bones by means of petroleum benzine. Noticing that benzine vapour was escaping from the extractor through the lid which had been incorrectly left open he tried, with the help of a fellow workman, to close it. This second man was affected by the fumes and left the room, only to discover later that he had not been followed by his companion. Mr. Lloyd, who was not on duty, but was passing the works on his way home, heard what had happened and, putting a scarf round his mouth, ran to the upper floor of the building where he found the unconscious man near the lid of the extractor. Mr. Lloyd succeeded in dragging him down three steps to a lower floor but was himself overcome and collapsed and was later taken out of the building by other men. The rescue was completed later but the man had been so badly affected by fumes that he died.

LOCKE   218
George
Rank/Title: Mr.
Unit/Force/Occupation: Leading hand, steelwork erectors employed by Dorman Long & Co. Ltd.
Other Decorations: Carnegie Medal for Bravery
Date of Gazette: 2 Mar. 1926
Place/Date of Birth: — 1891
Place/Date of Death: Dovercourt, Essex — 10 Jun. 1974
Place of Memorial: —
Town/County Connections: Dovercourt, Essex
Remarks: (EM)

Account of Deed: On 8th October 1925 Mr. Locke was engaged in the erection of steel work for the rebuilding of the premises of Bourne & Hollingsworth in Oxford Street, London. He and another workman were standing on the parallel girders on the fourth floor level when the other man tripped and fell, striking his head in his fall and lying stunned on the girder. The girders on which the men were working were only 7 inches in width and were no less than 7 feet apart. Mr. Locke, on seeing his comrade fall, with great presence of mind immediately leapt across the intervening space and throwing himself upon the legs of the fallen man, pinned him to the girder until help arrived and they were dragged back to safety. Mr. Locke's action in springing from one girder to another at a great height was no small feat and he must have recognised in holding down his comrade that any struggle on the latter's part would endanger the lives of both.

LOW 219

John Niven Angus
Rank/Title: Lieutenant
Unit/Force/Occupation: Royal Navy
Other Decorations: —
Date of Gazette: 16 Aug. 1940
Place/Date of Birth: — 25 Aug. 1910
Place/Date of Death: North Sea — 29 Apr. 1940
Place of Memorial: Portsmouth Naval Memorial, Hampshire
Town/County Connections: —
Remarks: (EGM)

Account of Deed: On 29th April 1940 the submarine *Unity* on patrol duty in the North Sea, was in collision in the dark with the Norwegian freighter *Atle Jarl*, and sank a few minutes later. Lieutenant Low and Able Seaman Miller* were the two men on duty in the submarine control room. When the order to abandon ship was given by the submarine commander they were instrumental in helping every member of the submarine to escape — except themselves. (*See also entry for MILLER, H.J.)

LOWE 220

Alfred Raymond
Rank/Title: Boy First Class (later Petty Officer)
Unit/Force/Occupation: Royal Navy
Other Decorations: —
Date of Gazette: 8 Feb. 1949
Place/Date of Birth: London — 14 Jun. 1931
Place/Date of Death: —
Place of Memorial: —
Town/County Connections: Wickham, Hampshire
Remarks: (AM); served in Korean War; left Navy in 1959 and went to New Zealand; became a sales representative with a marine boat building company in Auckland.

Account of Deed: At 2245 hours on 17th October 1948 a liberty boat returning from Weymouth Pier to HMS *Illustrious* in Portland Harbour overturned and sank 50 to 100 yards from the ship's stern with 51 men on board. Boy Lowe was trapped under the canopy, struggled free and surfaced. He saw a life-belt a short distance from him and swam to it, and having removed his overcoat and shoes, swam towards the ship. When he was under the stern a line was thrown to him but at that moment he heard a cry for help and saw a midshipman about 10 yards away in great difficulty. He grabbed the line and swam to the midshipman who was now unconscious, and managed to pull him to the ship's side. A fog buoy was then lowered and he dragged the midshipman on to this and held on to him until a petty officer came down the rope to help him. Together they secured the midshipman who was then hoisted on board. The accident took place in eight fathoms of water, in a rough sea with a strong wind blowing.

LUNGLEY 221

Alfred
Rank/Title: Lance-Sergeant (later Battery Sergeant Major)
Unit/Force/Occupation: 24th Mountain Brigade, Royal Artillery
Other Decorations: —
Date of Gazette: 19 Nov. 1935
Place/Date of Birth: Colchester, Essex — 20 Oct. 1905
Place/Date of Death: Norwich, Norfolk — 31 Dec. 1989
Place of Memorial: —
Town/County Connections: Norwich, Norfolk
Remarks: (EGM); served in Second World War

Account of Deed: At the time of the earthquake in Quetta, India (31 May/1 June 1935) men of the 24th Mountain Brigade were soon on the scene of the disaster. The men stacked their rifles and set to work — some with tools and others with their bare hands — to put out fires and rescue any survivors they could find. Lance-Sergeant Lungley located a survivor in a house in Bruce Road. In order to extricate him he had to tunnel down deep beneath tottering masonry, some of which had already collapsed. Although he had sustained severe injury to his foot, Lance-Sergeant Lungley persisted in this dangerous work until he had rescued the trapped man alive.

LYNCH

222

Joseph
Rank/Title: Chief Petty Officer
Unit/Force/Occupation: Royal Navy
Other Decorations: BEM
Date of Gazette: 15 Jun. 1948
Place/Date of Birth: — 6 Nov. 1912
Place/Date of Death: —
Place of Memorial: —
Town/County Connections: Wallasey, Cheshire
Remarks: (AM); later Customs Officer at Liverpool Airport

Account of Deed: While HMS *Nigeria* was lying at anchor at Port Stanley, Falkland Islands on the night of 26th February 1948 a rating missed his footing on the Jacob's ladder while disembarking from the motor cutter at the port boom and fell into the sea. It was after dark and the sea was rough and at a temperature of 42°F with the wind blowing a fresh gale. The rating managed to hold on to the ladder but being dressed in heavy oilskins, was not able to pull himself up nor could he make for the cutter owing to the cold state of the sea. Chief Petty Officer Lynch heard the pipe for the lifeboat while sitting in his mess. Dressed only in a singlet and trousers he at once went on deck, made his way out along the boom, down the ladder and into the water, where he persuaded the rating to let go of the ladder and then supported him to the motor cutter. To keep out of the way CPO Lynch then swam back to the ladder and waited until the rating had been hauled safely into the boat before he himself swam to the cutter and was hauled aboard.

McALONEY

223

William Simpson
Rank/Title: Aircraftman (later Group Captain)
Unit/Force/Occupation: Royal Australian Air Force
Other Decorations: OBE
Date of Gazette: 18 Feb. 1938
Place/Date of Birth: Adelaide, South Australia — 12 May 1910
Place/Date of Death: —
Place of Memorial: —
Town/County Connections: —
Remarks: (AM); served in Second World War and retired in 1967.

Account of Deed: On 31st August 1937 Aircraftman McAloney attempted to rescue an officer from the burning wreckage of an aircraft at Hamilton, Victoria, Australia. Despite the fact that the aircraft was ablaze from nose to rudder, Aircraftman McAloney dashed into the flames and continued his efforts at rescue until pulled away in an unconscious condition, having received severe burns which necessitated his removal to hospital.

McAVOY

224

Thomas
Rank/Title: Private
Unit/Force/Occupation: 1st Bn., The Green Howards (Alexandra, Princess of Wales's Own Yorkshire Regiment)
Other Decorations: —
Date of Gazette: 25 Jul. 1939
Place/Date of Birth: Glasgow, Scotland — 11 Dec. 1909
Place/Date of Death: Glasgow — 20 May 1977
Place of Memorial: Maryhill Crematorium, Glasgow
Town/County Connections: Glasgow, Scotland
Remarks: (EGM); worked for the Post Office in Glasgow on leaving the army after the Second World War.

Account of Deed: On 15th March 1939 a truck belonging to the 1st Bn., The Green Howards caught fire at Jinsafut Camp, Palestine. The corporal* in charge of the mechanised transport, with great initiative and leadership, rallied the drivers and managed to avoid a general conflagration spreading throughout the camp. Private McAvoy of the same battalion also behaved with great gallantry in preventing the fire from spreading. (*See also entry for ATKINSON, T.)

McCABE   225

John
Rank/Title: Mr.
Unit/Force/Occupation: Assistant foreman, Royal Ordnance Factory
Other Decorations: —
Date of Gazette: 31 May 1940
Place/Date of Birth: —
Place/Date of Death: Royal Ordnance Factory — 2 Apr. 1940
Place of Memorial: —
Town/County Connections: —
Remarks: (EGM)

Account of Deed: On 2nd April 1940 when a fire was discovered at the factory Mr. McCabe did all that was possible to prevent it from spreading. When he realised that these measures were likely to be unsuccessful, he warned everyone to escape, but he himself stayed working on the job until an explosion occurred and he was killed instantly.

McCABE   226

John
Rank/Title: Mr.
Unit/Force/Occupation: Drawer, Stanrigg Colliery, Airdrie, Lanarkshire
Other Decorations: —
Date of Gazette: 13 Jun. 1919
Place/Date of Birth: — 6 Dec. 1901
Place/Date of Death: Caldercruix, Lanarkshire, Scotland — 29 Jan. 1974
Place of Memorial: —
Town/County Connections: Caldercruix, Lanarkshire, Scotland
Remarks: (EM); also awarded a silver watch of the Carnegie Hero Fund.

Account of Deed: On 9th July 1918 there was an inrush of moss into the workings at Stanrigg Colliery. Seventeen-year-old John McCabe, with two other drawers and three miners, was at the bottom of number 3 shaft when they were told that the moss had broken in. The other two drawers and the three men at once escaped. John McCabe, however, knowing that there were men at the face who might be cut off, returned for a quarter of a mile and warned the men. They were all ultimately collected and raised by another shaft. When he returned to the face, John McCabe did not know where the break had occurred, or whether the moss might not at any moment fill the workings through which he returned, as in fact it did soon afterwards. He faced grave and unknown danger, which might have been fatal, in order to enable others to escape.

McCARTHY   227

William Henry Debonnaire
Rank/Title: Boatswain (later Lieutenant-Commander)
Unit/Force/Occupation: Royal Navy
Other Decorations: —
Date of Gazette: 27 Jul. 1943
Place/Date of Birth: — 2 Apr. 1911
Place/Date of Death: Portsmouth, Hampshire — 21 Jul. 1978
Place of Memorial: —
Town/County Connections: Portsmouth, Hampshire
Remarks: (AM)

Account of Deed: In January 1943 Mr. McCarthy dived into a tempestuous sea from the Mole at Benghazi to save some Indian seamen who had been thrown into the sea from a raft. When a line was thrown he swam with it to the Indians, caught hold of one of them and successfully brought him ashore. He then returned to the rescue of another. There was grave danger that Mr. McCarthy would be dashed against the rocks by the gale and the high sea.

McCLYMONT

228

John McIntosh
Rank/Title: Corporal
Unit/Force/Occupation: Auxiliary Air Force
Other Decorations: —
Date of Gazette: 19 Jul. 1940
Place/Date of Birth: — 15 Oct. 1903
Place/Date of Death: —
Place of Memorial: —
Town/County Connections: —
Remarks: (EGM)

Account of Deed: On 18th January 1940 an aircraft with two occupants crashed during a snowstorm near 18 Balloon Centre at Bishopbriggs, Glasgow and immediately caught fire. Several of the Auxiliary airmen at the centre ran out to look for the plane and the first to find it was Corporal McClymont. He went as close as he could, saw one man through the flames and climbed into the burning fuselage. He pulled him clear of the wreckage and as he was doing so saw another man aboard. Although badly burnt himself Corporal McClymont entered the plane again and brought the second man out. Both men, however, were dead.

McCORMACK

229

Thomas William
Rank/Title: Mr.
Unit/Force/Occupation: Workman at a dry dock at Jarrow, Co. Durham
Other Decorations: Carnegie Hero Medal (probably the first Carnegie award)
Date of Gazette: 23 Jul. 1909
Place/Date of Birth: — 23 Feb. 1886
Place/Date of Death: Jarrow, Co. Durham — 6 Mar. 1973
Place of Memorial: —
Town/County Connections: Jarrow, Co. Durham
Remarks: (AM)

Account of Deed: On 27th November 1908 workmen were engaged in painting the inside of an iron tank in the stokehold of a steamer lying in dry dock at Jarrow. Because of the very strong fumes which were given off by the anti-corrosive paint used, the men worked in relays, each squad of three being relieved after 10 or 15 minutes. One workman was overcome by the fumes and the chargeman sacrificed his life in trying to save the man. Mr. McCormack, who had already been affected by the fumes while working in the tank, went to the chargeman's assistance, but was himself overcome and had to be rescued by the works manager, who, having pulled Mr. McCormack out, re-entered the tank to try to save the first man overcome by the fumes, but was himself overcome. The rescue of both these men was eventually effected from the top of the tank.

McKECHNIE

230

William Neil
Rank/Title: Flight Cadet (later Group Captain)
Unit/Force/Occupation: Royal Air Force
Other Decorations: —
Date of Gazette: 18 Oct. 1929
Place/Date of Birth: — 27 Aug. 1907
Place/Date of Death: Germany — 30 Aug. 1944
Place of Memorial: The Runnymede Memorial, Surrey
Town/County Connections: —
Remarks: (EGM). He was killed in action during flying operations over Germany.

Account of Deed: On 20th June 1929 Flight Cadet McKechnie had just landed his aircraft at Cranwell aerodrome when another machine crashed on landing some 200 yards away. The cadet left his aircraft and ran over to the scene of the accident where he found the pilot of the crashed aircraft lying semi-conscious in a pool of burning fuel. He ran into the flames, pulled the injured pilot out and extinguished his burning clothing, although he himself was badly burnt.

McTEAGUE
Thomas Patrick
Rank/Title: Corporal
Unit/Force/Occupation: Royal Air Force
Other Decorations: DCM
Date of Gazette: 12 Apr. 1929
Place/Date of Birth: — 2 Oct. 1893
Place/Date of Death: — 12 Apr. 1962
Place of Memorial: —
Town/County Connections: —
Remarks: (EGM); served in Second World War

231

Account of Deed: On 10th December 1928 an RAF pilot, whilst flying off Leysdown, Sheerness, crashed into the sea 200 yards from the shore. Corporal McTeague and Flying Officer Anderson* at once plunged into the sea and swam to his assistance. Between them they brought the pilot safely to shore in spite of a rough and bitterly cold sea. (*See also entry for ANDERSON, W.)

MADDEN
Horace William
Rank/Title: Private
Unit/Force/Occupation: 3rd Bn., Royal Australian Regiment
Other Decorations: —
Date of Gazette: 30 Dec. 1955
Place/Date of Birth: Cronulla, Sydney, New South Wales, Australia — 14 Feb. 1924
Place/Date of Death: Korea — 6 Nov. 1951
Place of Memorial: —
Town/County Connections: —
Remarks: Served in Second World War (Australian Motor Ambulance Convoy Platoon) and as a member of the British Commonwealth Occupation Force in Japan after the war.

232

Account of Deed: Private Madden was captured by Chinese Communists on 24th April 1951 near Kapyong. During the period of his captivity he resisted all enemy efforts to force him to collaborate, to such a degree that his name and example were widely known throughout the various groups of prisoners. In spite of repeated beatings and other forms of ill-treatment, Private Madden remained cheerful and undismayed. It must have been abundantly clear to him that his unco-operative attitude would result in his death, but as he got progressively weaker he remained undaunted in his resistance. He finally died of malnutrition and brutal ill-treatment.

MAHONEY
Herbert John
Rank/Title: Stoker Petty Officer
Unit/Force/Occupation: Royal Navy
Other Decorations: —
Date of Gazette: 23 Dec. 1927
Place/Date of Birth: — 4 Jun. 1892
Place/Date of Death: — 1 Dec. 1942
Place of Memorial: Plymouth Naval Memorial, Devon
Town/County Connections: —
Remarks: (EGM)

233

Account of Deed: In July 1927 HMS *Taurus* was steaming at high speed when the supports to the starboard fore turbo-fan fractured, causing the fan to drop; this in turn severed the main auxiliary exhaust steam pipe and several smaller exhaust pipes. Stoker Petty Officer Mahoney ordered the boiler room to be cleared at once, but remained himself, at great personal danger, to close stop-valves and take other necessary action. The boiler room was enveloped in steam, and large pieces of metal were being hurled about by the turbo-fan which was still running.

The only George Cross which was not gazetted. The award was made by His Majesty King George VI to the Governor of Malta by letter dated 15th April 1942:

THE MALTESE ISLANDS

The Citation read by President Roosevelt when he visited Malta in December 1943:

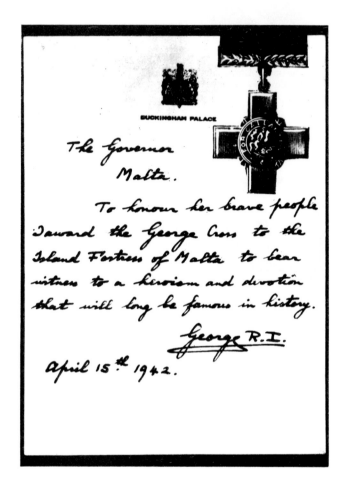

BUCKINGHAM PALACE

The Governor
Malta.

To honour her brave people I award the George Cross to the Island Fortress of Malta to bear witness to a heroism and devotion that will long be famous in history.

George R.I.

April 15th 1942.

"To honour her brave people I award the George Cross to the Island Fortress of Malta to bear witness to a heroism and devotion that will long be famous in history. *George R.I.*"

(NWMA Collection)

"In the name of the people of the U.S.A. I salute the Island of Malta, its people and its defenders, who, in the cause of freedom and justice and decency throughout the world, have rendered valorous service far above and beyond the call of duty.

"Under repeated fire from the skies Malta stood alone and unafraid in the centre of the sea, one tiny, bright flame in the darkness — a beacon of hope in the clearer days which have come.

"Malta's bright story of human fortitude and courage will be read by posterity with wonder and gratitude through all the ages.

"What was done in this island maintains all the highest traditions of gallant men and women who from the beginning of time have lived and died to preserve civilisation for all mankind."

7th December 1943

Franklin D. Roosevelt

MALTBY
235

Reginald Harry
Rank/Title: Staff Sergeant
Unit/Force/Occupation: 11th Armoured Car Company
Other Decorations: —
Date of Gazette: 3 Jul. 1926
Place/Date of Birth: —
Place/Date of Death: — 17 Dec. 1943
Place of Memorial: —
Town/County Connections: —
Remarks: (EGM)

Account of Deed: Staff Sergeant Maltby was awarded the Empire Gallantry Medal in recognition of the heroism he displayed in saving a child from drowning in a disused well in Lahore, India.

MANWARING
236

Thomas George
Rank/Title: Mr.
Unit/Force/Occupation: Miner, Arthur & Edward Colliery, Forest of Dean, Gloucestershire
Other Decorations: —
Date of Gazette: 1 Nov. 1949
Place/Date of Birth: — 11 Dec. 1916
Place/Date of Death: —
Place of Memorial: —
Town/County Connections: Lydbrook, Gloucestershire
Remarks: (EM)

Account of Deed: On the 10th June 1949 the Arthur and Edward Colliery, Forest of Dean, was flooded by a sudden inrush of water. Evacuation of the mine was ordered as soon as the water broke in and the escape of the men who were underground was organised by officers of the mine. At one point during the evacuation it was found that two men who were old and feeble had been left in the workings. Mr. Manwaring, who had voluntarily stayed to help these men, together with one of the mine officials, assisted them towards the main shaft. By this time, however, the flood had completely cut them off from the main shaft so the party had to find a way to the second shaft. The going was difficult and dangerous and the air in places very bad; they had to wade through torrents of water and sometimes clamber over falls of ground. One of the old men was very exhausted and had to be pushed along in a truck, but eventually after about 7 hours underground, the party reached the second shaft and were hauled to safety.

MARCH
237

Frederick Hamilton
Rank/Title: Mr.
Unit/Force/Occupation: Chauffeur to Sir Lee Stack, Governor-General of the Sudan
Other Decorations: MBE
Date of Gazette: 5 Dec. 1924
Place/Date of Birth: Bowning, Yass, New South Wales, Australia — 6 Aug. 1891
Place/Date of Death: Khartoum, Sudan — 31 Oct. 1977
Place of Memorial: —
Town/County Connections: —
Remarks: (EGM); served in First and Second World Wars.

Account of Deed: On 19th November 1924 Mr. March was acting as chauffeur to Sir Lee Stack, Governor-General of the Sudan and Sirdar of the Egyptian Army, when near the Ministry of Public Instruction in Cairo, seven Egyptians opened fire simultaneously on the car from the pavement. The Sirdar and his ADC and Mr. March himself were all wounded and had it not been for the great gallantry and presence of mind displayed by Mr. March both his passengers would almost certainly have been killed outright.

MARTIN

238

Cyril Arthur Joseph
Rank/Title: T/Major
Unit/Force/Occupation: Corps of Royal Engineers
Other Decorations: MC
Date of Gazette: 11 Mar. 1943
Place/Date of Birth: Derby, Derbyshire — 23 Jul. 1897
Place/Date of Death: South Cadbury, Yeovil, Somerset — 27 Nov. 1973
Place of Memorial: —
Town/County Connections: South Cadbury, Yeovil, Somerset
Remarks: Served in First World War; first GC winner to hold office in the VC & GC Association (Hon. Sec.) 1961-70.

Account of Deed: Major Martin was concerned with bomb disposal work in the London area from the beginning of the Blitz, and in the heavy raids of 1940 and 1941 he personally dealt with a large number of unexploded bombs. He continued with this dangerous work right into 1943 when on the night of 17/18 January a large calibre bomb fell on the warehouse of the Victoria Haulage Company at Battersea. At that time the warehouse was filled with new and heavy machinery tools from the USA and it was obvious that the disposal of the bomb must be of first priority. Upon examination it was discovered that it contained a new type of fuse which made it not only more formidable as an anti-handling and booby trap than any other type so far produced, but was intended to make it proof against any known disarming technique or equipment. It was decided that the best method of dealing with it would be to remove the base-plate and extract the main explosive filling. Major Martin was called to undertake this task, but when he had succeeded in removing the base-plate he found that the bomb contained solid cast TNT which could only be removed by high pressure steam. It was too risky to use the normal steaming out process by remote control, so it was decided to apply the steam nozzle by hand, only using enough steam at a time to soften the TNT sufficently to allow it to be scraped away in small quantities. This slow and nerve-wracking task took Major Martin and another officer from the afternoon of the 20th January to 8.30am next day, by which time they had succeeded in removing the entire main filling of TNT from the bomb. The work had to be carried out in a cramped hole filled with steam and water in which they had to lie alongside the bomb. Throughout this long and highly dangerous operation and on two other occasions during that period when he was called on to deal with similar types of bomb, Major Martin displayed almost unbelievable and cold-blooded courage.

MASON

239

Dudley William
Rank/Title: Captain
Unit/Force/Occupation: Merchant Navy (Master, SS *Ohio*)
Other Decorations: —
Date of Gazette: 4 Sep. 1942
Place/Date of Birth: Surbiton, Surrey — 7 Oct. 1901
Place/Date of Death: Lymington, Hampshire — 26 Apr. 1987
Place of Memorial: —
Town/County Connections: Sway, Hampshire
Remarks: —

Account of Deed: In August 1942, the *Ohio*, a 14,000 ton tanker belonging to the Texas Oil Company on loan to the British Ministry of War Transport and under the command of Captain Mason, was one of a fleet of 14 merchant vessels being sent to the aid of Malta. The convoy, with its naval and air escort, first met enemy action on 11th August and next day when the expected air attacks began, it became apparent that the *Ohio* was to be the main target of the enemy. For the next four days she suffered continuous attacks from enemy aircraft and submarines. She sustained grave damage from a torpedo, two sticks of bombs lifted her right out of the water and another exploded in her boiler room, a Stuka crashed and exploded on her deck, her back was broken and she was twice abandoned and twice re-boarded. In spite of all this she finally reached Malta on 15th August and was literally carried into Valetta harbour, lashed between two destroyers and it was not until the last of her fuel had been pumped out that she finally sank. Captain Mason's award of the George Cross was not only for the master's personal indomitable courage and determination, but for every member of his crew.

MATA DIN

240

Rank/Title: Lance-Naik
Unit/Force/Occupation: 4th Bn., 19th Hyderabad Regiment
Other Decorations: —
Date of Gazette: 19 Nov. 1935
Place/Date of Birth: —
Place/Date of Death: —
Place of Memorial: —
Town/County Connections: —
Remarks: (EGM)

Account of Deed: At the time of the Quetta earthquake (31st May/1st June 1935) Lance-Naik Mata Din showed great gallantry and conspicuous devotion to duty in his rescue work, and in particular in managing to extricate a man who was buried in a very dangerous place, and for whom three unsuccessful rescue attempts had previously been made.

MATTHEWS

241

Lionel Colin
Rank/Title: Captain
Unit/Force/Occupation: Corps of Signals, Australian Military Forces
Other Decorations: MC
Date of Gazette: 28 Nov. 1947
Place/Date of Birth: Stepney, South Australia — 15 Aug. 1912
Place/Date of Death: Kuching, Borneo — 2 Mar. 1944
Place of Memorial: Labuan War Cemetery, Sabah; Lionel Matthews Signals Memorial Scholarship (to help educate children of ex-servicemen).
Town/County Connections: —
Remarks: —

Account of Deed: Captain Matthews was captured by the Japanese when Singapore fell on 15th February 1942. During his imprisonment, he was continually interrogated and tortured in an attempt to make him give information which would have implicated his colleagues and been beneficial to the Japanese. He steadfastly refused to give them any help at all and was finally executed.

MAY

242

Phillip Robert Stevens
Rank/Title: Leading Seaman
Unit/Force/Occupation: Royal Navy
Other Decorations: —
Date of Gazette: 25 Nov. 1947
Place/Date of Birth: — 6 Aug. 1922
Place/Date of Death: —
Place of Memorial: May Road, Daget's Wood, Chatham, Kent named after him.
Town/County Connections: Whitley Bay, Northumberland; Herne Bay and Broadstairs, Kent.
Remarks: (AM); served throughout the Second World War, taking part in the evacuations from Dunkirk and Burma and in the landings in Madagascar, North Africa, Sicily, Italy and Greece.

Account of Deed: On 20th June 1947 HM Cable Ship *St. Margarets* was lying at Hay Wharf, Malta when a chief petty officer, entering No. 2 cable tank, was overcome by gas. The First Lieutenant, the Boatswain and four ratings all tried to rescue him and were themselves overcome. Leading Seaman May then entered the tank and in a series of rescues in which he tied a line round each of the men, so enabling them to be hauled on deck, he saved the lives of the six who had gone to the rescue of the chief petty officer, although the latter died later. After his third venture, Leading Seaman May was himself so exhausted by the fumes and exertion that a ship-mate offered to relieve him, but this man was overcome by gas and needed to be rescued. The leading seaman therefore continued his gallant work single handed until the task was completed.

MEADOWS   243
Albert John
Rank/Title: Mr.
Unit/Force/Occupation: Assistant store keeper at the distillery of W.A. Gilbey Ltd., Camden Town, London
Other Decorations: —
Date of Gazette: 29 Dec. 1931
Place/Date of Birth: — 6 Jun. 1904
Place/Date of Death: Selby, West Sussex — 19 Mar. 1988
Place of Memorial: —
Town/County Connections: Bognor Regis, Sussex
Remarks: (EM)

Account of Deed: On 18th September 1931 an employee of the distillery, who was cleaning out the residue in an empty cherry brandy vat, was discovered unconscious in the vat by a mate, having apparently been gassed by the carbon dioxide generated by the fermentation of the residue. Several unsuccessful attempts were made by various people, including one of the firm's analysts who was himself overcome by the gas. Mr. Meadows then volunteered to go into the vat and at the second attempt, with a wet cloth round his mouth and a rope round his body he succeeded in rescuing the analyst. His third attempt to rescue the first victim was unsuccessful, but having asked for a length of rubber gas piping, he put it into his mouth to breathe through and taking a looped rope he went down a fourth time. This time he managed to put the rope round the unconscious man and they were both drawn up from the vat.

MERRIMAN   244
Arthur Douglas
Rank/Title: Dr.
Unit/Force/Occupation: Part-time Experimental Officer, Directorate of Scientific Research, Ministry of Supply
Other Decorations: OBE
Date of Gazette: 3 Dec. 1940
Place/Date of Birth: — 25 Nov. 1892
Place/Date of Death: Streatham, London — 4 Nov. 1972
Place of Memorial: Streatham Cemetery, London
Town/County Connections: Streatham, London
Remarks: DL, London, 1955

Account of Deed: Dr. Merriman was an Experimental Officer in the Directorate of Scientific Research who tackled some of the first of the unexploded bombs in the early summer of 1940. Although he was supposed to be a part-time experimental officer with duties mainly in the office, he did, in fact, on many occasions, volunteer to carry out personally very dangerous bomb disposal tasks at the request of the War Office and Air Ministry. On 11th September 1940 he and the Director General of Scientific Research tackled a bomb which had fallen in Regent Street, London. As they started work they heard the bomb ticking and knew that all they could do was to get out as much of the explosive as possible so that when the bomb did explode the bang would be comparatively subdued and harmless. Their timing was perfect. They went on working to the last possible minute, made their getaway successfully, and when the explosion did occur, it only caused some broken windows.

MAXWELL-HYSLOP, Alexander Henry — see HYSLOP, Alexander Henry MAXWELL-

MILES   245
Alfred
Rank/Title: Able Seaman
Unit/Force/Occupation: Royal Navy
Other Decorations: —
Date of Gazette: 29 Apr. 1941
Place/Date of Birth: — 12 Jun. 1899
Place/Date of Death: Gillingham, Kent — 27 May 1989
Place of Memorial: —
Town/County Connections: Gillingham, Kent
Remarks: (AM); served in First World War.

Account of Deed: On 1st December 1940 when HMS *Saltash* was passing from one dock basin to another in Grimsby, a wire was run out from the starboard bow to the weather corner of the gate so as to hold the bow up to the wind. The wire was taken to the windlass, but this was too slow, and men were picking up the slack by hand, leaving some loose turns on the deck. As the ship drew level the order was passed to turn up and the wire was taken from the windlass to the bollards. Able Seaman Miles saw another able seaman standing in the bight of wire and called out to him to get clear, but he failed to do so and the wire drew taut round his ankles. Able Seaman Miles knew that the other man might be hauled through the bullring and that if he himself were caught in the wire he would be in the same danger; yet he tried to force the bight open with his hands. His right hand was jammed between the wire and the other man's foot but he said nothing and still tried to free his shipmate. The hurt which caused the loss of his hand was not known until later. The trapped man was dragged along the deck to the bullring but way was taken off the ship just in time to save him.

MILES
246

Leonard John
Rank/Title: Mr.
Unit/Force/Occupation: ARP Warden
Other Decorations: —
Date of Gazette: 17 Jan. 1941
Place/Date of Birth: —
Place/Date of Death: Ilford, Essex — 22 Sep. 1940
Place of Memorial: —
Town/County Connections: St. Bride's Magor, Gwent, Wales; Ilford, Essex
Remarks: —

Account of Deed: On the night of 21st/22nd September 1940 at Ilford, Essex, Mr. Miles was on duty when he was warned of the imminent danger of a bomb exploding nearby. He left his own shelter to run out to warn other people whom he knew were in the danger area. He had succeeded in warning several of them when the explosion occurred. Although fatally injured, he refused to be attended to and directed his ARP workers to deal first with a fire which had been caused by a fractured gas main. His action saved the lives of many who had received his warning in time.

MILLER
247

Henry James
Rank/Title: Able Seaman
Unit/Force/Occupation: Royal Navy
Other Decorations: —
Date of Gazette: 16 Aug. 1940
Place/Date of Birth: Poole, Dorset — 28 Nov. 1900
Place/Date of Death: North Sea — 29 Apr. 1940
Place of Memorial: Portsmouth Naval Memorial, Hampshire and in Memorial Chapel, Church Hanborough Parish Church, Oxfordshire
Town/County Connections: Church Hanborough, Oxfordshire
Remarks: (EGM)

Account of Deed: On 29th April 1940 the submarine *Unity* on patrol duty in the North Sea, was in collision in the dark with the Norwegian freighter *Atle Jarl,* and sank a few minutes later. Lieutenant Low* and Able Seaman Miller were the two men on duty in the submarine control room. When the order to abandon ship was given by the submarine commander they were instrumental in helping every member of the submarine to escape — except themselves. (*See also entry for LOW, J.N.A.)

MILLER
248

John Bryan Peter Duppa-
Rank/Title: T/Sub-Lieutenant
Unit/Force/Occupation: Royal Naval Volunteer Reserve
Other Decorations: —
Date of Gazette: 14 Jan. 1941
Place/Date of Birth: Posbury, Devon — 22 May 1903
Place/Date of Death: —
Place of Memorial: —
Town/County Connections: Posbury, Crediton, Devon
Remarks: Inspector-General, Min. of Education, Addis Ababa, 1945-47; Education Dept., Kenya 1947-57; author of *Saints and Parachutes*.

Account of Deed: Sub-Lieutenant Miller, who, with Able Seaman Tuckwell*, had been engaged in the dangerous work of mine disposal since the early days of the Blitz, was called to deal with a mine which had fallen into the soft mud in Roding River, which runs into Barking Creek. Sub-Lieutenant Miller decided to borrow a canoe and having put this on a fire-float with the kit, he and Able Seaman Tuckwell went off up the creek to where the mine was thought to be lying. They then left the River Fire Service fire-float and went on in the canoe until they sighted the black rim of the mine which was stuck in the mud by the nose. They worked together — Able Seaman Tuckwell handing the necessary tools to Sub-Lieutenant Miller who was working under about a foot of water. They managed to get out one fuse, but could not reach the other, so appealed to several crane-drivers who had come to see what was happening, and they at once volunteered to help. The two experts got back into the water, put ropes round the mine, and with the assistance of the crane-drivers, the huge cylinder was dragged slowly out of the creek, over the muddy bank and up on to the wharf. The final stages of the operation were then completed in comparative comfort. (*See also entry for TUCKWELL, S.J.)

MILLER 249
Thomas Frank
Rank/Title: Private
Unit/Force/Occupation: 2nd Bn., The Dorset Regiment
Other Decorations: —
Date of Gazette: 2 Jun. 1923
Place/Date of Birth: Portland, Dorset — 7 Oct. 1887
Place/Date of Death: Birmingham — 13 Dec. 1974
Place of Memorial: —
Town/County Connections: Portland, Dorset; Birmingham
Remarks: (EGM); served in First World War.

Account of Deed: At Nilambur, Malabar, India on the 24th September 1921 Private Miller displayed great gallantry by going forward towards a rebel ambush and firing on it at close range. He was instrumental in dislodging several snipers who were causing casualties to the British troops. He and Sergeant Hand* subsequently showed great courage in clearing up the situation. (*See also entry for HAND, W.G.)

MIRGHANY 250
Ahmed Muhammad
Rank/Title: —
Unit/Force/Occupation: —
Other Decorations: —
Date of Gazette: 2 Jan. 1933
Place/Date of Birth: —
Place/Date of Death: — 25 Aug. 1961
Place of Memorial: —
Town/County Connections: —
Remarks: (EGM)

Account of Deed: On 18th September 1932, at the height of the Nile flood, and at a point where the river is particularly dangerous, even for the strongest swimmer, Mirghany Ahmed Muhammad rescued three girls, the eldest only fifteen years of age, from drowning.

MITCHELL 251
John Henry
Rank/Title: Acting Second Hand (later Lieutenant-Commander RNVR)
Unit/Force/Occupation: Royal Naval Reserve
Other Decorations: BEM
Date of Gazette: 29 Apr. 1941
Place/Date of Birth: — 1 Jan. 1917
Place/Date of Death: West Norwood, Middlesex — 12 Apr. 1972
Place of Memorial: —
Town/County Connections: West Norwood, Middlesex
Remarks: (AM); became a Detective Inspector, Metropolitan Police.

Account of Deed: On 27th September 1940, in an Icelandic harbour a chief engineman fell into the sea between two trawlers. He could not swim and was soon unconscious. An unknown seaman jumped in to save him but was soon in difficulties. Second Hand Mitchell, hearing shouts, clambered over a vessel to the quay, ran 100 yards, climbed across two other ships and jumped into the water. He seized the first man by the hair and held up the other man until a rope was passed down from the trawler. This he secured round the now helpless seaman, using one hand, while he supported both men and himself by gripping the rope with his teeth. The seaman was then hauled out of the water and Mr. Mitchell, although fully clad and wearing sea boots, supported the chief engineman by treading water until a pilot ladder could be lowered. Mr. Mitchell had been in very cold water for 35 minutes and was unconscious when rescued.

MOHI-ud-DIN, Ghulam — see GHULAM MOHI-ud-DIN

MOORE
Richard Valentine
Rank/Title: T/Sub-Lieutenant (later Lieutenant-Commander)
Unit/Force/Occupation: Royal Naval Volunteer Reserve
Other Decorations: CBE
Date of Gazette: 27 Dec. 1940
Place/Date of Birth: London — 14 Feb. 1916
Place/Date of Death: —
Place of Memorial: —
Town/County Connections: Appleton, Cheshire
Remarks: AERE, Harwell 1946-53; Dept. of Atomic Energy, Risley 1953; Design and Construction of Calder Hall 1953-57; Chief Design Enginer 1955; UKAEA 1955; Dir. of Reactor Design 1958-61; Faraday Lecturer 1966; Hon. DTech. Bradford 1970.

252

Account of Deed: Sub-Lieutenant Moore was awarded the George Cross for gallantry and undaunted devotion to duty in connection with bomb disposal. Although he had had no practical training, he was called upon in an emergency and disarmed five mines.

MORRIS
Alfred Ernest
Rank/Title: Mr.
Unit/Force/Occupation: Mill foreman, Ashanti Goldfields Corporation Ltd.
Other Decorations: —
Date of Gazette: 4 Jul. 1924
Place/Date of Birth: — 19 Aug. 1881
Place/Date of Death: Bulawayo, Rhodesia — 24 Nov. 1973
Place of Memorial: —
Town/County Connections: —
Remarks: (EM); served in Boer War, First and Second World Wars.

253

Account of Deed: On 29th May 1923 at Obuasi, Ashanti, while a cyanide solution was being prepared in a vat on the premises of the Ashanti Goldfields Corporation, a native who was working in the vat contrary to orders was overcome by the fumes. Three people tried to rescue him but were overcome. Mr. Morris and the shift engineer arrived and between them managed to drag one of the men out of the vat. The shift engineer then collapsed and Mr. Morris tied a rope round himself, re-entered the vat and eventually succeeded in bringing out the other three men still alive. Unfortunately three of the victims did not survive but Mr. Morris had risked his life no less than three times in his work of rescue.

MORTESHED
Francis Austin
Rank/Title: Police Constable
Unit/Force/Occupation: Royal Ulster Constabulary
Other Decorations: —
Date of Gazette: 3 Jun. 1924
Place/Date of Birth: —
Place/Date of Death: — ?1940s
Place of Memorial: —
Town/County Connections: Londonderry, Ireland
Remarks: (EGM); later joined the Royal Air Force and reached the rank of sergeant.

254

Account of Deed: In March 1924 an attempt was made by three armed men to carry out a robbery in an office in Belfast. During the course of the robbery, the raiders shot, and mortally wounded, the manager of the office. They then fled, but were pursued by Police Constable Morteshed, and though one of the criminals turned and, at close range, endeavoured to shoot the constable, the latter effected his arrest single-handed without drawing his revolver.

MOSEDALE 255

William
Rank/Title: Mr.
Unit/Force/Occupation: Station Officer & Rescue Officer, Birmingham Fire Brigade
Other Decorations: —
Date of Gazette: 28 Mar. 1941
Place/Date of Birth: Birmingham — 28 Mar. 1894
Place/Date of Death: Nailsea, Somerset — 27 Mar. 1971
Place of Memorial: Arno's Vale Crematorium, Bristol
Town/County Connections: Upper Killamarsh, Derbyshire
Remarks: —

Account of Deed: On the night of 12th December 1940 an Auxiliary Fire Station in Birmingham was completely demolished by a very large high explosive bomb. A number of firemen were trapped in the station and civilians were buried in an adjoining house which had also been demolished. Hundreds of tons of debris covered the site and Station Officer Mosedale of Birmingham Fire Brigade immediately began tunnelling through to the control room, where he found that he could not reach some of the victims, so he tunnelled from another direction and found five men, one dead and the others injured. He gave them oxygen and they were taken to safety through the tunnel. He then went to direct operations for removing the debris from the cellar of the private house, only to find that the cellar itself had collapsed. He persevered and eventually reached the people who were trapped; three had been killed outright when the roof caved in, but he gave oxygen to the other four before they too were taken to safety. It was then necessary to begin tunnelling again to reach four other victims in the cellar under the Fire Station. Although badly injured, they were still alive and Mr. Mosedale was able to get them to safety. The cellar collapsed completely shortly after the removal of the last victim. These rescue operations had lasted twelve hours and had been carried out under intense bombardment.

MOSS 256

Brandon
Rank/Title: Special Constable
Unit/Force/Occupation: Coventry Constabulary
Other Decorations: —
Date of Gazette: 13 Dec. 1940
Place/Date of Birth: Brandon, Norfolk — 5 Jun. 1909
Place/Date of Death: —
Place of Memorial: —
Town/County Connections: Coventry, Warwickshire
Remarks: —

Account of Deed: In the bombing raid on Coventry on 14th November 1940, Special Constable Moss was on duty when a house was struck by a high explosive bomb and completely demolished, burying its three occupants. He led a rescue party into the building under extremely dangerous conditions, owing to collapsing debris and leaking gas. When conditions became even more critical he worked his way, alone, through a space he managed to clear and was able to save the three people. It was then discovered that other people were still buried in adjoining premises and Special Constable Moss again led the rescue. He worked unceasingly for over seven hours, with falling beams and debris round him and as a result of his superhuman efforts one more person was brought out alive and four bodies were recovered. During the whole of this time bombs were dropping and it was known that there was a delayed action bomb in the doorway of an inn 20 yards away.

MOTT 257

Joseph Edward
Rank/Title: Private
Unit/Force/Occupation: 1st Bn., The Essex Regiment
Other Decorations: —
Date of Gazette: 25 Feb. 1938
Place/Date of Birth: — 30 Mar. 1913
Place/Date of Death: Basildon, Essex — 12 Jan. 1983
Place of Memorial: —
Town/County Connections: Dagenham, Essex
Remarks: (EGM)

Account of Deed: At 8.20pm on 25th December 1937 a bomb was thrown into the Jordania Café, Haifa, which was crowded with soldiers and civilians at the time. The bomb fell at the feet of Private Mott, who was seated at a table with some other men of his battalion. With the utmost coolness and presence of mind he picked it up and hurled it through the window just before it exploded with great violence.

MOULD   258
John Stuart
Rank/Title: Lieutenant (later Lieutenant-Commander)
Unit/Force/Occupation: Royal Australian Naval Volunteer Reserve
Other Decorations: GM
Date of Gazette: 3 Nov. 1942
Place/Date of Birth: Gosforth, Newcastle upon Tyne, Northumberland — 1910
Place/Date of Death: Sydney, New South Wales, Australia — 9 Aug. 1957
Place of Memorial: —
Town/County Connections: —
Remarks: Became Chief Architect, New South Wales Housing Commission after the war.

Account of Deed: Lieutenant Mould joined HMS *Vernon* for enemy mining work in March 1941 and from that time was almost continuously employed on most dangerous operations. The work which resulted in his being awarded the George Cross was in the period 14th November 1941 to 30th June 1942 and included the successful handling of a wide range of disposal and clearance problems. For many of these he devised ingenious and unique solutions. A particularly dangerous phase was the stripping of the first magnetic-acoustic mine which had been fitted with delicate "anti-stripping" devices and which had caused the death of several other rendering-safe officers.

MOXEY   259
Eric Laurence
Rank/Title: A/Squadron Leader
Unit/Force/Occupation: Royal Air Force Volunteer Reserve
Other Decorations: —
Date of Gazette: 17 Dec. 1940
Place/Date of Birth: Sao Paulo, Brazil — 14 Apr. 1894
Place/Date of Death: Biggin Hill, Kent — 27 Aug. 1940
Place of Memorial: Churchyard of St. Peter & St. Paul, Cudham, Orpington, Kent
Town/County Connections: Leeds, Yorkshire; Birmingham
Remarks: Served in the First World War with The Yorkshire & Lancashire Regiment and the Royal Flying Corps.

Account of Deed: On 27th August 1940 two unexploded bombs were reported at Biggin Hill aerodrome. Squadron Leader Moxey, a Technical Intelligence Officer at the Air Ministry who had joined the Special Branch which dealt with the de-fusing of unexploded bombs, immediately volunteered to go to the site and remove them. He had already risked his life many times in rendering bombs safe and was well aware of the danger he was facing in this assignment. One of the bombs went off while he was examining it and he was killed.

MUHAMMAD   260
Muhammad Abdulla
Rank/Title: Nafar
Unit/Force/Occupation: Khartoum Police
Other Decorations: —
Date of Gazette: 12 Dec. 1924
Place/Date of Birth: —
Place/Date of Death: Khartoum — 23 Jun. 1978
Place of Memorial: —
Town/County Connections: —
Remarks: (EGM)

Account of Deed: On 27th and 28th November 1924 two platoons of the 11th Sudanese Regiment ran amok at Khartoum. Three British officers and two Syrian medical officers were killed by the mutineers and some nine other ranks were wounded. Nafar Muhammad Abdulla Muhammad and two other other members* of the Khartoum Police were recommended for great gallantry displayed during the disturbances. (*See also entries for NEGIB, Ibrahim and TAHA, El Jak Effendi).

MUNNELLY
Michael Joseph
Rank/Title: Mr.
Unit/Force/Occupation: Journalist
Other Decorations: —
Date of Gazette: 29 Jun. 1965
Place/Date of Birth: — 1941
Place/Date of Death: Regent's Park, London — 25 Dec. 1964
Place of Memorial: —
Town/County Connections: Regent's Park, London
Remarks: —

Account of Deed: On 24th December 1964 fourteen youths, who had been drinking, attacked the occupier of a flat in Regents Park Road, London, to which they had been refused entry. With milk bottles from a dairy opposite, they broke all the windows of the flat and when the dairyman went into the street to protect his property they set upon him. Mr. Munnelly, his brother and a friend, were the occupants of a third floor flat, and hearing the noise of breaking glass and shouting, went to help. They grabbed two of the youths, but Mr. Munnelly was hit on the head and released the one he was holding. The van in which some of the youths had left the scene then returned. Mr. Munnelly's friend followed it into a side street and banged on the window to make the driver stop. He managed to grab a youth sitting next to the driver, but was attacked and kicked unconscious. Mr. Munnelly, going to his friend's assistance, was kicked and fatally stabbed in the abdomen.

NAIRAC
Robert Laurence
Rank/Title: Captain
Unit/Force/Occupation: Grenadier Guards
Other Decorations: —
Date of Gazette: 13 Feb. 1979
Place/Date of Birth: Mauritius — 31 Aug. 1948
Place/Date of Death: Ireland — 15 May 1977
Place of Memorial: Window in the Guards Chapel, Wellington Barracks; Special Fund established in his memory, designed to assist adventurous training pursuits within the Regiment; room named after him at The Royal Military Academy, Sandhurst; chapel in St. Edward's House, Ampleforth, refurbished in his memory; a sports cup established by Lincoln College, Oxford, to be awarded annually to the best sportsman of the year; The Captain Robert Nairac Award Scheme, instituted by The Royal Society of St. George (Gloucestershire Branch); memorial plaque at The Boys' Club, Denmark Road, Gloucester.
Town/County Connections: Stonehouse, Gloucestershire; Sunderland, Co. Durham
Remarks: —

262

Account of Deed: During his four tours of duty in Northern Ireland Captain Nairac made an outstanding contribution. His quick analytical brain, resourcefulness, physical stamina and above all, his courage and dedication inspired admiration in everyone who knew him. On his fourth tour of duty he was a Liaison Officer at Headquarters, 3 Infantry Brigade. His task was connected with surveillance operations. On the night of 14/15th May 1977 he was abducted from a village in South Armagh by at least seven men. Despite his fierce resistance he was overpowered and taken across the border into the Republic of Ireland, where he was subjected to a succession of exceptionally savage assaults in an attempt to extract information which would have put other lives and future operations at serious risk. These efforts to break Captain Nairac's will failed entirely. Weakened as he was in strength — though not in spirit — by the brutality, he yet made repeated and spirited attempts to escape, but each time was eventually overpowered by the weight of numbers against him. After several hours in the hands of his captors, he was callously murdered by a gunman of the Provisional Irish Republican Army who had been summoned to the scene.

NANDLAL THAPA
Rank/Title: Naik (later Havildar)
Unit/Force/Occupation: 2nd Bn., 8th Gurkha Rifles, Indian Army
Other Decorations: —
Date of Gazette: 19 Nov. 1935
Place/Date of Birth: —
Place/Date of Death: Dhaulagiri, West Nepal — 27 Jun. 1987
Place of Memorial: —
Town/County Connections: —
Remarks: (EGM)

263

Account of Deed: At the time of the earthquake at Quetta (31st May/1st June 1935) Naik Nandlal Thapa was in one of the leading detachments of his battalion which was taken from the lines to Quetta City. There was no time for the party to collect any tools. On arrival in the city the detachment was split up into small parties and worked with their hands for three hours, extricating men and women from the debris. The area in which they were working was one of those which had suffered the greatest damage. During this period minor shocks frequently occurred, causing further falls of masonry in the houses in which they were digging. Naik Nandlal Thapa displayed conspicuous courage in entering tottering buildings, and rescued ten people alive at considerable risk to himself.

NAUGHTON
264

Frank
Rank/Title: Private (later Captain)
Unit/Force/Occupation: 10th Light Tank Coy., Royal Tank Corps
Other Decorations: —
Date of Gazette: 1 Feb. 1937
Place/Date of Birth: Burton-on-Trent, Staffordshire — 13 Mar. 1915
Place/Date of Death: —
Place of Memorial: —
Town/County Connections: Plympton, Devon
Remarks: (EGM); served in Second World War (Royal Armoured Corps)

Account of Deed: On 5th August 1936 two men of the 10th Light Tank Company were engaged in recovering an armoured car which had broken down on the Irish Bridge over the flooded River Indrayani, near Moshi when they were swept off the bridge into the water below, where there were very swift and dangerous currents. Private Naughton, who was fully clothed, except for his boots, immediately dived off the bridge to render assistance. Exhausted by the strong cross and underwater currents and unable to find either of the men, he had managed to regain shallow water when he saw one of the soldiers appear on the surface about 40 yards away. He again entered the river and by superhuman efforts succeeded in bringing the man ashore about 100 yards downstream.

NEGIB
265

Ibrahim
Rank/Title: Sol
Unit/Force/Occupation: Khartoum Police Force
Other Decorations: —
Date of Gazette: 12 Dec. 1924
Place/Date of Birth: —
Place/Date of Death: —
Place of Memorial: —
Town/County Connections: —
Remarks: (EGM)

Account of Deed: On 27th and 28th November 1924 two platoons of the 11th Sudanese Regiment ran amok at Khartoum. Three British officers and two Syrian medical officers were killed by the mutineers and some nine other ranks were wounded. Sol Ibrahim Negib and two other members* of the Khartoum Police were recommended for great gallantry displayed during the disturbances. (*See also entries for MUHAMMAD, Muhammad Abdulla and TAHA, El Jak Effendi)

NEWGASS
266

Harold Reginald
Rank/Title: T/Lieutenant (later Lieutenant-Commander)
Unit/Force/Occupation: Royal Naval Volunteer Reserve
Other Decorations: —
Date of Gazette: 4 Mar. 1941
Place/Date of Birth: — 3 Aug. 1896
Place/Date of Death: West Stafford, Dorchester, Dorset — 17 Nov. 1984
Place of Memorial: —
Town/County Connections: Dorchester, Dorset
Remarks: Served in the Territorial Army 1918-34 (Royal Artillery)

Account of Deed: On 28th November 1940 a German mine fell in Garston Gas Works, Liverpool and paralysed industry over a large area. The mine had fallen through the top of a large gasometer and the parachute had become entangled in the hole in the roof. The hole torn by the mine had allowed some of the gas to escape and the roof to sink, until the mine rested on the floor nearly upright, nose down in some seven feet of foul, oily water, and leaning against one of the brick pillars six feet high, on which the iron pillars supporting the roof were based. The bomb fuse was against the pillar and in order to get to it the mine had to be turned. Lieutenant Newgass who dealt with this assignment, one of the most dangerous ever undertaken, tackled the job entirely on his own. He could only breathe at all with oxygen supplied in cylinders, six of which he used during the operation. On the first cylinder he did his inspection and made his plan. On the second he took down his tools and a ladder. On the third he put sandbags round the nose of the mine, climbed to the top of a brick pillar and lashed the top of the mine to the iron roof support. On the fourth he turned the mine, removed the bomb fuse and unit primer and detonater. On the fifth he turned the mine again and undid the clock keep ring and on the last cylinder he withdrew the clock — and the mine was safe.

NEWMAN
267

Alfred William
Rank/Title: Acting Mate (later Commander)
Unit/Force/Occupation: Royal Navy
Other Decorations: —
Date of Gazette: 1 Mar. 1918
Place/Date of Birth: Empingham, Rutland — 8 Apr. 1888
Place/Date of Death: East Grinstead, Sussex — 1 Sep. 1984
Place of Memorial: —
Town/County Connections: Empingham, Rutland; East Grinstead, Sussex
Remarks: (AM)

Account of Deed: On 10th October 1917 an alarm of fire was given in the after magazine of HMS *Tetrarch*. Mr. Newman, who was on the upper deck, went to the magazine as soon as he heard the alarm and, seeing smoke issuing from a box of cordite, opened the lid and passed the cartridges on to the upper deck, where they were thrown overboard. One cartridge in the middle of the box was very hot and smoke was issuing from the end. This prompt and gallant action probably saved the magazine from blowing up and the loss of many lives.

NEWNHAM
268

Lanceray Arthur
Rank/Title: T/Colonel
Unit/Force/Occupation: The Middlesex Regiment
Other Decorations: MC
Date of Gazette: 18 Apr. 1946
Place/Date of Birth: — 3 Aug. 1889
Place/Date of Death: Sham Shui Po Prison Camp, Hong Kong — 18 Dec. 1943
Place of Memorial: Stanley Military Cemetery, Hong Kong
Town/County Connections: —
Remarks: —

Account of Deed: Colonel Newnham, whilst a prisoner of war in Japanese hands, tried to gain contact with British agents, and early in 1943 he succeeded in doing so. While correspondence was being exchanged and plans for a general break-out being arranged, the Japanese discovered the organisation and on 10th July 1943 Colonel Newnham and a number of others* were arrested. He was constantly interrogated, starved, tortured and finally sentenced to death in an endeavour to make him talk, but he remained absolutely silent and was executed on 18th December 1943. (*See also entry for FORD, D.)

NICHOLLS
269

Arthur Frederick Crane
Rank/Title: A/Brigadier
Unit/Force/Occupation: Coldstream Guards
Other Decorations: —
Date of Gazette: 1 Mar. 1946
Place/Date of Birth: Bexhill-on-Sea, Sussex — 8 Feb. 1911
Place/Date of Death: Albania — 11 Feb. 1944
Place of Memorial: Phaleron War Cemetery, Athens, Greece
Town/County Connections: Bexhill-on-Sea, Sussex
Remarks: —

Account of Deed: In October 1943 Brigadier Nicholls was parachuted into Albania as General Staff Officer to the Allied Military Mission, which was organising resistance activities against the Germans in that country. The Mission was attacked and dispersed by the Germans in December and from then until the end of January 1944 Brigadier Nicholls was a fugitive in the mountains in bitter weather and conditions of extreme hardship. He suffered so severely from frost-bite that he ordered an inexperienced man to amputate both his legs without an anaesthetic, and was then towed along over the mountains on his greatcoat by two members of his party. He was determined to make contact with the nearest British Mission and he succeeded in making his report, upon which important questions of Allied strategy and policy depended. He had, however, taxed his body beyond its limit and he died of gangrene and heart failure early in February 1944.

NIGHTALL
James William
Rank/Title: Mr.
Unit/Force/Occupation: Fireman, London & North Eastern Railway
Other Decorations: LNER Medal for courage and resource, Order of Industrial Heroism
Date of Gazette: 25 Jul. 1944
Place/Date of Birth: Littleport, Cambridgeshire — 1922
Place/Date of Death: Soham, Cambridgeshire — 2 Jun. 1944
Place of Memorial: Memorial plaque formerly at Soham Station, Cambridgeshire now in Soham Village College; locomotive named after him.
Town/County Connections: Littleport and Soham, Cambridgeshire
Remarks: —

270

Account of Deed: In the early hours of 2nd June 1944, an ammunition train of 51 trucks, filled with unfused bombs destined for the American Air Force bases in East Anglia, was approaching Soham station in Cambridgeshire. Suddenly the driver* saw that the wagon next to the engine, containing forty 500lb. bombs, was on fire. He at once began to apply the steam brake very gradually, so as not to precipitate an explosion, and sounded two blasts on the engine whistle to give the fire warning to the guard and the signalman. When the train finally came to a halt just outside the station, Fireman Nightall jumped down, ran back to the burning wagon and attacked the coupling with a hammer. Within a minute he had uncoupled the burning truck from the rest of the train and rejoined the driver in the cab. The engine was then urged gently into motion, slowly pulling the burning truck away from the rest of the train. As they approached the signal box and the driver leant out of the cab to shout another warning to the signalman, the bombs in the blazing wagon exploded. A massive crater some 20 feet deep and 60 feet wide was blown in the middle of the railway track and all the buildings of Soham station and many more were obliterated or badly damaged. The engine lay on its side and beneath it lay the dead body of Fireman Nightall. The signalman later died of his injuries, but the driver, although blown sky-high, was not killed. (*See also entry for GIMBERT, B.)

NIVEN
George Paterson
Rank/Title: Able Seaman
Unit/Force/Occupation: Royal Navy
Other Decorations: —
Date of Gazette: 1 Jan. 1930
Place/Date of Birth: —
Place/Date of Death: — 2 Jan. 1947
Place of Memorial: —
Town/County Connections: —
Remarks: (EGM)

271

Account of Deed: On 26th July 1929 HMS *Devonshire* was carrying out full calibre firing with all eight guns (twin turrets) together. At the first salvo there was a heavy explosion which blew off the roof of one of the turrets. A midshipman* immediately took stretcher parties aft and ordered one crew to follow him and the other to rig hoses. When he reached the turret some very badly burnt men with their clothes still on fire were falling out of the hatch in the rear. He and Able Seaman Niven did what they could for them and then went into the gunhouse, where there was still a lot of cordite burning fiercely, and pulled out more bodies, after which they turned on the hoses and helped to cool things down. Though they did not realise it at the time they had both inhaled a large quantity of cordite fumes which had a most unpleasant delayed action effect. (*See also entry for COBHAM, A.J.)

NIX
Frank Emery
Rank/Title: Mr.
Unit/Force/Occupation: Miner
Other Decorations: —
Date of Gazette: 21 Nov. 1944
Place/Date of Birth: — 22 Apr. 1914
Place/Date of Death: —
Place of Memorial: —
Town/County Connections: Chesterfield, Derbyshire
Remarks: (EM)

272

Account of Deed: On 18th April 1944 a 'Bump' occurred at the coal face on which two miners were cutting coal with a compressed air machine, as a result of which the flamper over the bars from the left side end of the machine was broken for a distance of 35 yards, the roof lowering about 8 inches. The bar over one of the men lowered under the weight of the flamper and pinned his head against the edge of the conveyor pans. The trapped man shouted and signalled by knocking on the pans and his workmate stopped the machine and, as he was unable to go past the machine to help, shouted to Mr. Nix who had three men with him behind the machine. Two of these men slid down the pans and placed a prop to take the weight off the trapped man's head; Mr.

Nix followed them down and with the aid of the third man worked his way down the face side, resetting all the broken props (about 12) until he got to within three yards of the trapped man who was now hidden by a fall of earth. By this time the roof had lowered to about 15 inches from the floor making the rescue work more difficult and dangerous. When two of them had cleared away the earth it was obvious that the only way to effect a rescue was to lighten the bar and this Mr. Nix did by breaking the flamper with a hammer. When the bar was sufficiently uncovered he then sawed off the end and the trapped miner was released suffering only from severe shock and bruises.

OAKES   273
Wallace Arnold
Rank/Title: Mr.
Unit/Force/Occupation: Locomotive driver, British Rail
Other Decorations: Bronze Medal of the Carnegie Hero Trust
Date of Gazette: 18 Oct. 1965
Place/Date of Birth: Barbridge, Nantwich, Cheshire — 23 April 1932
Place/Date of Death: Withenshawe, Manchester — 12 June 1965
Place of Memorial: Buried at Haslington, near Crewe; memorials at Crewe Station and in Acton Primary School, near Nantwich; electric locomotive named after him.
Town/County Connections: Sandbach, Crewe, Cheshire
Remarks: —

Account of Deed: On 5th June 1965 Mr. Oakes was driving the locomotive of a relief passenger train. This train consisted of ten coaches and was reasonably well filled with passengers. About seven miles from Crewe, travelling at about 60mph the engine cab was suddenly filled with smoke, with flames blowing back from the fire box. The fireman at once climbed back through the window and managed to get onto the cab steps where he extinguished his burning clothing by rubbing himself against the plating. He could not get into the cab, but realising that the brakes had been applied, remained on the steps until the train stopped. The flames subsided and he re-entered the cab to find that Mr. Oakes was missing. He saw him lying on the cutting slope just ahead of the cab; his clothing was partly burnt and it was found later that 80% of his body was burnt. Instead of leaving the cab as soon as the blow-back occurred, Mr. Oakes had apparently remained to apply the brakes, open the blower and close the regulator partly. He had obviously not left the engine until it had come to rest, although he must have been aware that to remain at the controls was to risk his own life. Nevertheless he applied the brakes fully and took all measures he could to retain the effects of the blow-back. His action ensured the safety of his passengers but the terrible burns he suffered caused his death a week later.

O'HAGAN   274
Leo Francis
Rank/Title: Mr.
Unit/Force/Occupation: Explosive worker, Royal Gunpowder Factory, Waltham Abbey, Essex
Other Decorations: —
Date of Gazette: 6 Feb. 1940
Place/Date of Birth: —
Place/Date of Death: — 1968
Place of Memorial: —
Town/County Connections: Earlswood, Redhill, Surrey
Remarks: (EGM); joined the Royal Navy in 1943

Account of Deed: On 18th January 1940 an explosion occurred at the Royal Gunpowder Factory. At the time when the explosion took place Mr. O'Hagan and another explosive worker* — generally known as hillmen — were engaged on the nitration of glycerine, the most critical stage in the process of manufacture when the liability to detonation is greatest. The building in which the process was carried out was only 150 yards from the scene of the explosion and was also damaged. Over 1,000 lbs of nitroglycerine were under process and in a condition of instability. Mr. O'Hagan and the other hillman, realising the damage to life and property which would be caused by a further explosion, stood by their posts for some two hours, until the services were restored, and then calmly continued with their work until the whole charge had been brought to a state of stability. (*See also entry for SEWELL, S.W.)

O'LEARY (real name **GUERISSE**)
Patrick Albert (real names Albert Marie Edmond)
Rank/Title: Lieutenant-Commander
Unit/Force/Occupation: Royal Navy
Other Decorations: DSO
Date of Gazette: 5 Nov. 1946
Place/Date of Birth: Brussels, Belgium — 5 Apr. 1911
Place/Date of Death: Waterloo, Belgium — 26 Mar. 1989
Place of Memorial: —
Town/County Connections: —
Remarks: Officier Légion d'Honneur & Grand Officier Ordre Léopold (Belgium); Croix de Guerre (France & Poland); Medal of Freedom with golden palm (USA); Medical Officer; re-joined Belgian Army after 1946 (1st Lancers); joined Belgian Volunteer Bn. 1951 as Chief of Medical Service in Korea; Major-General in Belgian Army; Director General, Medical Service, Belgian Forces; retired 1970.

Account of Deed: Albert Guerisse was a doctor in the Belgian Army at the outbreak of war, but when Belgium fell, he managed to escape to England and joined the Royal Navy in the assumed name of Patrick O'Leary and was employed on the task of landing agents in France. He was captured by the French police during operations off the south coast of France in April 1941. He escaped whilst en route to a French prison and set up an organisation to help the escape of Allied prisoners of war and evaders. This organisation was so successful that it soon had to be expanded and Lieutenant-Commander O'Leary travelled frequently between the Dutch border and the south of France, escorting numbers of escapers himself. In March 1943 he was betrayed to the Gestapo by a member of his group and subjected to many forms of torture in an attempt to make him reveal the names, whereabouts and duties of the other members of the organisation. He never gave any information and after more ferocious experiments the Germans gave him up as hopeless and sent him to a concentration camp where he was again tortured. He was a prisoner in Mauthausen, Natzweiler, Newbremm and finally Dachau, where he stayed until liberation. From the time of its inception to the end of the war his group had been responsible for the rescue of over 600 British and American officers and men, and over 250 of these owed their safety directly to Lieutenant-Commander O'Leary.

OLIVER
Dick
Rank/Title: Leading Seaman
Unit/Force/Occupation: Royal Navy
Other Decorations: BEM
Date of Gazette: 2 Aug. 1928
Place/Date of Birth: — 6 Aug. 1901
Place/Date of Death: Christchurch, Dorset — 5 Feb. 1986
Place of Memorial: —
Town/County Connections: Mudeford, Hampshire
Remarks: (AM)

Account of Deed: On 23rd May 1928 whilst HMS *Warspite* was lying alongside Parlatorio Wharf, Malta, an examination of the bulge compartments situated on the port side aft was being carried out. The man-hole door of the lower bulge compartment was removed and the compartment tested and it was found that the air was foul and poisonous. A chief stoker attempted to enter the compartment and was overcome by gas and fell unconscious to the bottom, a distance of about 20 feet. The alarm was given and an officer* immediately went to the aid of the chief stoker, but the rescue attempt was unsuccessful and he had to be hauled to safety in an unconscious condition. At this point Leading Seaman Oliver, who was standing by with a shallow diving helmet, volunteered to attempt a rescue. Donning the helmet he was passed with considerable difficulty through the man-holes of the upper and lower bulge compartments and eventually succeeded in reaching the unconscious man and passing a line round his body so that he could be drawn up through the man-hole to the pontoon abreast the ship. (*See also entry for ARMYTAGE, R.W.)

OMARA

277

Edwardo
Rank/Title: Mr.
Unit/Force/Occupation:
Other Decorations: —
Date of Gazette: 9 Oct. 1934
Place/Date of Birth: — Uganda 1910
Place/Date of Death: —
Place of Memorial: —
Town/County Connections: —
Remarks: (EGM)

Account of Deed: A game scout who was anxious to punish a herd of marauding elephants, had wounded two bulls when one of them charged him and pinned him to the ground. Mr. Omara pulled out the scout's rifle from between the elephant's feet, but, being unable to reload it, attacked the elephant with his spear. He drove the animal off and eventually killed it and then carried the scout, whose injuries proved fatal, for three hours, to Adilang. Again, on another occasion, an elephant which had been burnt in a bush fire, and was consequently in a most dangerous temper, took possession of a village water-hole and terrorised the local population. Mr. Omara, at great risk to himself, killed it with a heavy hunting spear.

ORR

278

Samuel
Rank/Title: Special Head Constable (later Harbour Constable)
Unit/Force/Occupation: Royal Irish Constabulary
Other Decorations: —
Date of Gazette: 3 Jun. 1924
Place/Date of Birth: —
Place/Date of Death: — 14 Apr. 1958
Place of Memorial: —
Town/County Connections: Belfast, Ireland
Remarks: (EGM)

Account of Deed: Early in 1922 Special Head Constable Orr effected the capture of an armed criminal. Later in the same year, though unarmed himself, he tried to arrest two armed robbers. He succeeded in grappling with one, but while doing so was severely wounded by the other.

OSBORNE

279

Albert Matthew
Rank/Title: Leading Aircraftman
Unit/Force/Occupation: Royal Air Force Volunteer Reserve
Other Decorations: —
Date of Gazette: 10 Jul. 1942
Place/Date of Birth: — 19 Oct. 1906
Place/Date of Death: Malta — 1 Apr. 1942
Place of Memorial: Capuccini Naval Cemetery, Malta GC
Town/County Connections: Belfast, Ireland
Remarks: —

Account of Deed: Leading Aircraftman Osborne was fearless in fire-fighting and rescue operations during the fierce enemy attacks on Malta. Among his many acts of bravery were making safe the torpedo of a burning plane, working three feet from the main petrol tank for ten minutes, and extinguishing the fire on a burning plane during a heavy bombing attack. In one day alone he fought fires in two aircraft and saved one, freed the parachute of a burning flare caught in a plane, enabling the pilot to taxi clear, and checked the fire in another burning aircraft. He was killed on 1st April 1942 whilst leading a party to extinguish the flames in yet another burning plane.

O'SHEA
280

John Michael
Rank/Title: The Reverend
Unit/Force/Occupation: Parish Priest
Other Decorations: RNLI Gold Medal, Sea Gallantry Medal (Silver)
Date of Gazette: 30 Jun. 1924
Place/Date of Birth: —
Place/Date of Death: — ? after 1940
Place of Memorial: —
Town/County Connections: Ardmore, Co. Waterford, Ireland
Remarks: (EGM)

Account of Deed: On 18th March 1911 when the schooner *Teaser* was lost during a very heavy gale in Ardmore Bay, off the south coast of Ireland, The Reverend John Michael O'Shea led several very gallant attempts, in a small boat, to save the lives of the three members of the crew.

PARISH
281

Graham Leslie
Rank/Title: Sergeant
Unit/Force/Occupation: Royal Air Force Volunteer Reserve
Other Decorations: —
Date of Gazette: 2 Apr. 1943
Place/Date of Birth: Sheffield — 29 Aug. 1912
Place/Date of Death: Sudan — 16 Sep. 1942
Place of Memorial: Khartoum War Cemetery, Sudan
Town/County Connections: Sheffield, Yorkshire
Remarks: —

Account of Deed: In September 1942 Sergeant Parish was the navigator of an aircraft during a delivery flight from the United Kingdom to the Middle East Command. Shortly after taking off from an airfield in Anglo-Egyptian Sudan one morning, the port engine failed and the pilot attempted to turn round and land on the airfield, but the aircraft struck a building and immediately burst into flames. All the crew, with the exception of Sergeant Parish and a passenger, who had both legs broken, managed to get free from the blazing bomber. Sergeant Parish carried the helpless man to the rear turret in an endeavour to get him through, but the fire had become so fierce that they were both burnt to death. Sergeant Parish could have made his own escape, but his unselfish desire to save the passenger cost him his own life.

PARKER
282

Edward Donald J.
Rank/Title: Pilot Officer (later Squadron Leader)
Unit/Force/Occupation: Royal Air Force Volunteer Reserve
Other Decorations: DFC
Date of Gazette: 6 Aug. 1940
Place/Date of Birth: 20 May 1910
Place/Date of Death: Berlin — 16 Jan. 1943
Place of Memorial: Berlin 1939-1945 War Cemetery, Germany
Town/County Connections: —
Remarks: (EGM)

Account of Deed: On the night of 8th June 1940 Pilot Officer Parker was first pilot of an aircraft detailed for bombing operations. Just after taking off in complete darkness the port engine failed and a forced landing had to be made in a field. The aircraft crashed and immediately burst into flames. Pilot Officer Parker jumped out and got clear, to find that his navigator and air gunner were also safe but that the wireless operator was lying stunned near the burning aircraft. Knowing that there were four 500lb. bombs in the wreckage which might explode at any second Pilot Officer Parker returned and carried his wireless operator to a place of safety — and was able to protect the injured man when one of the bombs did in fact explode.

PATTON   283
John MacMillan Stevenson
Rank/Title: Lieutenant
Unit/Force/Occupation: 1st Bn., Corps of the Royal Canadian Engineers
Other Decorations: CBE
Date of Gazette: 17 Dec. 1940
Place/Date of Birth: Warwick, Bermuda — 29 Aug. 1915
Place/Date of Death: —
Place of Memorial: —
Town/County Connections: —
Remarks: —

Account of Deed: Lieutenant Patton was not a member of the established Bomb Disposal Unit, but was called upon urgently to help when a large bomb fell in an aircraft factory at Weybridge on 21st September 1940. Not being able to discover any obvious method of disarming it, he wisely decided that his best course was to remove it to a safe place as soon as possible and as carefully as possible. He towed the bomb away on a skid behind a lorry and dumped it in a bomb crater, where it exploded violently but harmlessly a few hours later.

PEARSON   284
Joan Daphne Mary
Rank/Title: Corporal (later Section Officer)
Unit/Force/Occupation: Women's Auxiliary Air Force
Other Decorations: —
Date of Gazette: 19 Jul. 1940
Place/Date of Birth: Mudeford, Hampshire — 26 May 1911
Place/Date of Death: —
Place of Memorial: —
Town/County Connections: Mudeford, Hampshire
Remarks: (EGM)

Account of Deed: On 31st May 1940 an hour after midnight, an aircraft crashed near the Women's Auxiliary Air Force quarters at Detling in Kent, the pilot being seriously injured, another officer killed outright and two airmen slightly injured. Upon hearing the crash Corporal Pearson rushed out and although she knew that there were bombs aboard she stood on the wreckage, roused the pilot, who was stunned, released his parachute harness and helped him to get clear. When she had got him about 30 yards from the wreckage a 120lb. bomb went off and Corporal Pearson threw herself on top of the pilot to protect him from blast and splinters. She remained with him until a stretcher party arrived and then returned to the burning aircraft to look for the fourth member of the crew. She found him — the wireless operator — dead in the bomber.

PEARSON   285
Robert
Rank/Title: Mr.
Unit/Force/Occupation: Workman at H. Marsland Ltd., Stockport, Cheshire
Other Decorations: Order of Industrial Heroism
Date of Gazette: 20 Oct. 1925
Place/Date of Birth: Stockport, Cheshire — 4 Jul. 1896
Place/Date of Death: Stockport, Cheshire — 17 Mar. 1973
Place of Memorial: —
Town/County Connections: Stockport, Cheshire
Remarks: (EM)

Account of Deed: On 11th July 1925 while two boys were working in a vat at the works of H. Marsland Ltd. there was a sudden inrush of scalding liquid and steam owing to a mistake made in opening the pipe of another vat. The screams of the scalded boys attracted the attention of other workers and attempts were made to extricate them through the man-holes. One boy was successfully rescued, but the other, after reaching the man-hole, fell back into the vat owing to the burnt flesh of his hand giving way. Mr. Pearson then came on the scene. He had seen the one boy pulled out terribly scalded and on hearing that the other was still in the vat he immediately jumped down the man-hole and after groping about found the lad and hoisted him up sufficiently to enable those outside to drag him to the surface. Mr. Pearson's feet were severely scalded during his efforts and he was practically unconscious when he was drawn to the top. He had attempted the rescue without any regard for his own safety, while neither the scalding he experienced nor the intense pain which he suffered deterred him from persisting in his efforts to get the lad out of the vat.

PIR KHAN

286

Rank/Title: Subedar-Major
Unit/Force/Occupation: Indian Army (Jemadar Badragga to the Commander, Royal Enginers)
Other Decorations: —
Date of Gazette: 28 Jun. 1940
Place/Date of Birth: —
Place/Date of Death: —
Place of Memorial: —
Town/County Connections: —
Remarks: (EGM)

Account of Deed: Subedar-Major Pir Khan was escorting a party of officers of the Royal Engineers up the Tochi road, some three miles from Bannu in the Waziristan District on the North-West Frontier of India on 3rd February 1940 when they were ambushed by 30 hostile tribesmen. After the first volley the colonel, a major and Subedar-Major Pir Khan managed to take cover behind a low irrigation culvert by the side of the road and the latter opened fire on the advancing tribesmen with such effect that they started to retreat. His gallant conduct undoubtedly saved the lives of the two officers and prevented the tribesmen from looting the cars and mutilating the bodies of the dead and dying which were lying in the road.

POLLITT

287

James
Rank/Title: Mr.
Unit/Force/Occupation: Miner, South Kirkby Colliery, Yorkshire
Other Decorations: —
Date of Gazette: 17 Apr. 1936
Place/Date of Birth: Wigan, Lancashire — 2 Dec. 1896
Place/Date of Death: Wigan, Lancashire — 8 Sep. 1972
Place of Memorial: —
Town/County Connections: South Kirkby, Yorkshire; Wigan, Lancashire
Remarks: (EM)

Account of Deed: On 22nd/23rd August 1935 explosions occurred at South Kirkby Colliery and a number of men were injured. Later in the evening of the 23rd August, after the rescue parties had left the mine, it was found that a member of one of the rescue parties was still missing. There were reasons for fearing that another explosion might shortly occur and that a fresh search might only swell the casualty roll, but volunteers were anxious to go down into the mine and make a further attempt. A rescue party, captained by Mr. Pollitt, entered the district and succeeded in finding the missing man and brought him safely to the surface. Great courage and pertinacity were displayed by the men who took part in the rescue operations, and in particular services of outstanding merit were rendered by Mr. Pollitt and others who took charge at each stage. (See also entries for BASTER, N. and BEAMAN, G.W.)

PRATT

288

Michael Kenneth
Rank/Title: Constable
Unit/Force/Occupation: Victoria Police, Melbourne, Australia
Other Decorations: —
Date of Gazette: 4 Jul. 1978
Place/Date of Birth: East Melbourne, Victoria, Australia — 13 Nov. 1954
Place/Date of Death: —
Place of Memorial: —
Town/County Connections: —
Remarks: —

Account of Deed: On the morning of 4th June 1976, Constable Pratt, who was off duty and unarmed, was driving in his car past a bank in Clifton Hill when he saw three masked men entering the bank. He noticed that they were carrying firearms and realised that they were about to commit an armed robbery. He immediately turned his car, switched up the lights and, sounding his horn, mounted the kerb and blocked the bank entrance, at the same time shouting to a passer-by to get police assistance. The raiders were taken by surprise, but one of them threatened the constable with a gun and told him to remove the car. He refused, removed the ignition key and armed himself with the handle of a car jack. The men then tried to leave the bank and Constable Pratt managed to grab one of them, and during the violent struggle which ensued, the raider was knocked unconscious. A second gunman had now left the bank and was threatening to shoot the officer at close range. Constable Pratt was by this time grappling again with the first man who had recovered consciousness, and while he was trying to retain his hold on his captive, he was shot and seriously wounded. He had displayed outstanding bravery and complete disregard for his own safety when, unarmed and single-handed, he faced and attempted to arrest three dangerous armed criminals.

PUGH
289

Herbert Cecil
Rank/Title: Squadron Leader The Reverend
Unit/Force/Occupation: Royal Air Force Volunteer Reserve, Chaplains' Branch
Other Decorations: —
Date of Gazette: 1 Apr. 1947
Place/Date of Birth: Johannesburg, Transvaal, South Africa — 2 Nov. 1898
Place/Date of Death: Atlantic — 5 July 1941
Place of Memorial: The Runnymede Memorial, Surrey
Town/County Connections: —
Remarks: Served as a Private with the South African Field Ambulance 1917-1919.

Account of Deed: The Rev. Herbert Pugh was a passenger on board the Troop Carrier *Anselm* when the ship was torpedoed on 5th July 1941. It was soon obvious that she was sinking rapidly and the Padre did everything in his power to comfort and help the injured without thought of his own safety. When it was clear that the ship could only remain afloat for a few more minutes, it was discovered that a number of airmen were still trapped in part of the ship which had been badly damaged, and the Padre insisted on being lowered into the damaged hold, and knelt with them in prayer as the ship sank.

PURVES, Mrs. J.W. — see **VAUGHAN,** Margaret

PURVIS
290

James Sidney
Rank/Title: Mr.
Unit/Force/Occupation: Pit lad, South Garesfield Colliery, Durham
Other Decorations: —
Date of Gazette: 22 Nov. 1929
Place/Date of Birth: Northumberland — 2 Jul. 1904
Place/Date of Death: —
Place of Memorial: —
Town/County Connections: Durham, Co. Durham
Remarks: (EM)

Account of Deed: On 17th May 1929 a colliery deputy was injured during blasting operations. An overman set off down the pit and, collecting James Purvis and another lad* at the bottom of the shaft and a tram and stretcher, went in search of the deputy. They were joined by two hewers. Meanwhile five other men had attempted a rescue, but four of them were overcome by gas while the fifth managed to crawl out just in time. The overman organised his party and by repeated efforts they succeeded in extricating the five men, of whom three were dead. The rescue party were all affected by the fumes. For an hour, during the whole of which time the atmosphere was thick with smoke and gas, the overman with James Purvis and his other three helpers, know- ingly and repeatedly risked their lives in determined efforts to save the lives of their fellows, and there is no doubt that but for their courageous action the death-toll would have been heavier than it was. (*See also entry for BAKER, J.T.)

QUINTON
291

John Alan
Rank/Title: Flight Lieutenant
Unit/Force/Occupation: 228 Operational Conversion Unit, Royal Air Force
Other Decorations: DFC
Date of Gazette: 23 Oct. 1951
Place/Date of Birth: — 2 Feb. 1921
Place/Date of Death: Yorkshire — 13 Aug. 1951
Place of Memorial: Annual prize awarded at the Halton School of Technical Training.
Town/County Connections: Cuffley, Hertfordshire
Remarks: Served in Second World War

Account of Deed: On 13th August 1951 Flight Lieutenant Quinton was a navigator under instruction in a Wellington aircraft which was involved in a mid-air collision. An Air Training Corps cadet was with him in the rear compartment of the aircraft when the force of the impact caused the Wellington to break up and plunge to earth out of control. Flight Lieutenant Quinton picked up the only parachute he could see, clipped it on to the cadet's harness, showed him how to pull the rip-cord and ordered him to jump. The cadet landed safely and was the only survivor of the disaster.

RACKHAM
Geoffrey
Rank/Title: Second Lieutenant
Unit/Force/Occupation: Royal Army Service Corps, attd. 545th Siege Bty., Royal Horse Artillery
Other Decorations: —
Date of Gazette: 3 Jan. 1919
Place/Date of Birth: — 7 Aug. 1896
Place/Date of Death: Welwyn, Hertfordshire — 10 Jan. 1982
Place of Memorial: —
Town/County Connections: Welwyn, Hertfordshire
Remarks: (AM)

292

Account of Deed: At Le Cateau on 27th October 1918 a lorry (one of a convoy of seven) laden with shells and cartridges caught fire. Second Lieutenant Rackham, who was awakened by the fire alarm, hurried to the scene of the fire in his pyjamas to find that flames three to four feet high were issuing from the petrol tank. He put the cap on the tank, jumped into the driver's seat, started up the blazing lorry and drove it while cartridges were exploding, to a place of safety. He then helped to extinguish the flames. This prompt and courageous action averted what might have been great loss of life, for there were other loaded lorries close by and some 130 men of the battery were only 30 yards away.

RAHMAN
Abdul
Rank/Title: Havildar
Unit/Force/Occupation: 3rd Bn., 9th Jat Regiment, Indian Army
Other Decorations: —
Date of Gazette: 10 Sep. 1946
Place/Date of Birth: —
Place/Date of Death: Kletek, Java — 22 Feb. 1945
Place of Memorial: The Rangoon Memorial, Burma
Town/County Connections: —
Remarks: —

293

Account of Deed: On 22nd February 1945 a jeep in which Havildar Rehman was travelling with five other Indian soldiers, hit a mine and was hurled into a ditch where it burst into flames. Havildar Rehman was thrown clear but three of his comrades were pinned underneath the vehicle. His task of trying to extricate them was made more difficult as the ammunition carried in the jeep began to explode, but he got two of the men out and was attempting to rescue the third when the petrol tanks exploded. Before he died he called out to the ambulance party which was approaching that they should finish the task.

RAM DITTO — see DITTO RAM

RAM KIRPA — see KIRPA RAM

RANGIT SINGH
Rank/Title: Babu
Unit/Force/Occupation: Revenue Officer, United Provinces, India
Other Decorations: —
Date of Gazette: 1 Jan. 1935
Place/Date of Birth: —
Place/Date of Death: — Oct. 1942
Place of Memorial: —
Town/County Connections: —
Remarks: (EGM)

294

Account of Deed: This Revenue Officer was one night in the neighbourhood of the village of Jharvan in the Saharanpur District when he received information that a gang of 25 dacoits armed with shot guns and lathis were attacking the house of a wealthy Bania. He collected four men and went at once to the village where he attacked the dacoits, his only weapon being a pistol. When two of his men had been wounded and his pistol had temporarily jammed, Babu Rangit Singh still continued to attack. Eventually, after wounding one of the dacoits, he succeeded in driving them off.

REED 295

Henry Herbert
Rank/Title: Bombardier
Unit/Force/Occupation: 1 Maritime A.A. Regt., Royal Artillery
Other Decorations: Lloyd's War Medal for Bravery at Sea
Date of Gazette: 23 Sep. 1941
Place/Date of Birth: Sunderland, Co. Durham — 1911
Place/Date of Death: North Sea — 21 Jun. 1941
Place of Memorial: Bishopwearmouth Cemetery, Sunderland, Co. Durham
Town/County Connections: Sunderland, Co. Durham
Remarks: —

Account of Deed: While sailing in convoy from Blyth to London on 20th/21st June 1941 the SS *Cormount* was attacked by E-boats and aircraft and although sustaining a direct hit under the navigating bridge amidships, replied at once with defensive armament, and the men on the guns went on firing despite the hail of bullets and cannon shells. Bombardier Reed was badly wounded but refused to leave his anti-aircraft gun. Then, seeing that the Chief Officer was also badly wounded, the bombardier carried him from the bridge down two ladders to the deck below and put him in a shelter, before falling dead himself. It was afterwards discovered that his stomach had been ripped open by machine gun bullets.

REEVES 296

James Arthur
Rank/Title: Chief Officer (later Captain)
Unit/Force/Occupation: Merchant Navy
Other Decorations: Lloyd's War Medal for Bravery at Sea
Date of Gazette: 25 May 1943
Place/Date of Birth: — 15 Jun. 1911
Place/Date of Death: — 26 Dec. 1984
Place of Memorial: —
Town/County Connections: Darwen, Lancashire
Remarks: (AM); Deputy Secretary, Albert Medal Association 1966-72; Assistant County Commissioner for Scouts, Lancashire.

Account of Deed: Two men were seen floating in the oily water which flooded the engine-room to a depth of 25 feet after a ship had been torpedoed in the Arctic and was being abandoned. Both men were helpless, one being badly injured and the other overcome by oil fumes. All the engine-room ladders had been destroyed, but using a boat ladder, Chief Officer Reeves descended into the engine-room and tied lines round both men. While being hauled to safety one of the men slipped back into the oily water and Mr. Reeves again went down into the engine-room, which was rapidly filling with surging oil and water, and tied another rope round the injured man who was then brought up on deck.

REHMAN, Abdul — see RAHMAN, Abdul

RENNIE 297

John
Rank/Title: A/Sergeant
Unit/Force/Occupation: The Argyll and Sutherland Highlanders of Canada
Other Decorations: —
Date of Gazette: 26 May 1944
Place/Date of Birth: Aberdeen, Scotland — 13 Dec. 1920
Place/Date of Death: Slough, Buckinghamshire — 29 Oct. 1943
Place of Memorial: Brookwood Military Cemetery, Surrey
Town/County Connections: —
Remarks: —

Account of Deed: Sergeant Rennie was supervising grenade throwing by members of his unit at a Canadian Training Camp at Slough, Buckinghamshire on 29th October 1943. One grenade had been successfully thrown but a second failed to clear the protective embankment and rolled back into the throwing area. Despite the fact that he had the time and opportunity to escape from danger Sergeant Rennie without the slightest hesitation dashed forward, putting himself between the grenade and his comrades, and attempted to pick it up and throw it clear. Before he could do so, however, the grenade exploded and Sergeant Rennie was fatally injured. By his action he prevented serious and possibly fatal injuries to three other soldiers who were within five yards of the explosion.

REYNOLDS

298

Edward Womersley
Rank/Title: Lieutenant (later Major)
Unit/Force/Occupation: 101 & 102 Bomb Disposal Sections, Corps of Royal Engineers
Other Decorations: —
Date of Gazette: 17 Sep. 1940
Place/Date of Birth: — 27 Jun. 1917
Place/Date of Death: — 16 Dec. 1955
Place of Memorial: —
Town/County Connections: Birmingham
Remarks: (EGM)

Account of Deed: On 17th August 1940 a 250 kilo bomb fell in a garden among some council houses and did not explode. Lieutenant Reynolds was a member of one of the newly formed Bomb Disposal Sections and was sent to investigate. On digging down 17 feet he found that the bomb had a new type of fuse concerning which no instructions had been issued. After traffic had been stopped and the people had been cleared out of the neighbouring houses, he removed the fuse. Again on 3rd September 1940 he successfully dealt with another unexploded bomb.

RHOADES

299

William Ernest
Rank/Title: Sergeant
Unit/Force/Occupation: 6 Squadron, Royal Flying Corps
Other Decorations: MSM
Date of Gazette: 1 Jan. 1918
Place/Date of Birth: — 6 Feb. 1888
Place/Date of Death: Eastbourne, Sussex — 4 Mar. 1972
Place of Memorial: —
Town/County Connections: Eastbourne, Sussex
Remarks: (AM)

Account of Deed: At an aerodrome in France on 14th October 1916 a bomb accidentally exploded in the mouth of a dug-out forming a bomb store which contained a large number of bombs packed in wooden cases and a quantity of rockets. Two men were killed by the explosion, and another man, who was severely injured, was thrown down into the store. Dense volumes of smoke issued from the dug-out, and there was great risk of a further explosion. A young officer, on hearing a call for help, immediately entered the dug-out, followed by Sergeant Rhoades and between them they succeeded in rescuing the wounded man who would otherwise have been suffocated.

RICHARDS

300

Richard Walter
Rank/Title: Mr.
Unit/Force/Occupation: Member of Ross Sea Party of the Shackleton Trans-Antarctic Expedition
Other Decorations: The Polar Medal & Bar
Date of Gazette: 6 Jul. 1923 and 2 May 1924
Place/Date of Birth: Bendigo, Victoria, Australia — 14 Nov. 1893
Place/Date of Death: Victoria, Australia — 8 May 1985
Place of Memorial: Medal awarded annually to the best student at the Ballarat School of Mines
Town/County Connections: —
Remarks: (AM); Principal of Ballarat School of Mines & Industry 1946-58; author of *The Ross Sea Shore Party*.

Account of Deed: The Shackleton Trans-Antarctic Expedition of 1914-17 had for its object the crossing of the Antarctic Continent from the Weddell Sea to the Ross Sea via the South Pole, a distance of about 1700 miles. As sufficient supplies for the journey could not be carried, a chain of depots on the Ross Sea side had to be established as far southwards as possible. With this end in view the ship *Aurora* was sent to McMurdo Sound at the southern extremity of the Ross Sea to winter there so that only a portion of the stores and equipment needed to be disembarked. The *Aurora* reached McMurdo Sound in January 1915 but during a blizzard in May was blown out to sea and was unable to return, leaving the nine members of the expedition who were on shore stranded. They recognised that failure to establish the depots would result in the loss of the main body and decided that they must carry out the allotted programme. This party, of which Mr. Richards was a member, started off on 9th October with two sledges and four dogs and 162 days later the surviving members arrived back with their mission accomplished. One member of the party had to be dragged on a sleigh for 42 days, mainly by hand labour, over a distance of 350 miles and he died when only 19 miles remained to be covered. The leader of the party collapsed at one point and all suffered from scurvy and snow blindness.

RICHARDSON

301

Gerald Irving
Rank/Title: Superintendent
Unit/Force/Occupation: Lancashire Constabulary
Other Decorations: —
Date of Gazette: 13 Nov. 1972
Place/Date of Birth: Blackpool, Lancashire — 2 Nov. 1932
Place/Date of Death: Blackpool, Lancashire — 23 Aug. 1971
Place of Memorial: —
Town/County Connections: Blackpool, Lancashire
Remarks: Served with the Royal Corps of Military Police for his National Service, 1956-57.

Account of Deed: Following an armed raid on a jeweller's shop in Blackpool, Lancashire on 23rd August 1971, there was a prolonged chase by a number of police cars and a running gun battle against unarmed police. Superintendent Richardson, who had chased and tried to persuade one of the raiders to give up his gun, was shot in the stomach and sustained injuries from which he died the same day in hospital. Throughout the pursuit, all the police officers concerned were aware that they faced the threat of death or serious injury, but gave no thought to their own safety in their efforts to effect the arrest of armed and dangerous criminals. (See also entry for WALKER, C.)

RIDLING

302

Randolph Gordon
Rank/Title: Lieutenant (later Captain)
Unit/Force/Occupation: New Zealand Rifle Brigade
Other Decorations: —
Date of Gazette: 9 Dec. 1919
Place/Date of Birth: Auckland, New Zealand — 17 Mar. 1888
Place/Date of Death: Wellington, New Zealand — 13 Jan. 1975
Place of Memorial: —
Town/County Connections: —
Remarks: (AM); employed by Dept. of Education as supervisor in agricultural manual and technical work after First World War; Director, Wellington Technical College 1931-50; member of Consultative Committee on Recruitment, Education and Training of Teachers 1948.

Account of Deed: At Brocton Camp, Staffordshire on 19th April 1918 a recruit who was under instruction in bombing, dropped a live Mills' grenade in the throwing bay after pulling out the pin. Lacking the presence of mind to attempt to escape, he kicked the bomb towards the entrance and retreated to the inner end of the bay. Lieutenant Ridling, the bombing officer, seeing the man's danger, went to his rescue. Seizing him in his arms, he started to carry him out, but the bomb exploded before he could get clear of the bay, and he was wounded severely in the groin. The recruit, who was only slightly wounded, would have in all probability lost his life but for Lieutenant Ridling's coolness and bravery.

RILEY

303

Geoffrey
Rank/Title: Mr.
Unit/Force/Occupation: 14-year-old schoolboy
Other Decorations: —
Date of Gazette: 3 Oct. 1944
Place/Date of Birth: — 20 Nov. 1929
Place/Date of Death: —
Place of Memorial: —
Town/County Connections: Huddersfield, Yorkshire
Remarks: (AM)

Account of Deed: On 29th May 1944 a thunderstorm, followed by a cloudburst, broke over the Digley Valley, near Holmfirth, Yorkshire and the River Holme became a raging torrent 80 feet wide and over 15 feet deep, flooding surrounding land and buildings. Geoffrey Riley, aged 14, saw that an elderly woman had taken refuge on a low wall, surrounded by flood water which was rising rapidly. He first attempted a rescue by walking to her along the wall, but she would not leave her position. He then entered the flood water, rescued her from the wall, which later collapsed, and though only a moderate swimmer, struggled to bring her to safety through the flood until he became exhausted. His father went to his assistance but all three were swept away into the river, Geoffrey being the sole survivor.

RIMMER

304

Reginald
Rank/Title: Sergeant (later Sub-Inspector)
Unit/Force/Occupation: Bombay Police
Other Decorations: —
Date of Gazette: 3 Jun. 1931
Place/Date of Birth: Chester — 21 Nov. 1902
Place/Date of Death: —
Place of Memorial: —
Town/County Connections: Chester, Cheshire
Remarks: (EGM); served with The Cheshire Regiment. 1919-27; served with The Royal Welch Fusiliers 1939-42; transferred to Occupied Enemy Territory Administration (Civil Police), Tripolitania and then Eritrea 1942-50.

Account of Deed: Sergeant Rimmer was decorated not for one act of gallantry, but because on numerous occasions he showed great courage and coolness. His pluck and presence of mind evoked the highest praise from his superiors and he consistently set a fine example to the constabulary under him.

ROBERTSON

305

Paul Douglas
Rank/Title: A/Flight Commander (later Group Captain with the Royal Air Force)
Unit/Force/Occupation: Royal Naval Air Service
Other Decorations: CBE
Date of Gazette: 18 Jun. 1918
Place/Date of Birth: Willesden, Middlesex — 30 Apr. 1891
Place/Date of Death: Auckland, New Zealand — 4 Aug. 1975
Place of Memorial: —
Town/County Connections: —
Remarks: (AM); served in Royal Air Force in Second World War; retired to New Zealand in 1966.

Account of Deed: On 28th February 1918 at Hornsea Mere, Lincolnshire, a seaplane got out of control and spun to the ground. Flight Commander Robertson, the observer, jumped from the machine just before it reached the marshy ground and landed safely. The pilot was imprisoned in the aircraft, which, on striking the ground, burst into flames and quickly became a furnace of burning petrol. In spite of the fact that the bombs, a number of rounds of ammunition and the reserve petrol tank were all likely to explode, Flight Commander Robertson returned and tried to rescue the pilot and only gave up when he had been so severely burned in the face, hands and leg that his recovery was for some time in doubt.

ROBINSON

306

Harry
Rank/Title: Mr.
Unit/Force/Occupation: Deputy, Louisa Colliery, Durham
Other Decorations: —
Date of Gazette: 20 Jul. 1948
Place/Date of Birth: North Kyo, Co. Durham — 27 Dec. 1916
Place/Date of Death: Stanley, Co. Durham — 16 Oct. 1987
Place of Memorial: —
Town/County Connections: Durham, Co. Durham
Remarks: (EM)

Account of Deed: Shortly before midnight on 22nd August 1947 a serious explosion of firedamp and coal dust occurred in the Louisa Colliery. Mr. Robinson and two other deputies*, who with their intimate knowledge of the geography of the mine could have made their way to safety, went at once to the scene of the disaster, where they were soon joined by an overman* who came down from the surface. Twenty-four men, all of whom were either injured or incapacitated by carbon-monoxide poisoning, were in the district at the time; 19 of them died and but for the prompt and continuous heroic work performed by the three deputies and the overman, there is little doubt that not one would have survived. The atmosphere was so thick that the beams of the cap lamps could only penetrate a foot or so, which meant that the rescuers could do nothing to guard against danger from falls of ground, a very real danger after an explosion, and the road in places was almost completely blocked by tubs derailed by blast. (*See also entries for HUTCHINSON, J., SHANLEY, J. and YOUNGER, W.)

RODRIQUES

307

George David
Rank/Title: Mr.
Unit/Force/Occupation: Assistant Surgeon, Indian Medical Department
Other Decorations: —
Date of Gazette: 2 Jun. 1923
Place/Date of Birth: —
Place/Date of Death: Bangalore, India — 21 Aug. 1962
Place of Memorial: —
Town/County Connections: —
Remarks: (EGM)

Account of Deed: Mr Rodriques was awarded the Empire Gallantry Medal for services rendered in connection with military operations in Malabar, India in 1921/22.

ROGERS

308

Jonathan
Rank/Title: Chief Petty Officer
Unit/Force/Occupation: Royal Australian Navy
Other Decorations: DSM
Date of Gazette: 12 Mar. 1965
Place/Date of Birth: Pen-y-Cae, Wrexham, Wales — 16 Sep. 1920
Place/Date of Death: Jervis Bay, off Australian coast — 10 Feb. 1964
Place of Memorial: —
Town/County Connections: Pen-y-Cae, Wrexham, Clwyd, Wales
Remarks: —

Account of Deed: On 10th February 1964, HMAS *Voyager* sank after a collision. Chief Petty Officer Rogers kept up the morale of junior ratings, organised the escape of as many as possible, and stayed with those who could not escape and encouraged them to meet their death with dignity and honour. He upheld the highest tradition of the Service at sea and of his rating as a Chief Petty Officer.

ROGERSON

309

Sidney George
Rank/Title: A/Staff Sergeant
Unit/Force/Occupation: Royal Army Ordnance Corps
Other Decorations: —
Date of Gazette: 11 Oct. 1946
Place/Date of Birth: Mitcham, Surrey — 14 May 1915
Place/Date of Death: —
Place of Memorial: —
Town/County Connections: Caterham, Surrey; Ramsgate, Kent
Remarks: —

Account of Deed: On 2nd January 1946, men from the RAOC, the Pioneer Corps and the RASC were completing the loading of a train with American and German ammunition in Savernake Forest, Wiltshire. In the same siding another British ammunition train was standing — there were 96 wagons in all. There was a sudden flash and explosion and two railway wagons and a 3-ton lorry literally disappeared, fire swept the yard and more wagons burst into flames. More explosions followed and altogether 27 railway wagons and two lorries blew up; there was a great risk that fire would spread to all the remainder of the loaded wagons, causing more explosions and widespread damage. Eight men died in the original explosion and six more were badly hurt. Major Biggs* was commanding the Sub-Depot and he and Staff Sergeant Rogerson together uncoupled a burning wagon and extinguished the flames. With complete disregard for their own safety they worked with their men all through the night and succeeded in preventing any more wagons catching fire. Next day the remains of wagons, lorries, shells, mines, detonators, packages and telegraph poles could be seen strewn all over the countryside, and there were two huge craters, but 69 of the wagons had been saved from exploding. (*See also entry for BIGGS, K.A.)

ROSS

310

Arthur Dwight
Rank/Title: Air Commodore
Unit/Force/Occupation: Royal Canadian Air Force
Other Decorations: CBE
Date of Gazette: 27 Oct. 1944
Place/Date of Birth: Winnipeg, Manitoba, Canada — 18 Mar. 1907
Place/Date of Death: Kingston, Ontario, Canada — 27 Sep. 1981
Place of Memorial: —
Town/County Connections: —
Remarks: Air Adviser to Canadian High Commission in London 1954-56; later commanded 5th Canadian Air Force; retired 1959.

Account of Deed: In June 1944 a Halifax bomber, in making a night landing at the RAF Station, Tholthorpe, Yorkshire, crashed into another bomber which was just taking off. The crashed aircraft broke into three parts and was burning furiously. Air Commodore Ross was at the airfield to attend the return of aircraft from operations and the interrogation of their crews. With the assistance of a corporal he rescued the pilot who had sustained severe injuries. At that moment a 500lb. bomb in the second aircraft about 80 yards away exploded and Air Commodore Ross and the airman were thrown to the ground. When the hail of debris had subsided cries were heard from the rear turret of the crashed aircraft. Despite explosions from bombs and petrol tanks Air Commodore Ross and the corporal returned to the blazing wreckage and tried to release the rear gunner. The Air Commodore hacked at the blazing perspex with an axe and while he was doing this a second bomb exploded which practically severed his arm. The rear gunner was rescued and Air Commodore Ross calmly walked to the ambulance, and an emergency amputation was performed on arrival at the station sick quarters.

ROWLANDS

311

John Samuel (later Sir John)
Rank/Title: A/Wing Commander (later Air Marshal)
Unit/Force/Occupation: Royal Air Force Volunteer Reserve
Other Decorations: KBE
Date of Gazette: 10 Aug. 1943
Place/Date of Birth: — 23 Sep. 1915
Place/Date of Death: —
Place of Memorial: —
Town/County Connections: Sheffield, Yorkshire
Remarks: Permanent commission in RAF 1945; British Defence Staff, Washington 1961-63; Imperial Defence College 1964; RAF College, Cranwell 1965-68; First Director General of Training, RAF 1968-70; AOC-in-C, RAF Maintenance Command 1970-73; Assistant Principal, Sheffield Polytechnic 1974-80.

Account of Deed: Wing Commander Rowlands was awarded the George Cross for his conspicuous courage in bomb disposal over a period of two years. During this time he dealt with several hundred weapons of various kinds — his duties included the rendering safe and dismantling of new types of enemy weapons and also dealing with Allied weapons in crashed aircraft, or those which had been jettisoned over Britain. On one occasion a bomb in a large bomb dump at Bomber Command had accidentally detonated and severely damaged large numbers of incendiary and high explosive bombs, many of which were already fully fused for operational use. These damaged bombs were highly dangerous and had to be rendered safe by Wing Commander Rowlands, despite intense fire and exploding ammunition.

RUSSELL

312

David
Rank/Title: Lance-Corporal
Unit/Force/Occupation: 22nd Bn., 2nd New Zealand Expeditionary Force
Other Decorations: —
Date of Gazette: 24 Dec. 1948
Place/Date of Birth: Ayr, Scotland — 30 Mar. 1911
Place/Date of Death: Italy — 28 Feb. 1945
Place of Memorial: Udine War Cemetery, Italy; ward at Napier Hospital, Hawke's Bay, New Zealand named after him.
Town/County Connections: —
Remarks: —

Account of Deed: Lance-Corporal Russell escaped from a prisoner of war camp in Italy in 1943, obtained civilian clothes and was befriended by an Italian peasant. He became well-known and liked by the people of the locality and he was able to maintain contact with a number of other ex-prisoners of war. This went on for two years and then he was arrested by a patrol of German and Italian Fascist troops and the peasant with whom he was living was also arrested on suspicion of having harboured him. He was beaten up in an attempt to make him incriminate the peasant, but he denied ever having seen the man who was therefore released. The Germans, however, were convinced that Lance-Corporal Russell had been in contact with other ex-prisoners of war and partisans and were determined to make him disclose their whereabouts. He was chained to a wall in a stable, constantly beaten up and told that if he did not give the information within three days he would be shot. He steadfastly refused to say anything and was finally shot.

RYAN
313

Richard John Hammersley
Rank/Title: Lieutenant-Commander
Unit/Force/Occupation: Royal Navy
Other Decorations: —
Date of Gazette: 20 Dec. 1940
Place/Date of Birth: — 23 Jul. 1903
Place/Date of Death: Dagenham, Essex — 21 Sep. 1940
Place of Memorial: Haslar Royal Naval Cemetery, Gosport, Hampshire
Town/County Connections: Alverstoke, Hampshire
Remarks: —

Account of Deed: Lieutenant-Commander Ryan was one of the two officers who stripped the first magnetic mine of Type C found in a German aircraft which had crashed at Clacton. When magnetic mines were first dropped over London he came forward without hesitation for the perilous work of making them safe, although, with his unrivalled knowledge of this work, he was well aware of the dangers he so readily accepted. The clock of the bomb-fuse was normally timed to explode the mine about 22 seconds after its fall. If it failed to do so, it might be re-started by the slightest movement, even a footfall. The amount of the clock already run off could not be known, and once it was re-started time for escape could not be more than a few seconds. Lieutenant-Commander Ryan tackled six of these mines with his own hands, one of them in a canal where he worked waist deep in mud and water which would have made escape impossible. Here he found and removed the bomb-fuse only by groping for it under water. At Hornchurch he made safe a very hazardous mine which threatened the aerodrome and an explosives factory, and then he and his assistant, Chief Petty Officer Ellingworth* with whom he had shared many dangerous assignments, went on to Dagenham. Here they tackled a mine hanging by a parachute in a warehouse and both were killed by its explosion. (*See also entry for ELLINGWORTH, R.V.)

SANSOM (later Churchill, now Hallowes)
314

Odette Marie Céline
Rank/Title: Mrs.
Unit/Force/Occupation: Women's Transport Service (FANY)
Other Decorations: MBE
Date of Gazette: 20 Aug. 1946
Place/Date of Birth: 28 Apr. 1912
Place/Date of Death: —
Place of Memorial: —
Town/County Connections: Weybridge and Walton-on-Thames, Surrey
Remarks: Légion d'Honneur (France); Vice-President, Women's Transport Service (FANY); Founder Vice-President, Woman of the Year Luncheon; Member of Committee, VC and GC Association; President, 282 (East Ham) Air Cadet Squadron; Vice-President, Military Medallist League.

Account of Deed: Mrs. Sansom was infiltrated into enemy-occupied France in October 1942 and worked with great courage and distinction until April 1943 when she and her commanding officer were arrested. On their way to prison at Fresnes they managed to talk together and agreed that for their mutual protection they should maintain that they were married. She stuck to this story and even succeeded in convincing her captors, in spite of considerable contrary evidence and through at least fourteen interrogations. She also drew Gestapo attention from her commanding officer to herself, saying that he had only come to France on her insistence and even agreed that it should be herself and not her commanding officer who should be shot. The Gestapo were most determined to discover the whereabouts of a wireless operator and another British officer whose lives were of the greatest value to the Resistance organisation. Mrs. Sansom was the only person who had this information but although she was subjected to every sort of indignity and cruelty, she never gave anything away and by her bravery and determination not only saved the lives of the two officers but also enabled them to carry on their most valuable work. She was in solitary confinement for two years and whilst in the prison of Ravensbrück Concentration Camp was kept in complete darkness for three months and eleven days, as a punishment for the Allied landings in the south of France. Ultimately, she was taken by the German Camp Commandant to the nearest American unit in May 1945.

SAUNDERS

Robert Benjamin
Rank/Title: Dr.
Unit/Force/Occupation: Doctor
Other Decorations: —
Date of Gazette: 19 Aug. 1937
Place/Date of Birth: — 1905
Place/Date of Death: — 14 Sep. 1981
Place of Memorial: —
Town/County Connections: —
Remarks: (EM)

Account of Deed: On 4th January 1937 an accident occurred in the Tebekwe Mine, Salisbury, Southern Rhodesia, in which one of the miners was trapped underground by a fall of rock and completely buried. Dr. Saunders arrived on the scene at 3.15pm by which time the rescue party had removed most of the spillage from the imprisoned man's body but his left hand was firmly held between two timbers. He remained in this dangerous position until 12.30pm the following day. During most of this time Dr. Saunders stayed underground giving medical assistance under extremely difficult and dangerous conditions. To attend his patient he had to lie on top of him with his back in close proximity to a dangerously shaky roof, any disturbance of which would have resulted in a fall sufficient to crush them both. After a period of 16 hours when all attempts to free the trapped man had failed it was decided to amputate his arm. The conditions were such that the operation had to be performed by a left-handed amputator and this was done under the personal supervision of Dr. Saunders. The man was then taken to the surface and fortunately recovered from the effects of his long ordeal, owing, undoubtedly, to the example and devotion to duty displayed by the doctor.

SCHOFIELD

Carl Mallinson
Rank/Title: Mr.
Unit/Force/Occupation: Overman, Bold Colliery, St. Helens
Other Decorations: —
Date of Gazette: 8 Oct. 1940
Place/Date of Birth: — 5 Jan. 1902
Place/Date of Death: Bold, St. Helens, Lancashire — 7 Jan. 1978
Place of Memorial: —
Town/County Connections: Bold, St. Helens, Lancashire
Remarks: (EM)

Account of Deed: On 14th February 1940 at about 8.45pm a serious fall of roof occurred in the main loading level of the Bold Colliery, completely burying five men. Rescue work was immediately begun and in a little over an hour one of the men was rescued. He was able to tell the agent*, who had arrived and taken charge, the position of the other four men. The agent and Mr. Schofield, whose father was one of the men buried, worked with their hands, removing stones and dirt, and sawed through a conveyor chain and a rail. After prolonged efforts one of the men was rescued by 2am next morning and a third man was released an hour later. The other two men could be seen but appeared to be dead. The rescue had to be carried out in a very confined space and in conditions of extreme difficulty and danger, owing to the risk of further falls as the debris which covered the buried men was removed. (*See also entry for JAMESON, T.)

SCULLY

James Patrick
Rank/Title: Corporal
Unit/Force/Occupation: Royal Pioneer Corps
Other Decorations: —
Date of Gazette: 8 Jul. 1941
Place/Date of Birth: Dublin — 20 Oct.1909
Place/Date of Death: Rangoon — 28 Dec. 1974
Place of Memorial: —
Town/County Connections: Streatham, London
Remarks: —

Account of Deed: On 8th March 1941 at the time of the Liverpool Blitz, Corporal Scully was a member of a rescue party that went to look for survivors after a bombing incident. He risked his life in circumstances of extreme danger in rescuing people buried under the debris, and worked unceasingly for seven hours.

SEAGRIM 318

Hugh Paul
Rank/Title: T/Major
Unit/Force/Occupation: 19th Hyderabad Regiment, attd. Force 136
Other Decorations: DSO, MBE
Date of Gazette: 12 Sep. 1946
Place/Date of Birth: Ashmansworth, Hampshire — 1909
Place/Date of Death: Rangoon — 14 Sep. 1944
Place of Memorial: Rangoon War Cemetery, Burma
Town/County Connections: Whissonsett, Norfolk
Remarks: The only instance to date of the GC and VC being awarded to the same family. His brother, Lieutenant Colonel D.A. Seagrim, was posthumously awarded the VC for gallantry in Tunisia, 20/21 Mar. 1943.

Account of Deed: Major Seagrim was the leader of a party which included two other British and one Karen officer, operating in the Karen hills (Burma), from February 1943 to February 1944. Towards the end of 1943 the presence of this party became known to the Japanese, who started a wide-spread campaign of arrests and torture to discover their whereabouts. In February 1944 the other two British officers were ambushed and killed, but Major Seagrim and the Karen officer escaped. The Japanese then arrested 270 Karens, including elders and headmen, and tortured and killed many of them, but they continued to assist and shelter Major Seagrim. In order, however, to save them further suffering, Major Seagrim surrendered himself to the Japanese on 15th March 1944. He was taken to Rangoon and, with eight others, was sentenced to death. He pleaded that only he should be executed, as the others had only obeyed his orders, but such was the devotion he had inspired that they all expressed their willingness to die with him and they were executed on 22nd September 1944.

SEWELL 319

Stanley William
Rank/Title: Mr.
Unit/Force/Occupation: Explosive worker, Royal Gunpowder Factory, Waltham Abbey, Essex
Other Decorations: —
Date of Gazette: 6 Feb. 1940
Place/Date of Birth: Enfield, Middlesex — 16 Dec. 1906
Place/Date of Death: Enfield, Middlesex — 25 May 1969
Place of Memorial: —
Town/County Connections: Enfield, Middlesex
Remarks: (EGM)

Account of Deed: On 18th January 1940 an explosion occurred at the Royal Gunpowder Factory. At the time when the explosion took place Mr. Sewell and another explosive worker* — generally known as hillmen — were engaged on the nitration of glycerine, the most critical stage in the process of manufacture when the liability to detonation is greatest. The building in which the process was carried out was only 150 yards from the scene of the explosion and was also damaged. Over 1,000lbs. of nitroglycerine were under process and in a condition of instability. Mr. Sewell and the other hillman, realising the damage to life and property which would be caused by a further explosion, stood by their posts for some two hours, until the services were restored, and then calmly continued with their work until the whole charge had been brought to a state of stability. (*See also entry for O'HAGAN, L.F.)

SHANLEY 320

Joseph
Rank/Title: Mr.
Unit/Force/Occupation: Deputy, Louisa Old Section, Louisa Colliery, Durham
Other Decorations: —
Date of Gazette: 20 Jul. 1948
Place/Date of Birth: — 8 Jan. 1907
Place/Date of Death: Rainworth, Nottinghamshire — 23 Apr. 1980
Place of Memorial: —
Town/County Connections: Durham, Co. Durham
Remarks: (EM)

Account of Deed: Shortly before midnight on 22nd August 1947 a serious explosion of firedamp and coal dust occurred in the Louisa Colliery. Mr. Shanley and two other deputies*, who with their intimate knowledge of the geography of the mine could have made their way to safety, went at once to the scene of the disaster, where they were soon joined by an overman* who came down from the surface. Twenty-four men, all of whom were either injured or incapacitated by carbon-monoxide poisoning, were in the district at the time; 19 of them died and but for the prompt and continuous heroic work performed by the three deputies and the overman, there is little doubt that not one would have survived. The atmosphere was so thick that the beams of the cap lamps could only penetrate a foot or so, which meant that the rescuers could do nothing to guard against danger from falls of ground, a very real danger after an explosion, and the road in places was almost completely blocked by tubs derailed by blast. (*See also entries for HUTCHINSON, J., ROBINSON, H. and YOUNGER, W.)

SHEPHERD   321
John William Hersey
Rank/Title: Mr.
Unit/Force/Occupation: Workman, Palmers Shipbuilding & Iron Co. Ltd., Jarrow
Other Decorations: —
Date of Gazette: 14 Feb. 1930
Place/Date of Birth: — 20 Dec. 1898
Place/Date of Death: Jarrow, Co. Durham — 16 Mar. 1983
Place of Memorial: —
Town/County Connections: Jarrow, Co. Durham
Remarks: (EM)

Account of Deed: On 16th October 1929 Mr. Shepherd was about to follow another man into a boiler which they had been detailed to clean when he detected traces of gas. In reply to a call he only received a faint reply from his comrade and immediately climbed inside the boiler to go to his aid. He found the man semi-conscious some 25 feet away from the boiler man-hole and tried to drag him to the opening but had to give up as he was feeling the effects of the gas. He made his way out of the boiler, called for help and, though still seriously affected by the gas, returned with a rope which he tried to fasten round the now unconscious man. He collapsed, however, before he was able to do so and further help had to be called for. Compressed air was used to clear the gas out of the boiler and eventually a rescue party wearing respirators succeeded in extricating the two men. The man who went first into the boiler unfortunately died a few hours later.

SILK   322
Joseph Henry
Rank/Title: Private
Unit/Force/Occupation: Somerset Light Infantry
Other Decorations: —
Date of Gazette: 13 Jun. 1944
Place/Date of Birth: — 14 Aug. 1916
Place/Date of Death: Burma — 4 Dec. 1943
Place of Memorial: Taukkyan War Cemetery, Rangoon, Burma
Town/County Connections: Finsbury, London
Remarks: —

Account of Deed: On 4th December 1943 the men of the platoon to which Private Silk belonged were sitting down on a slope in the jungle cleaning their weapons. The latter included grenades, all of which were fused. Some of Private Silk's comrades were sitting round him, and below on the slope were other soldiers cleaning their weapons. Owing to the thickness of the jungle Private Silk would have been unable to see anybody except the men immediately around him, although he could hear talking above and below him on the slope. For some reason unknown, a grenade belonging to Private Silk ignited and the fuse began to hiss. He shouted a warning, rolled over, clutching the grenade to his stomach and putting his body between the grenade and the majority of the men immediately around him. The grenade exploded, killing him instantly and slightly injuring two other men. There is little doubt that this soldier appreciated at once that he could not safely throw the grenade away because of the men above and below him on the slope and that in order to minimize injury to his comrades his body was the best shield. His level-headedness, resourcefulness and cool courageous action undoubtedly saved many lives.

SINCLAIR

323

Laurence Frank (later Sir Laurence)
Rank/Title: Wing Commander (later Air Vice-Marshal)
Unit/Force/Occupation: 110 Squadron, Royal Air Force
Other Decorations: KCB, CBE, DSO & Bar
Date of Gazette: 21 Jan. 1941
Place/Date of Birth: — 23 Oct. 1908
Place/Date of Death: —
Place of Memorial: —
Town/County Connections: Great Brickhill, Bletchley, Buckinghamshire
Remarks: Legion of Merit (USA); Légion d'Honneur (France); Partisan Star (Yugoslavia). Comd. RAF Watton 1941; Comd. Tactical Light Bomber Force N. Africa and Italy 1943-44; ADC to King George VI 1943-44; subsequently Senior Air Staff Officer, Balkan Air Force; commanded No. 2 Light Bomber Group (Germany) 1948-49; Assistant Commmandant, RAF Staff College 1949-50; Commandant, RAF College, Cranwell 1950-52; Commandant, School of Land/Air Warfare, Old Sarum, Wiltshire 1952-53; Assistant Chief of the Air Staff (Operations) 1953-55; Comdr. British Forces, Arabian Peninsula 1955-57; Commandant, Joint Services Staff College 1958-60; retired from RAF; Controller of Ground Services, Min. of Aviation 1960-61; Controller, Nat. Air Traffic Control Services, Min. of Aviation and Min. of Defence 1962-66.

Account of Deed: On 30th September 1940 an aircraft burst into flames whilst taking off from the RAF Station at Wattisham. Wing Commander Sinclair immediately went to the rescue of the trapped airmen, and despite the fact that two 250lb. bombs had exploded before he reached the aircraft and he knew that it carried two more, he dashed into the fire and succeeded in dragging the air gunner to safety. Unfortunately the airman later died of his injuries.

SMITH

324

Anthony
Rank/Title: Mr.
Unit/Force/Occupation: Chimney sweep. Civil Defence Rescue Service, Chelsea
Other Decorations: —
Date of Gazette: 30 May 1944
Place/Date of Birth: — 1899
Place/Date of Death: —1964
Place of Memorial: —
Town/County Connections: Chelsea, London
Remarks: Served with Royal Marines in First World War.

Account of Deed: On 23rd February 1944 a string of bombs fell at World's End, Chelsea, demolishing a 4-storey block of flats. Escaping gas ignited and set fire to the wreckage and the building became an inferno; two floors collapsed, forming a huge pile of burning rubble. Mr. Smith, a member of the Heavy Rescue Squad, dug his way into the debris and found a man trapped in the front basement. He managed to extricate the casualty, but found the way blocked by a wall of fire, with the upper walls collapsing and so cutting off his escape route. He burrowed his way through the burning debris and brought the man out safely, just as the remaining wall fell into the area. Although almost overcome by the smoke and fumes, he went back and spent another hour with a comrade rescuing another victim trapped in the basement of an adjoining building.

SMITH

325

Charles
Rank/Title: Mr.
Unit/Force/Occupation: Miner, Askern Main Colliery, Yorkshire
Other Decorations: —
Date of Gazette: 28 Jun. 1940
Place/Date of Birth: — 17 Dec. 1908
Place/Date of Death: Blaydon, Co. Durham — 25 Oct. 1987
Place of Memorial: —
Town/County Connections: Askern, Doncaster, Yorkshire
Remarks: (EM)

Account of Deed: At 10am on 3rd January 1940 a fall of roof occurred at a coal face in Warren House Seam and a miner was buried by the fall. He was rescued some three hours later, without having suffered serious injury, through the gallantry displayed by a rescue party. The trapped man was completely buried except for his head and shoulders and his arms were pinned by fallen rocks and by a steel bar. The agent, who took charge of the operations, succeeded in removing a stone which was pinning one arm and eventually managed to work his way through to free the man and to pass him out to the other rescuers. Mr. Smith and another miner* were both close at hand when the fall occurred and at once started rescue operations, taking a prominent part in the dangerous work of clearing a way under the fall, and both were able to remove some of the debris which was pinning the trapped man down. (*See also entry for THOMPSON, M.)

SMITH   326
Francis Haffey BROOKE-
Rank/Title: Sub-Lieutenant (later Lieutenant-Commander)
Unit/Force/Occupation: Royal Naval Reserve
Other Decorations: —
Date of Gazette: 27 Jun. 1941
Place/Date of Birth: Hasketon, near Woodbridge, Suffolk — 21 Sep. 1918
Place/Date of Death: Woodbridge, Suffolk — 3 Dec. 1952
Place of Memorial: Hasketon, Suffolk (churchyard)
Town/County Connections: Hasketon, Suffolk
Remarks: —

Account of Deed: In December 1940 an unexploded bomb fell inside the deck locker alongside the engine-room on the fire-float *Firefly* in the Manchester Ship Canal. When Sub-Lieutenant Brooke-Smith arrived to deal with the weapon, he found it was firmly wedged, but by using a rope he was able to pull the mine slightly clear of the engine-room casing and then, lying on the sloping engine casing, head downwards, he managed to place a safety gag in the bomb-fuse. The clock of the fuse then started to tick, but he stayed where he was and finally managed to stop it before the inevitable explosion occurred. He had dealt successfully with many unexploded bombs, but this was the first time that he had used a safety gag on a bomb-fuse and he had to do so in most difficult circumstances as he was compelled to work by touch, without being able to see the bomb fuse at all, and his chances of succeeding and of escaping with his life were regarded as very small.

SMITH   327
George Stewart BAIN
Rank/Title: Lieutenant (later Lieutenant Colonel)
Unit/Force/Occupation: Royal Regiment of Artillery, seconded to Indian Army Ordnance Corps
Other Decorations: —
Date of Gazette: 30 Sep. 1927
Place/Date of Birth: Grampound, Truro, Cornwall — 1 Dec. 1898
Place/Date of Death: Cartmel, Lancashire — 22 Jan. 1972
Place of Memorial: Lancaster & Morecambe Crematorium
Town/County Connections: Cartmel, Lancashire
Remarks: (AM); bursar of Sedbergh School, Yorkshire on retirement from Army.

Account of Deed: On 3rd June 1927 an army major and two Gurkha companions were descending an ice slope on a mountain in the Himalayas when at a height of about 14,000 feet the party lost their foothold and slid some 1,000 feet on to a snow slope below. The major and one of his companions were so badly injured that they were unable to move, but the third managed to make his way to Lakka, some 3,000 feet lower where he met Lieutenant Bain Smith and told him of the accident. Although the Lieutenant had no knowledge or experience of mountaineering he set out at once to the rescue. He had no ice axe and was wearing smooth-soled boots so had to travel across the snow-field in his stockinged feet, and he was alone, as the coolie who had started out with him, would not cross the snow-field. When he reached the two injured men he made a sledge of his coat and, helped a little by the Gurkha who was just able to move, dragged the major some 500 feet lower. He then had to get help from two shepherds and they managed to move down another 500 feet when progress became impossible again because of the roughness of the snow. He sent one of the shepherds for more help, but the man failed to return so Lieutenant Bain Smith set off again by himself and found four more shepherds. He was so exhausted by this time that he could only get along by crawling, but when he managed to get back to the injured men he sent the Gurkha down with two of the shepherds before making several unsuccessful attempts to continue the descent. At sunset the remaining shepherds deserted him, so after staying (clad only in shirt, shorts and stockings) for half an hour with the major, who was unconscious, if not already dead, he made his way to a fire below the glacier where he found the major's wife and a party of men. They could not tackle the mountain side in the dark, but early next morning Lieutenant Bain Smith escorted them to a point from where the major's body could be seen. He was then on the verge of collapse and both feet were frost-bitten.

SMITH

328

Kenneth
Rank/Title: Signalman
Unit/Force/Occupation: Royal Corps of Signals
Other Decorations: —
Date of Gazette: 19 Oct. 1945
Place/Date of Birth: Humby, Grantham, Lincolnshire — 7 Dec. 1920
Place/Date of Death: Island of Ist, Adriatic — 10 Jan 1945
Place of Memorial: Belgrade War Cemetery, Yugoslavia
Town/County Connections: Grantham, Lincolnshire
Remarks: —

Account of Deed: On 10th January 1945, at a time when acts of sabotage were of daily occurrence, Signalman Smith found a time-bomb in a house where members of his detachment were billeted with civilians and children on the Adriatic island of Ist. Realising from its ticking that it might explode at any moment and that there were a number of partisans in the room and young children elsewhere in the house, his one thought was to remove it as far as possible from the house and its occupants. He did so, and was the only casualty as it blew him to pieces.

SOULSBY

329

Oliver
Rank/Title: Mr.
Unit/Force/Occupation: Miner, Bentley Colliery, Yorkshire
Other Decorations: —
Date of Gazette: 30 Sep. 1932
Place/Date of Birth: — 1910
Place/Date of Death: 14 Jan. 1977
Place of Memorial: —
Town/County Connections: Bentley, Doncaster, Yorkshire
Remarks: (EM)

Account of Deed: On 20th November 1931 in the afternoon, a violent explosion of firedamp, followed by fires, occurred in the North East District of the Bentley Colliery. Of some 47 men working at or near the coal face, 45 were either killed or died later. A number of miners rendered heroic assistance at the work of rescue, among them Mr. Soulsby who displayed great gallantry and perseverance in extricating the injured and conveying them to a place of safety. They had to work in an atmosphere which was hot and vitiated and there was always risk of further explosion. One such explosion actually occurred at 10.30pm injuring members of one of the rescue parties, and this was followed by yet another. (See also entries for ALLPORT, E., DARKER, R.E., SYKES, F., TEMPERLEY, S.J. and YATES, P.W.)

SOUTHWELL

330

Bennett
Rank/Title: Able Seaman
Unit/Force/Occupation: Royal Navy
Other Decorations: —
Date of Gazette: 23 Jan. 1941
Place/Date of Birth: — 21 Mar. 1913
Place/Date of Death: Hoxton, London — 17 Oct. 1940
Place of Memorial: Gilroes Cemetery, Leicester
Town/County Connections: —
Remarks: —

Account of Deed: On 17th October 1940, an unexploded bomb had fallen in Hoxton in the East End of London and a large area of tenement property had been evacuated. Sub-Lieutenant Easton*, together with Able Seaman Southwell set off down the empty street to deal with it, along the slate-littered pavement to the house where the mine had crashed through the roof and was hanging suspended through a hole in the ceiling, its nose within six inches of the floor. The Sub-Lieutenant decided to dismantle the mine as it hung, and told Able Seaman Southwell that he wanted him to stay in the passage outside the room and hand him the necessary tools. They started work but had only been at it for about a minute when the bomb slipped and there was a sound of falling brickwork as the chimney pot overhead collapsed. Sub-Lieutenant Easton heard the whirr of the bomb mechanism and knew that there were exactly twelve seconds in which to get away. He shouted a warning to Able Seaman Southwell, who at once ran down the street to what he thought was safety, but he was killed by the blast when the explosion occurred. The mine destroyed six complete streets and it was six weeks before his body was found amongst the rubble. (*See also entry for EASTON, J.M.C.)

SPILLETT
331

Brian
Rank/Title: Mr.
Unit/Force/Occupation: Detail fitter
Other Decorations: Bronze Medal of Carnegie Hero Fund Trust
Date of Gazette: 29 Jun. 1965
Place/Date of Birth: —
Place/Date of Death: Enfield, Middlesex — 16 Jan. 1965
Place of Memorial: Buried at Waltham Cross
Town/County Connections: Waltham Cross, Hertfordshire
Remarks: Mr. Spillett was a member of 'P' Battery, 298th Parachute Regiment, RHA (TA).

Account of Deed: At 5.30am on 9th January 1965 a fire broke out in a house at Waltham Cross, Hertfordshire. Mr. Spillett, attracted by the shouting, arrived there only partially dressed and was told that a man was still trapped in the house which was now blazing furiously. Despite attempts to hold him back, Mr. Spillett insisted on going into the house, but he failed to get the man out and he himself died a week later from his injuries.

SPOONER
332

Kenneth Gerald
Rank/Title: Leading Aircraftman
Unit/Force/Occupation: Royal Canadian Air Force
Other Decorations: —
Date of Gazette: 7 Jan. 1944
Place/Date of Birth: Smiths Falls, Ontario, Canada — 24 May 1922
Place/Date of Death: Lake Erie, Canada — 14 May 1943
Place of Memorial: Hillcrest Cemetery, Smiths Falls, Ontario, Canada
Town/County Connections: —
Remarks: —

Account of Deed: On 14th May 1943 Leading Aircraftman Spooner was on an instructional flight as a student navigator. Shortly after the aircraft in which he was flying left the Training School the pilot fainted at the controls. None of the other students in the plane were capable of flying it, but LAC Spooner, with great initiative, seized the controls and told the other three to bale out, which they did and all landed safely. He then attempted to land the aircraft, a thing which he had never done before, but he was unsuccessful, and he and the still unconscious pilot were killed.

SPOORS
333

Robert
Rank/Title: Private (later Sergeant)
Unit/Force/Occupation: 1st Bn., The West Yorkshire Regiment
Other Decorations: MM
Date of Gazette: 19 Nov. 1935
Place/Date of Birth: — 11 Jul. 1910
Place/Date of Death: Norwich — 28 Feb. 1984
Place of Memorial: —
Town/County Connections: Newcastle upon Tyne, Northumberland
Remarks: (AM)

Account of Deed: After the earthquake at Quetta, on the morning of 31st May 1935 Private Spoors, at very considerable risk to himself from falling debris, entered an army officer's house which was in a dangerous condition. He was successful in clearing a path for the officer's wife and was mainly responsible for saving her life. He then re-entered the house to save the nurse and baby, but was himself caught in the debris and was later rescued by two other men and brought out in an exhausted condition. He subsequently worked for many hours at the British Military Hospital.

STANNERS

334

John George
Rank/Title: Mr.
Unit/Force/Occupation: Deckhand, Royal Naval Reserve
Other Decorations: —
Date of Gazette: 16 May 1918
Place/Date of Birth: — 2 Oct. 1890
Place/Date of Death: Newcastle upon Tyne, Northumberland — 23 Feb. 1974
Place of Memorial: —
Town/County Connections: Gateshead, Co. Durham
Remarks: (AM)

Account of Deed: On 29th December 1917 at Trinidad some cotton waste, which had been stored in a wooden cupboard in the magazine of HM Motor Launch No. 289 caught fire from an unknown cause. As soon as the fire was discovered by the smell of burning and the sight of smoke coming from the magazine hatch when opened, Deckhand Stanners, without hesitation, went down into the magazine and brought up a quantity of the burning waste. A Leading Deckhand from ML 285 went down and extinguished the remainder of the ignited cotton waste. The promptitude of action and the high courage of these men in the face of very grave danger averted a serious fire and probably saved both Motor Launches and the lives of those on board.

STEVENS

335

Henry William
Rank/Title: Police Constable (later Chief Inspector)
Unit/Force/Occupation: Metropolitan Police
Other Decorations: —
Date of Gazette: 21 Oct. 1958
Place/Date of Birth: Upton Park, London — 24 Jan. 1928
Place/Date of Death: —
Place of Memorial: —
Town/County Connections: Ilford, Essex
Remarks: —

Account of Deed: On 29th March 1958 Police Constable Stevens was in a police wireless car, doing duty as 'Aid' to the CID in plain clothes. While patrolling with a detective constable and another officer, they received a message to go to an address in Bickley Park Road, Bickley, Kent on receiving an alarm of a suspected break-in. When they got to the house the other two officers approached from the front and Constable Stevens went round to the back where he saw a man jump over the fence and run towards the railway bridge, and he gave chase. The man continued running but Constable Stevens was gaining on him and was only a few yards away when the man turned and, as the constable ran straight at him, shot him in the mouth. The criminal then turned and ran back along the road, still pursued by Constable Stevens who caught up with him and grabbed him. In the struggle that followed, the man managed to slip out of his coat, leaving it, his gun and hat in Constable Stevens' hands. The latter was now getting weak from loss of blood but continued the chase until the other two policemen came to his assistance. He was then taken to hospital where he underwent an operation. It was entirely due to Constable Stevens' tenacity and courage that the man was captured and brought to justice.

STEWART

336

Jamest Ernest
Rank/Title: Lieutenant Colonel
Unit/Force/Occupation: Corps of Royal Engineers
Other Decorations: DSO, MC
Date of Gazette: 26 Jun. 1928
Place/Date of Birth: — 1882
Place/Date of Death: Fulham, London — Jun. 1946
Place of Memorial: —
Town/County Connections: Fulham, London
Remarks: (EGM); served in the Home Guard in the Second World War.

Account of Deed: Lieutenant Colonel Stewart was awarded the Empire Gallantry Medal for his bravery in attempting to trace the whereabouts of a young officer of the East Yorkshire Regiment who had disappeared in the mountains while on a holiday journey from Peking to Ta T'ung Fu.

STOVES

John
Rank/Title: Mr.
Unit/Force/Occupation: Principal Officer, Pentonville Prison
Other Decorations: —
Date of Gazette: 23 Oct. 1928
Place/Date of Birth: —
Place/Date of Death: —
Place of Memorial: —
Town/County Connections: —
Remarks: (EGM)

337

Account of Deed: Principal Officer Stoves was awarded the Empire Gallantry Medal for services in connection with the attempted escape of a prisoner from an express train.

STRONACH

George Preston
Rank/Title: Chief Officer
Unit/Force/Occupation: Merchant Navy
Other Decorations: —
Date of Gazette: 23 Nov. 1943
Place/Date of Birth: — 4 Dec. 1914
Place/Date of Death: —
Place of Memorial: —
Town/County Connections: Glasgow, Scotland
Remarks: —

338

Account of Deed: On 19th March 1943 the SS *Ocean Voyager* which was anchored in Tripoli Harbour was struck by enemy bombs and caught fire. She had a cargo of petrol and ammunition which exploded, and in spite of strenuous efforts to fight the fire, she had to be abandoned. The Master was killed by the explosion and the Chief Officer, Mr. Stronach, was rendered temporarily unconscious, but as soon as he recovered he took command of the situation, rallied the crew and led a number of them to a boat alongside which took them to safety. He then braved the heat and flames to go back to rescue one of the officers who had been badly burnt, returning to fetch two other officers who had been so badly injured that they were unable to move. Again continuing his search for survivors, he found a greaser lying unconscious in the scuppers. He dragged this man to the side of the ship and, as there were now no lifeboats, he put a lifebelt round him and threw him overboard. In the full knowledge that the vessel was likely to blow up at any minute, Chief Officer Stronach stayed searching for survivors for a further hour and twenty minutes.

STYLES

Stephen George
Rank/Title: Major (later Lieutenant Colonel)
Unit/Force/Occupation: Royal Army Ordnance Corps
Other Decorations: —
Date of Gazette: 11 Jan. 1972
Place/Date of Birth: — 16 Mar. 1928
Place/Date of Death: —
Place of Memorial: —
Town/County Connections: Crawley, Sussex
Remarks: —

339

Account of Deed: As Senior Ammunition Technical Officer, Northern Ireland, Major Styles was responsible for the supervision of the Explosive Ordnance Disposal teams in the RAOC deployed to deal with explosive devices used in the terrorist campaign. On 20th October 1971 Major Styles was called to assist with a weapon of an apparently new design placed in the telephone kiosk in the Europa Hotel, Belfast. Having ensured that the area was cordoned off, and evacuated, Major Styles took charge of neutralising, removing and dismantling the bomb. Two days later he was again called to the same hotel where a second bomb had been laid by armed terrorists. This bomb was found to be an even larger weapon with a charge of over 30lbs. of explosive, an anti-handling device and a confusion of electrical circuits — it was clearly intended to defeat disarming techniques and to kill the operator trying to neutralise it. Major Styles again took charge of the situation and successfully disarmed, removed and dismantled the bomb, this time after nine hours of intense and dangerous work. Two determined and ingenious attempts by terrorists against life and property had thus been defeated, and technical information obtained to help save lives of operators faced with such devices in future.

SUBRAMANIAN

Rank/Title: Subedar
Unit/Force/Occupation: Queen Victoria's Own Madras Sappers & Miners
Other Decorations: —
Date of Gazette: 30 Jun.1944
Place/Date of Birth: —
Place/Date of Death: Mignano, Italy — 24 Feb. 1944
Place of Memorial: Sangro River Cremation Memorial, Italy
Town/County Connections: —
Remarks: IDSM (India)

Account of Deed: Subedar Subramanian was awarded the George Cross posthumously in recognition of most conspicuous gallantry in throwing himself on an exploding mine to save the lives of his comrades.

SUFFOLK & BERKSHIRE, Earl of

Charles Henry George HOWARD
Rank/Title: The Right Honourable
Unit/Force/Occupation: Research Officer, Ministry of Supply
Other Decorations: —
Date of Gazette: 18 Jul. 1941
Place/Date of Birth: — 2 Mar. 1906
Place/Date of Death: Erith Marshes, Kent — 12 May 1941
Place of Memorial: Memorial window in the Church of St. John the Baptist, Charlton, Malmesbury, Wiltshire.
Town/County Connections: Charlton, Wiltshire
Remarks: —

Account of Deed: Lord Suffolk was in charge of a Scientific Research Experimental Unit whose primary work was to investigate and make trials of the methods required for dealing with new types of unexploded bombs. In a special van equipped with all the necessary apparatus and with his driver/handyman and secretary, he would go straight to the spot where an incident had occurred and set to work dismantling and examining the weapon. He would then think out ways to defeat the effects of booby traps and other devices incorporated in the bomb. One of the most formidable and dangerous of the booby traps with which he dealt was the so-called ZUS 40, a device which gripped the inside end of the bomb-fuse and fired the main charge mechanically when the fuse was pulled out. In dealing with this booby trap the Earl cut a hole through the casing of the bomb itself and was then able to remove the whole core containing the ZUS 40 in one complete unit. His next step was to disregard the ZUS 40 altogether and remove the main charge by means of inserting a high-pressure steam jet. This was a tremendously important and life-saving development and although slow and tedious, meant that every type of bomb and mine could be handled with much increased safety, provided that the latter was not acoustic. On 12th May 1941 Lord Suffolk and his two assistants took an old and rusted bomb which had been collected from a bomb dump the previous day, and went to a spot in Erith Marshes to examine it. His senior officer, who visited the trio there, was amazed that all the usual precautions were being taken over this old bomb. But when he got back to London he heard that the seemingly harmless weapon had exploded, killing Lord Suffolk and his assistants.

SYKES

Frank
Rank/Title: Mr.
Unit/Force/Occupation: Miner, Bentley Colliery, Yorkshire
Other Decorations: —
Date of Gazette: 30 Sep. 1932
Place/Date of Birth: —
Place/Date of Death: Cleckheaton, Yorkshire — 9 Apr. 1982
Place of Memorial: —
Town/County Connections: Bentley, Doncaster, Yorkshire
Remarks: (EM)

Account of Deed: On 20th November 1931 in the afternoon, a violent explosion of firedamp, followed by fires, occurred in the North East District of the Bentley Colliery. Of some 47 men working at or near the coal face, 45 were either killed or died later. A number of miners rendered heroic assistance at the work of rescue, among them Mr. Sykes who displayed great gallantry and perseverance in extricating the injured and conveying them to a place of safety. They had to work in an atmosphere which was hot and vitiated and there was always risk of further explosion. One such explosion actually occurred at 10.30pm injuring members of one of the rescue parties, and this was followed by yet another. (See also entries for ALLPORT, E., DARKER, R.E., SOULSBY, O., TEMPERLEY, S.J. and YATES, P.W.)

SYLVESTER

343

William George
Rank/Title: Mr.
Unit/Force/Occupation: Explosive worker, Royal Gunpowder Factory, Waltham Abbey, Essex
Other Decorations: —
Date of Gazette: 6 Feb. 1940
Place/Date of Birth: Chadwell Heath, Romford, Essex — 6 Dec. 1914
Place/Date of Death: —
Place of Memorial: —
Town/County Connections: Queen's Park, London; Wrexham, Wales
Remarks: (EGM)

Account of Deed: On 18th January 1940 an explosion occurred at the Royal Gunpowder Factory. Mr. Sylvester was engaged on the work of purification of nitro-glycerine inside Number 2 Washing House. This building was only a hundred yards from the scene of the explosion and it suffered considerable damage; half the roof was torn off, two-thirds of the walls collapsed and the hot water and air services were interrupted. Mr. Sylvester was well aware of the conditions of acute danger which had arisen due to the possibility of the nitro-glycerine freezing, with the attendant risk of detonation, but he remained at his post for two hours until the charge had been processed and a condition of stability had been restored.

SYME

344

Hugh Randall
Rank/Title: Lieutenant
Unit/Force/Occupation: Royal Australian Naval Volunteer Reserve
Other Decorations: GM & Bar
Date of Gazette: 3 Aug. 1943
Place/Date of Birth: Melbourne, Australia — 12 Mar. 1903
Place/Date of Death: Melbourne, Australia — 7 Nov. 1965
Place of Memorial: Springvale Crematorium, Melbourne
Town/County Connections: —
Remarks: —

Account of Deed: During his 21 months of service in the Enemy Mining Section of HMS *Vernon*, Lieutenant Syme carried out 19 mine recovery or disposal operations, including five acoustic, eight magnetic and two acoustic magnetic mines. He was also responsible for the recovery of the first and only type T Sinker. Much importance was attached to his work on this mine when he located and recovered it intact, together with its sinker in November 1942. On that occasion, after removing the mine from the drifter *Noontide*, he had to insulate the detonator wires without earthing the weapon. This resulted in many painful shocks for him and he also had to operate up to his knees in mud and, at the vital stage, was hanging head downwards in a hole in the mud, so there was no chance of escape if the mine exploded. The information gained from this mine when it was dismantled was invaluable.

SZABO

345

Violette Reine Elizabeth
Rank/Title: Ensign
Unit/Force/Occupation: Women's Transport Service (FANY)
Other Decorations: —
Date of Gazette: 17 Dec. 1946
Place/Date of Birth: Brixton, London — 26 Jun. 1921
Place/Date of Death: Ravensbrück Concentration Camp, Germany — 25 Jan./5 Feb. 1945
Place of Memorial: The Brookwood Memorial, Surrey; plaque in Lambeth Town Hall, London
Town/County Connections: Brixton, London
Remarks: —

Account of Deed: Madame Szabo volunteered for a particularly dangerous mission in France in April 1944, when she acted as a courier to a Frenchman who had survived the break-up of his circuit based on Rouen and was trying to reconstitute a group in this strategically important area. She had to travel from Paris to Rouen, contacting certain people believed to have remained unmolested and report back to her chief in Paris. She accomplished this dangerous task successfully and after about six weeks returned to England. On D-Day plus one she was dropped into France again and soon afterwards, with her guide, a young French-man, was ambushed by a German patrol and wounded. She insisted that her guide should escape while he could, and she herself was captured and taken first to Limoges and then to Paris. After brutal interrogations over several weeks when she divulged nothing, she was put on a train for Germany. On the journey while an air raid was in progress and the guards ran for shelter, she managed, despite being chained by the ankle to another prisoner, to carry a bottle of water to badly wounded British officers in a cattle truck. Imprisonment at Ravensbrück followed and then two spells in labour camps, working under impossible conditions, but Madame Szabo was eventually returned to Ravensbrück and executed there.

TAHA
346

El Jak Effendi
Rank/Title: Shawish (later Sub-Mamom)
Unit/Force/Occupation: Khartoum Police Force
Other Decorations: —
Date of Gazette: 12 Dec. 1924
Place/Date of Birth: —
Place/Date of Death: —
Place of Memorial: —
Town/County Connections: —
Remarks: (EGM)

Account of Deed: On 27th and 28th November 1924 two platoons of the 11th Sudanese Regiment ran amok at Khartoum. Three British officers and two Syrian medical officers were killed by the mutineers and some nine other ranks were wounded. Shawish Jak Taha and two other members of the Khartoum Police were recommended for great gallantry displayed during the disturbances. (See also entries for NEGIB Ibrahim and MUHAMMAD Abdulla Muhammad)

TALBOT
347

Ellis Edward Arthur Chetwynd
Rank/Title: Second Lieutenant (later Lieutenant)
Unit/Force/Occupation: 103 Bomb Disposal Section, Corps of Royal Engineers
Other Decorations: MBE
Date of Gazette: 17 Sep. 1940
Place/Date of Birth: Newport, Shropshire — 22 Mar. 1920
Place/Date of Death: Sicily — 9 Oct. 1941
Place of Memorial: Catania War Cemetery, Sicily
Town/County Connections: —
Remarks: (EGM)

Account of Deed: At the beginning of the Blitz, on 24th/25th August 1940, Second Lieutenant Talbot, a member of one of the newly formed Bomb Disposal Units, had to deal with an unexploded bomb which was buried so deep that it took 12½ hours to dig down to it. He then diagnosed that it was of the delayed action type and ordered his men to a safe distance while he examined it. As the bomb appeared to be of a new type, he decided to move it to a new place where it would do no damage if it exploded. Still keeping his men under cover, he carried the bomb on his shoulder for some 200 yards and put it in a safe spot. From the start of the work there was a risk of explosion, and Second Lieutenant Talbot set a fine example of courage and devotion to duty.

TANDY-GREEN, Charles William — see **GREEN,** Charles William TANDY-

TAYLOR
348

George Anthony Morgan
Rank/Title: Mr.
Unit/Force/Occupation: Vulcanologist employed by the Commonwealth Bureau of Mineral Resources in Papua and New Guinea
Other Decorations: —
Date of Gazette: 22 Apr. 1952
Place/Date of Birth: Moree, New South Wales, Australia — 30 Oct. 1917
Place/Date of Death: New Guinea — 16 Aug. 1972
Place of Memorial: —
Town/County Connections: —
Remarks: Served in the Australian Army in the Pacific area 1942-47.

Account of Deed: Mr. Taylor was awarded the George Cross for his conspicuous courage in the face of great danger over a period of several months, following the violent eruption of Mount Lamington in Papua, which occurred on Sunday, 21st January 1951. The eruption was considered to be one of the most violent of its kind ever known — it devastated an area of about 90 square miles. Mr. Taylor arrived at Mount Lamington on the day following the main eruption and from that day onwards he visited the crater by aircraft almost daily and on many occasions on foot. Without regard for his personal safety he entered the danger area again and again, each time at greater risk, both in order to ensure the safety of the rescue and working parties and to obtain scientific information relating to this type of volcano, about which little was known. His work saved many lives in the danger zone where he was able to warn rehabilitation parties of the areas to be avoided.

TAYLOR 349

Patrick Gordon (later Sir Gordon)
Rank/Title: Captain
Unit/Force/Occupation: Navigator and relief pilot in civil aviation
Other Decorations: MC
Date of Gazette: 9 Jul. 1937
Place/Date of Birth: Mosman, Sydney, New South Wales, Australia — 20 Oct. 1896
Place/Date of Death: Honolulu, Hawaii — 14 Dec. 1966
Place of Memorial: —
Town/County Connections: —
Remarks: (EGM); served with RFC (later RAF) in First World War; resigned in 1919; was navigator and relief pilot for Sir Charles Kingsford-Smith including the flight from Australia to USA, Nov. 1934 — the first single-engined crossing of the Pacific; served as Squadron Leader in RAAF in Second World War until 1944, then with RAF.

Account of Deed: On 15th May 1935 the monoplane *Southern Cross* piloted by Sir Charles Kingsford-Smith, with Captain Taylor as navigator, left Sydney for an airmail flight across the Tasman Sea. About 600 miles from Sydney the starboard engine failed and the pilot had to turn back. The strain on the other two engines began to tell and the port engine began to use too much oil. Fuel and cargo were jettisoned but the aircraft lost height and at times was only a few feet above the water. It was in these hazardous conditions that Captain Taylor, six times at intervals of 35 minutes, climbed out of the cockpit, carrying oil by means of a vacuum flask to the overheating port engine. This almost incredible feat, and the skilful handling of the crippled aircraft by its pilot, resulted in the plane arriving safely back at the airport after 16 hours in the air.

TAYLOR 350

Robert George
Rank/Title: Mr.
Unit/Force/Occupation: Newspaper advertising representative
Other Decorations: —
Date of Gazette: 1 Aug. 1950
Place/Date of Birth: Fishponds, Bristol — 1920
Place/Date of Death: Bristol — 13 Mar. 1950
Place of Memorial: —
Town/County Connections: Manchester; Bristol
Remarks: Served in the Royal Artillery in the Second World War, attaining the rank of Sergeant.

Account of Deed: Two armed men entered a sub-branch of Lloyds Bank in Bristol on 13th March 1950. They threatened the cashier and the bank guard with a revolver, stole a great deal of money and escaped. The alarm was raised and the two men ran off. Mr. Taylor took up the chase and caught up with the man who was carrying the gun and tried to close with him. The criminal turned and fired point blank into Mr. Taylor's face, inflicting fatal injuries. Without any regard for the danger, Mr. Taylor had intervened out of a desire to help in the preservation of law and order and gave his life in a gallant attempt to apprehend an armed and dangerous criminal.

TAYLOR 351

William Horace
Rank/Title: Sub-Lieutenant (later Lieutenant-Commander)
Unit/Force/Occupation: Royal Naval Volunteer Reserve
Other Decorations: MBE
Date of Gazette: 14 Jan. 1941
Place/Date of Birth: — 23 Oct. 1908
Place/Date of Death: —
Place of Memorial: —
Town/County Connections: Blanefield, near Glasgow, Scotland; Axminster, Devon
Remarks: Commissioner, Scout Association 1946-; Field Commissioner for SW England Scout Association, 1952-74.

Account of Deed: Sub-Lieutenant Taylor was awarded the George Cross for great gallantry and undaunted devotion to duty in connection with mine disposal in late September/early October 1940, and in particular with an extremely dangerous operation at the RAF Depot, Uxbridge.

TEMPERLEY

352

Samuel Jarrett
Rank/Title: Mr.
Unit/Force/Occupation: Assistant Surveyor, Bentley Colliery, Yorkshire
Other Decorations: —
Date of Gazette: 30 Sep. 1932
Place/Date of Birth: — 21 Aug. 1899
Place/Date of Death: — 15 Dec. 1977
Place of Memorial: —
Town/County Connections: Bentley, Doncaster, Yorkshire
Remarks: (EM); later became an Area General Manager, National Coal Board.

Account of Deed: On 20th November 1931, in the afternoon, a violent explosion of firedamp, followed by fires, occurred in the North East District of the Bentley Colliery. Of some 47 men working at or near the coal face, 45 were either killed or died later. A number of miners rendered heroic assistance at the work of rescue, among them Mr. Temperley who was one of those concerned with rescues from the area of the fires, where the danger was extreme. Mr. Temperley volunteered to lead a rescue brigade to the return airway, where some men were still alive, by way of the face, there being a fire on the direct route. On the journey an explosion occurred severely burning three members of the party, who then turned back, but Mr. Temperley, though not equipped with breathing apparatus, went on, with one of the mines inspectors, as far as the entrance to the airway and subsequently helped to carry out an injured man past one of the fires, and also gave other assistance. (See also entries for ALLPORT, E., DARKER, R.E., SOULSBY, O., SYKES, F. and YATES, P.W.)

THOMAS

353

Arthur Devere
Rank/Title: Mr.
Unit/Force/Occupation: Railway flagman, London Underground
Other Decorations: —
Date of Gazette: 31 Mar. 1931
Place/Date of Birth: London — 5 Aug. 1895
Place/Date of Death: Harrow, Middlesex — 1 Nov. 1973
Place of Memorial: —
Town/County Connections: Harrow, Middlesex
Remarks: (EM); Later Inspector, British Transport Police

Account of Deed: On 14th January 1931 a workman who was engaged in dismantling a wooden staging fixed across the track of the Metropolitan Railway Station at Kings Cross, slipped and fell from a height of about 20 feet to the permanent way of the down Inner Circle line. He was unconscious and lay face downwards across one running rail with his head close to the negative rail of the electrified system. Mr. Thomas, who was acting as flagman for the protection of the workmen, saw the man fall and at the same time heard a down train approaching the station round the curve. Realising that a signal could not be seen by the driver in time for him to stop the train, Mr. Thomas immediately jumped down from the platform to the up line and, crossing two positive and two negative rails carrying 600 volts, snatched the unconscious man from almost under the wheels of the approaching train and held him in a small recess in the wall whilst the train passed within a few inches of them.

THOMAS

354

Dorothy Louise
Rank/Title: Miss
Unit/Force/Occupation: Nursing Sister, Middlesex Hospital, London
Other Decorations: —
Date of Gazette: 2 Mar. 1934
Place/Date of Birth: — 11 Aug. 1905
Place/Date of Death: Chelmsford, Essex — 22 Nov. 1989
Place of Memorial: —
Town/County Connections: Dovercourt and Chelmsford, Essex
Remarks: (EGM)

Account of Deed: On the morning of 26th January 1934, Miss Thomas was on duty as Theatre Sister in the main ground floor theatre at the Middlesex Hospital. At 8.45am an explosion suddenly occurred in a large oxygen cylinder. A stream of sparks and flames from the cylinder shot through the open door of the anaesthetic room across the theatre for a distance of about 15 feet. There was a state of considerable alarm and confusion and it was feared that the burning cylinder might explode at any moment, causing great damage and loss of life. All the staff were at once evacuated from the theatre. Sister Thomas remained behind until everyone was clear and then closed the door to minimise the effect of the explosion. However she then decided that it was her duty to try to avert the wrecking of the theatre by turning off the cylinder, so she went back into the anaesthetic room, rushed over to the cylinder and managed to turn off the oxygen supply — just in time.

THOMAS

355

Forest Frederick Edward YEO-
Rank/Title: Wing Commander
Unit/Force/Occupation: Royal Air Force Volunteer Reserve
Other Decorations: MC & Bar
Date of Gazette: 15 Feb. 1946
Place/Date of Birth: Holborn, London — 17 Jun. 1901
Place/Date of Death: Paris — 26 Feb. 1964
Place of Memorial: —
Town/County Connections: —
Remarks: Légion d'Honneur and Croix de Guerre (France); Cross of Merit (Poland).

Account of Deed: Wing Commander Yeo-Thomas ('The White Rabbit') was parachuted into France on 23rd February 1943 on his first mission which he completed successfully, bringing back with him a US Army Air Corps officer whom he had rescued after being shot down, and, speaking no French, was in danger of capture. He also completed a second mission successfully, the information which he had been able to obtain being instrumental in remedying a desperate situation. In February 1944 he was again parachuted into France, but he was betrayed to the Gestapo and was taken to their Headquarters in Paris where he underwent four days' continuous interrogation, interspersed with beatings and torture, including immersions, head downwards, in ice-cold water, with legs and arms chained. He was offered his freedom in return for information concerning the head of a Resistance Secretariat, but he remained silent. Owing to his wrist being cut by chains, he contracted blood poisoning and nearly lost his left arm, but in spite of this he made two daring attempts to escape, both unfortunately unsuccessful. On 17th July he was sent to Compeigne prison and then, with 36 other prisoners to Buchenwald, where 16 of them were executed. Wing Commander Yeo-Thomas had already started to organise resistance within the camp and remained undaunted by the threat of a similar fate. He accepted an opportunity of changing his identity with that of a dead French prisoner, on condition that other officers would also be able to do so, and in this way he was instrumental in saving the lives of two officers. Later he was transferred to a work Kommando for Jews, tried to escape but was re-captured and, claiming French nationality, was transferred to a camp near Marienburg. From this camp he led yet another escape party, in broad daylight, and was recaptured when only 800 yards from the American lines. A few days later he finally escaped with a party of ten prisoners whom he led through German patrols to the American lines. Wing Commander Yeo-Thomas had thus turned his final mission into a success by his determined opposition to the enemy, his strenuous efforts to maintain the morale of his fellow prisoners and his brilliant escape activities.

THOMAS

356

Thomas
Rank/Title: Mr.
Unit/Force/Occupation: Miner, Brynamman Colliery, Glamorgan
Other Decorations: —
Date of Gazette: 6 Feb. 1934
Place/Date of Birth: — 30 Jun. 1912
Place/Date of Death: — 19 Jul. 1984
Place of Memorial: —
Town/County Connections: Glamorgan, Wales
Remarks: (EM)

Account of Deed: On 21st September 1933 there was an inrush of water in the Brass Vein Slant of the Brynamman Colliery. Mr. Thomas was working underground at the time and at the risk of his own life helped a youth who had lost his lamp and was unable in the darkness and rush of water to make his way to safety, to reach a part of the working where several of the colliers had gathered. The men then divided into two groups, one group seeking a way out by an airway and the other by a roadway which was flooded and obstructed by a mass of timber and rails which had been washed down by the water. Mr. Thomas stayed at the rear of the group that took the roadway, and when they succeeded in reaching safety he returned to fetch the other group who then escaped by the same route.

THOMPSON

357

Jenkin Robert Oswald
Rank/Title: Captain
Unit/Force/Occupation: Royal Army Medical Corps
Other Decorations: —
Date of Gazette: 2 Feb. 1945
Place/Date of Birth: — 13 Jul. 1911
Place/Date of Death: Anzio, Italy (on board HM Hospital Carrier *St. David*) — 24 Jan. 1944
Place of Memorial: The Brookwood Memorial, Surrey
Town/County Connections: Claygate, Surrey
Remarks: —

Account of Deed: Captain Thompson spent most of the Second World War aboard hospital carriers and was awarded the

George Cross posthumously for his conspicuous gallantry and devotion to duty — particularly in HM Hospital Carrier *Paris* at Dunkirk in May 1940; in the *St. David* at Sicily from 10th to 14th July 1943; at Salerno from 10th to 15th September 1943 and at Anzio during 23rd/24th January 1944. On all these occasions, despite repeated dive-bombing attacks and enemy shell-fire, he showed indifference to danger and physical exhaustion in the care of his patients. On the night of 24th January 1944 HM Hospital Carrier *St. David* was sinking rapidly as the result of a direct hit from a dive-bombing attack. Captain Thompson organised parties to carry the seriously wounded to safety in the boats and by his efforts the lives of all the patients in his ward, except one, as well as those of many walking cases from other wards, were saved. Finally, when the ship was about to founder and all were ordered to save themselves, he himself did nothing of the sort, but returned alone in an endeavour to save the one remaining patient who was still lying trapped below decks. He could not save this man, so he remained with him and they went down with the ship together.

THOMPSON
Matthew
Rank/Title: Mr.
Unit/Force/Occupation: Miner, Askern Main Colliery, Yorkshire
Other Decorations: BEM
Date of Gazette: 28 Jun. 1940
Place/Date of Birth: — 24 Jan. 1898
Place/Date of Death: — 19 Apr. 1981
Place of Memorial: —
Town/County Connections: Askern, Doncaster, Yorkshire
Remarks: (EM)

358

Account of Deed: At 10am on 3rd January 1940 a fall of roof occurred at a coal face in Warren House Seam and a miner was buried by the fall. He was rescued some three hours later, without having suffered serious injury, through the gallantry displayed by a rescue party. The trapped man was completely buried except for his head and shoulders and his arms were pinned by fallen rocks and by a steel bar. The agent, who took charge of the operations, succeeded in removing a stone which was pinning one arm and eventually managed to work his way through to free the man and to pass him out to the other rescuers. Mr. Thompson and another miner* were both close at hand when the fall occurred and at once commenced rescue operations, taking a prominent part in the dangerous work of clearing a way under the fall, and both were able to remove some of the debris which was pinning the trapped man down. Mr. Thompson tried to get through to effect the final release, but was driven back by a further fall. (*See also entry for SMITH, C.)

TOLLEMACHE
Anthony Henry Hamilton
Rank/Title: Flying Officer (later Squadron Leader)
Unit/Force/Occupation: 600 Squadron, Auxiliary Air Force
Other Decorations: —
Date of Gazette: 6 Aug. 1940
Place/Date of Birth: — 3 Aug. 1913
Place/Date of Death: Paris — 20 Feb. 1977
Place of Memorial: Helmingham churchyard, Suffolk
Town/County Connections: Cambridge, Cambridgeshire
Remarks: (EGM); ADC to Field Marshal Earl Alexander, Governor-General of Canada, 1946.

359

Account of Deed: On 11th March 1940 at Manston, Kent, Flying Officer Tollemache was the pilot of an aircraft which carried a passenger and an air gunner and was engaged on a searchlight co-operation exercise. When approaching the flarepath to land, after completing the exercise shortly before midnight, the aircraft struck a tree and crashed into a field, where it immediately burst into flames. Flying Officer Tollemache was thrown clear of the wreckage and his air gunner also escaped. However, realising that his passenger was still in the aircraft, and despite the intense heat and the explosion of small arms ammunition, Flying Officer Tollemache tried to break through the forward hatch and rescue him. He persisted in his efforts until his own clothing was ablaze and he had suffered injuries which nearly cost him his life.

TOWNSEND

360

Emma José
Rank/Title: Miss
Unit/Force/Occupation: —
Other Decorations: —
Date of Gazette: 6 Sep. 1932
Place/Date of Birth: Leicester — 1879
Place/Date of Death: Wimbledon, Surrey — 8 Mar. 1965
Place of Memorial: —
Town/County Connections: Portlemouth, Devon
Remarks: (EGM)

Account of Deed: On 9th May 1932 a farmer of Kingsbridge, South Devon, having already murdered his wife and two children, made a brutal attack on his last surviving child in the South Hams Cottage Hospital at Kingsbridge. The boy, aged nine, was an in-patient at the hospital and his father attacked him as he lay in bed, first firing at him with a gun and then striking him with it several times. Miss Townsend, who was visiting her sister at the hospital, heard cries of 'Help' and went into the ward where she showed great courage in closing with the assailant and tried to prevent him from killing the boy. In the struggle she was struck with the barrel of the gun which cut her head open. The boy died two days later and the farmer was arrested and detained in a criminal lunatic asylum.

TROAKE

361

Frederick Henry
Rank/Title: Private
Unit/Force/Occupation: 2nd Bn., The Dorset Regiment
Other Decorations: —
Date of Gazette: 2 Jun. 1923
Place/Date of Birth: — 4 Sep. 1896
Place/Date of Death: Wellington, Somerset — 27 Apr. 1974
Place of Memorial: —
Town/County Connections: Wellington, Somerset
Remarks: (EGM)

Account of Deed: At Nilambur in September 1921 Private Troake showed conspicuous gallantry in advancing up to the fence round a house in which rebels had been located and in covering the rush of an officer and NCO who fired the roof. He and Private Chant* subsequently showed great courage in clearing the gardens and jungle round the house of the rebels who had taken possession of the area. (*See also entry for CHANT, F.)

TUCKWELL

362

Stephen John
Rank/Title: Able Seaman
Unit/Force/Occupation: Royal Navy
Other Decorations: —
Date of Gazette: 14 Jan. 1941
Place/Date of Birth: —
Place/Date of Death: Sompting, Lancing, Sussex — 2 Oct. 1966
Place of Memorial: —
Town/County Connections: Sompting, Lancing, Sussex
Remarks: —

Account of Deed: Able Seaman Tuckwell worked with Sub-Lieutenant Miller* on many occasions in the dangerous work of mine disposal and together they disposed of some ten of these deadly weapons. They were both awarded the George Cross for dealing with a mine that had fallen into the soft mud in Roding River, which runs into Barking Creek. Sub-Lieutenant Miller decided to borrow a canoe and having put this on a fire-float with the necessary kit, he and Able Seaman Tuckwell went off up the creek to where the mine was thought to be lying. They then left the River Fire Service fire-float and went on in the canoe, until they sighted the black rim of the mine which was stuck in the mud by the nose. They worked together — Able Seaman Tuckwell having refused a suggestion that he should retire to a place of safety. He pointed out that as Sub-Lieutenant Miller would be working under at least a foot of water he would need someone to hand him the tools — in short he preferred to take the same risks. They managed to get out one fuse, but could not reach the other, so appealed to several crane-drivers who had come to see what was happening, and they at once volunteered to help. The two experts got back into the water, put ropes round the mine, and with the assistance of the crane-drivers, the huge cylinder was dragged slowly out of the creek, over the muddy bank and up on to the wharf. The final stages of the operation were then completed in comparative comfort. (*See also entry for MILLER, J.B.P.Duppa-)

TUNNA

Norman
Rank/Title: Mr.
Unit/Force/Occupation: Shunter, Great Western Railway
Other Decorations: —
Date of Gazette: 24 Jan. 1941
Place/Date of Birth: Birkenhead, Cheshire — 29 Apr. 1908
Place/Date of Death: Birkenhead, Cheshire — 4 Dec. 1970
Place of Memorial: British Rail engine named after him (London-Midland Region)
Town/County Connections: Birkenhead, Cheshire
Remarks: —

Account of Deed: On 26th September 1940 when the Luftwaffe carried out their first big Blitz on Merseyside, in the Morpeth dock area of Birkenhead the scores of railway lines were crowded with trains. Some of the wagons were being discharged and reloaded, others loaded with shells and bombs of all sizes were waiting to be transferred to barges and ships next morning. Mr. Tunna knew that six of the wagons on one train contained high explosives, anything up to 500lb bombs. He walked the length of the train and suddenly noticed that burning debris was dropping from one of the HE wagons and discovered two incendiary bombs burning inside it. He ran back to the engine and got a bucket of water, raced back to the burning wagon and threw the water on the flames. This put the fire out under the wagon, but it seemed to him that there must be fire inside. He climbed on top of the wagon and found that an incendiary was wedged between two of the bombs which were becoming dangerously hot. With his shunting pole he managed to wedge the bombs apart and so release the incendiary which fell on the line, but the woodwork of the wagon was still burning and the bombs were in danger of exploding. He then got a stirrup pump and sprayed the bombs until the fire had been put out. To make assurance doubly sure he got the driver to pull the train under the water column and gave all the wagons a good soaking. There can be little doubt that but for Mr. Tunna's cool and courageous action a major explosion might well have occurred.

TURNER

Geoffrey Gledhill
Rank/Title: Sub-Lieutenant (later Commander)
Unit/Force/Occupation: Royal Naval Volunteer Reserve
Other Decorations: GM
Date of Gazette: 27 Jun. 1941
Place/Date of Birth: Sheffield, Yorkshire — 10 Sep. 1903
Place/Date of Death: Stambourne, Halstead, Essex — 9 Feb. 1959
Place of Memorial: Cremated Cambridge
Town/County Connections: Oldham, Lancashire; Stambourne, Essex
Remarks: Later in the war he took charge of a Marine Commando unit in the invasion of Normandy, took part in the capture of Brest and fought with the Commandos into Germany.

Account of Deed: Sub-Lieutenant Turner was called to deal with many unexploded mines in the early months of the Blitz. One fell near the LMS station at Sheffield, putting the station out of action, as it fell with its parachute draped over a railway coach. On 21st December 1940 another fell in the wool factory, Great Howard Street, Liverpool and was partly suspended by its parachute, with its nose on the ground floor and the bomb-fuse hidden. Great care had to be taken in the handling of this mine which weighed nearly a ton. Sub-Lieutenant Turner was successful in removing the fuses of both these mines before they could explode. He had more difficulty with one which fell in Seaforth, about 150 yards from the main Liverpool-Southport line and was almost completely buried in the small yard of a house in Cambridge Street. The mine was badly damaged and it was essential that it should be cleared as soon as possible. Sub-Lieutenant Turner rigged a wire and moved the mine so as to expose the bomb-fuse and fit the safety gag, but the fuse was damaged and only the top half came away, leaving the clockwork and operating mechanism in the mine. He then tried to pick out the remains of the bomb-fuse with his fingers. He had nearly managed this when the clock started and he retired hurriedly. When there was no explosion he waited five minutes and then returned to finish the work, not knowing, of course, how many more seconds the bomb-fuse had still to run. As soon as he touched the bomb-fuse the clock started again and almost at once the mine detonated. He was wounded and very severely shocked, but by some miracle he survived.

TURNER

365

James Gordon Melville
Rank/Title: Mr.
Unit/Force/Occupation: Radio Officer, Merchant Navy
Other Decorations: —
Date of Gazette: 13 Oct. 1939
Place/Date of Birth: — 1907
Place/Date of Death: Hither Green, Kent — 5 Nov. 1967
Place of Memorial: —
Town/County Connections: Staplecross, Robertsbridge, Sussex
Remarks: (EGM)

Account of Deed: Just after the outbreak of the Second World War on 6th September 1939 the SS *Manaar* was attacked by an enemy submarine 120 miles off Cape St. Vincent. After an action lasting about twenty minutes, during which the ship had been badly damaged, the order was given to abandon ship. Mr. Turner insisted on staying behind with two members of the native crew, both of whom were wounded, one severely. He tried to lower a lifeboat, which crashed into the sea, and then he carried the severely wounded lascar to another boat, which was blown to pieces by a shell with two wounded men inside it. Mr. Turner then swam out to the lifeboat, pulled it alongside and got the other injured lascar into it. Despite the continued enemy firing he and the lascar managed to join the Master's boat.

TUTTON

366

Cyril James
Rank/Title: Mr.
Unit/Force/Occupation: Prison Officer, Parkhurst, Isle of Wight
Other Decorations: —
Date of Gazette: 18 Mar. 1927
Place/Date of Birth: — 1892
Place/Date of Death: — 5 Jul. 1967
Place of Memorial: —
Town/County Connections: Wakefield, Yorkshire
Remarks: (EGM)

Account of Deed: Mr. Tutton was awarded the Empire Gallantry Medal for his action on 15th November 1926 when he effected single-handed and at great personal risk the arrest of an escaped convict on the ridge of the prison roof at Parkhurst Prison, Isle of Wight.

TWEEDDALE, Marquess of — see HAY, David George Montagu

TYLER

367

Albert
Rank/Title: Mr.
Unit/Force/Occupation: Workman
Other Decorations: Royal Humane Society's Silver Medal
Date of Gazette: 14 Feb. 1930
Place/Date of Birth: — 2 Apr. 1901
Place/Date of Death: Welwyn, Hertfordshire — 28 Dec. 1975
Place of Memorial: —
Town/County Connections: Welwyn, Hertfordshire
Remarks: (EM)

Account of Deed: On 19th October 1929 a workman and his two sons were engaged in cleaning and enlarging the cess pit of a factory at Burnham Green, near Welwyn. One of the sons who had been lowered to the bottom of the pit in a bucket attached to a rope became affected by gas and was being drawn up to the surface when he fell out of the bucket. His father at once went down the pit to his rescue but collapsed and became unconscious on reaching the bottom. Mr. Albert Tyler, the other son, in spite of having seen the collapse of his father and brother, made repeated attempts to rescue them, but was driven back by gas four times. At the fifth attempt he succeeded in reaching them and passing a rope round their bodies. They were then hauled to the surface, but unfortunately artificial respiration and the administration of oxygen failed to revive them. The rescue operations lasted over a period of about forty minutes and every time Mr. Tyler entered the pit he must have been fully aware that he was endangering his own life.

VAUGHAN (later PURVES)

368

Margaret
Rank/Title: Miss (later Mrs.)
Unit/Force/Occupation: 14-year-old schoolgirl
Other Decorations: —
Date of Gazette: 1 Nov. 1949
Place/Date of Birth: Cardiff, Wales — 25 Nov. 1934
Place/Date of Death: —
Place of Memorial: —
Town/County Connections: Cardiff, Wales; Bradford-on-Avon, Wiltshire
Remarks: (AM)

Account of Deed: On 28th May 1949 a party of Scouts aged between 11 and 15 years, visiting Sully Island off the coast of Glamorgan, were cut off by the rising tide from a causeway which led to the mainland. Most of the boys got safely across, but two of them were forced off the causeway by the strong tide. The leader of the party returned to help the elder boy but in the struggle he too became exhausted. Margaret Vaughan, a schoolgirl aged 14, saw from the beach the difficulties they were in, so she undressed and swam towards them over a distance of some 30 yards in cold rough water and against a strong current. On reaching them she managed to tow the boy, with the help of the Scout leader, towards the shore until a lifebelt was thrown to help them for the last ten feet. Margaret's action probably saved the life of the Scout leader as well as that of the elder boy. The younger boy was also rescued, with the help of a friend who unfortunately gave his own life in the attempt.

WALKER

369

Carl
Rank/Title: Police Constable (later Inspector)
Unit/Force/Occupation: Lancashire Constabulary
Other Decorations: —
Date of Gazette: 13 Nov. 1972
Place/Date of Birth: Kendal, Westmorland — 31 Mar. 1934
Place/Date of Death: —
Place of Memorial: —
Town/County Connections: Kendal, Westmorland; Blackpool, Lancashire
Remarks: Served with the Royal Air Force Police for his National Service; American Federation of Police Legion of Valor.

Account of Deed: On 23rd August 1971 an armed raid on a jeweller's shop occurred in Blackpool, Lancashire. During the chase which followed, involving a number of police cars, Police Constable Walker, with his Panda car, blocked the path of the getaway vehicle, which was stationary in a blind alley. The raiders, however, reversed their car at high speed down the alley, smashing into the side of the Panda. Constable Walker, although suffering from shock, did not give up the pursuit, but while running after the three raiders, was fired on at close range and was hit in the groin. Throughout the pursuit, all the police officers concerned were aware that they faced the threat of death or serious injury, but gave no thought to their own safety in their efforts to effect the arrest of armed and dangerous criminals. (See also entry for RICHARDSON, G.I.)

WALKER

370

Charles Henry
Rank/Title: Petty Officer Cook
Unit/Force/Occupation: Royal Navy
Other Decorations: —
Date of Gazette: 15 Dec. 1942
Place/Date of Birth: Portsmouth, Hampshire — 9 Mar. 1914
Place/Date of Death: —
Place of Memorial: —
Town/County Connections: Eastney, Portsmouth, Hampshire
Remarks: (AM)

Account of Deed: During a convoy to Malta in 1942 a vessel was hit by bombs in an air attack and burst into flames fore and aft. An escorting destroyer went very close, lowered her whaler and picked up survivors from the sea. Petty Officer Walker, seeing a man in difficulties, dived over the destroyer's side and rescued him. The heat was intense and he knew that his ship might have to turn away at any moment. Both rescued and rescuer were picked up.

WALTON 371

Eric William Kevin
Rank/Title: T/Lieutenant
Unit/Force/Occupation: Royal Navy — Member of Falkland Island Dependencies Survey Team
Other Decorations: DSC
Date of Gazette: 8 Jun. 1948
Place/Date of Birth: — 15 May 1918
Place/Date of Death: —
Place of Memorial: —
Town/County Connections: Colwall, Malvern, Worcestershire
Remarks: (AM); author of *Two Years in the Antarctic*

Account of Deed: At about 12 noon on 24th August 1946, while on a sledging journey, a member of the Falkland Islands Dependencies Survey Team fell through a badly-bridged crevasse and disappeared. He had fallen some 40 feet and was jammed in a narrow part of the crevasse. Ropes were lowered to him but he could not get them round himself properly and it was impossible to pull him up as he was jammed in the ice. Lieutenant Walton volunteered to be lowered into the crevasse to free him. It was not possible to use an ice axe in the restricted space, so a spike was sawn off and used as a hand tool to chip away at the ice. After three hours, during which period Lieutenant Walton had been lowered down the crevasse five times, gradually working his way along, he reached the trapped man and freed him so that he could be pulled to the surface.

WASTIE 372

Granville Charles
Rank/Title: Mr.
Unit/Force/Occupation: Farmer
Other Decorations: —
Date of Gazette: 6 & 10 Jun. 1930
Place/Date of Birth: — 29 Oct. 1902
Place/Date of Death: —
Place of Memorial: —
Town/County Connections: Long Hanborough, Oxfordshire
Remarks: (EM); served in Home Guard in Second World War.

Account of Deed: On 25th November 1929 at North Leigh, Oxfordshire, a bricklayer Hector Wastie, when descending a new well thirty feet deep and three feet wide, was overcome by gas half-way down and fell unconscious into thirty inches of water at the bottom. The man's brother (Stanley) went to his assistance but he also collapsed, unconscious. Another workman, in trying to help, became faint and had to be pulled up by a rope. By this time Mr. Granville Wastie, the brother of the two men, had arrived on the scene. After tying a handkerchief over his face and roping himself, he went down the well, and, tying a rope round Stanley, succeeded in bringing him alive to the surface. He then went down a second time and brought up his other brother, Hector, but it was found that he had been drowned after being rendered unconscious by inhaling carbon dioxide.

WATERFIELD 373

Albert
Rank/Title: Mr.
Unit/Force/Occupation: Park-keeper
Other Decorations: —
Date of Gazette: 30 Dec. 1922
Place/Date of Birth: — 1881
Place/Date of Death: Putney, London — 22 Aug. 1968
Place of Memorial: Cremated Mortlake Crematorium, Surrey
Town/County Connections: Putney, London
Remarks: (EGM); first recipient of an EGM (Civil Division). Served in First World War.

Account of Deed: At 2.05am on 10th May 1921 Mr. Waterfield, park-keeper, Richmond Park, saw two young men, each armed with a rifle. As he walked towards them they ran off and he gave chase. He followed them for about a mile to a spot not far from Robin Hood Gate when they stopped and called out that if he did not halt they would fire. He went on towards them and when he was about 50 yards away one of the men fired two shots, both of which missed. The men then turned and ran off, still followed by Mr. Waterfield. They scaled a wall into a lane and when captured some distance away were found to be carrying 76 cartridges between them. It was later revealed that they were trying to make an entry into White Lodge, Richmond Park, the home of The Duke and Duchess of York, later King George VI and Queen Elizabeth. Mr. Waterfield showed great courage and it was due to his persistence in giving chase that the two men were finally arrested.

WATERS

374

Terence Edward
Rank/Title: Lieutenant
Unit/Force/Occupation: The West Yorkshire Regiment, attd. 1st Bn., The Gloucestershire Regiment
Other Decorations: —
Date of Gazette: 13 Apr. 1954
Place/Date of Birth: — 1 Jun. 1929
Place/Date of Death: POW Camp, near Pyongyang, Korea — 22 Apr. 1951
Place of Memorial: —
Town/County Connections: Westbury-on-Trym, Bristol
Remarks: —

Account of Deed: Lieutenant Waters was wounded and taken prisoner at the battle of the Imjin River, in Korea, towards the end of April 1951. On the journey to Pyongyang with other captives he set a magnificent example of courage and fortitude in looking after the other wounded as best he could, despite the brutal treatment to which they were subjected by their Chinese captors. After a journey of immense hardship they arrived at an area west of Pyongyang known as 'The Caves'. Here they were imprisoned in a tunnel driven into the side of the hill through which a stream of water flowed continuously, flooding a great deal of the floor. The cavern was already packed with a great many South Korean and European prisoners of war in rags, filthy and crawling with lice. A large number died daily from wounds, sickness or merely malnutrition. There was no medical attention. It was obvious that few, if any, of the prisoners would survive in such conditions in view of their weakness and the complete lack of any attention to their wounds. After some days of this torment a Korean officer attempted to persuade Lieutenant Waters to join a pro-Communist formation called the Peace Fighters in return for better treatment, but this he refused to do and he died shortly afterwards.

WATERSON

375

William
Rank/Title: Mr.
Unit/Force/Occupation: Plant workman, General Electric Co. Ltd., Birmingham
Other Decorations: —
Date of Gazette: 2 Apr. 1946
Place/Date of Birth: — 1904
Place/Date of Death: Birmingham — 24 Mar. 1973
Place of Memorial: —
Town/County Connections: Birmingham
Remarks: (EM)

Account of Deed: At 4.30am on 18th August 1945 two workmen employed in the carbon-black plant at G.E.C. Co. Ltd. were engaged in collecting newly manufactured lamp black from a brick chamber. The men were unprotected and had to withstand a high temperature as well as an unpleasant atmosphere, while carbon monoxide was present from burning soot. After a short time one of the men collapsed and his companion, being unable to move him, sought assistance. Mr. Waterson was the first to arrive on the scene, and without awaiting the arrival of breathing apparatus, he and the man who had given the alarm entered the chamber and attempted to pull out the man who had collapsed. He was covered in sweat and carbon black and rescue work was difficult as it was impossible to get a proper grip on him. They were unsuccessful at first and on coming out Mr. Waterson's companion collapsed, but he, himself, continued to make rescue attempts — four in all. On his last entry he was accompanied by a member of the works' fire brigade and together they succeeded in bringing the unconscious man out, but unfortunately he was found to be dead.

WATSON

376

Victor Albert
Rank/Title: Flight Lieutenant
Unit/Force/Occupation: Royal Navy
Other Decorations: —
Date of Gazette: 8 Mar. 1918
Place/Date of Birth: — 1897
Place/Date of Death: London — 2 Oct. 1974
Place of Memorial: Golders Green Crematorium, London
Town/County Connections: London
Remarks: (AM)

Account of Deed: On the occasion of an accident to one of HM Airships, which resulted in a fire breaking out on board, Flight Lieutenant Watson, who was the senior officer on the spot, immediately rushed up to the car of the airship under the impression that one on the crew was still in it, although he was well aware that there were heavy bombs attached to the airship which it was impossible to remove owing to the nearness of the fire, and which were almost certain to explode at any moment on account of the heat. Having satisfied himself that there was in fact no one in the car, he turned away to render assistance elsewhere, and at that moment one of the bombs exploded, a portion of it shattering Flight Lieutenant Watson's right arm at the elbow. The arm had to be amputated almost immediately.

WATT-BONAR, Eric — see **BONAR,** Eric WATT-

WELLER, John — see **BROWN,** John Weller

WELLER 377
Percy Barnard
Rank/Title: Mr.
Unit/Force/Occupation: Workman
Other Decorations: —
Date of Gazette: 24 Oct. 1941
Place/Date of Birth: — 6 Jun. 1898
Place/Date of Death: — 22 Apr. 1979
Place of Memorial: —
Town/County Connections: —
Remarks: (EM)

Account of Deed: On 16th May 1941 an explosion accompanied by fire occurred in a building in which explosives were being broken down. A workman who was employed in the building was badly burnt. Mr. Weller, another workman, entered the burning building and succeeded in rescuing the injured man who died subsequently from the effects of his injuries. Mr. Weller ran great personal risks in effecting this rescue, not only from the fire but also from the danger of a further explosion which did in fact occur shortly afterwards, demolishing the building.

WESTERN 378
David Charles
Rank/Title: Mr.
Unit/Force/Occupation: 10-year-old schoolboy
Other Decorations: Royal Humane Society Medal
Date of Gazette: 13 Aug. 1948
Place/Date of Birth: 26 Apr. 1937
Place/Date of Death: —
Place of Memorial: —
Town/County Connections: Plymouth, Devon
Remarks: (AM); served with the Royal Navy. Youngest recipient of the Albert Medal, apart from an 8-year-old Canadian boy who did not live to exchange the medal for the George Cross (see entry for Ashburnham, D.)

Account of Deed: On the afternoon of 27th February 1948 David Western, aged 10, was walking on a frozen lake at Osterley Park, London with three other boys when the ice gave way and his companions fell through the ice. David immediately attempted the rescue of each in turn and in his efforts fell in himself. He succeeded in forcing a channel through the ice until he linked up with one of the boys who was in difficulties and they came out together. David then returned at once with a thin rope round his waist, to try to save the lives of the other two. Though only a moderate swimmer, he swam through the channel in the ice, beating the unbroken ice with his hands and leaning upon it to make it give way. The boys had slipped under the ice, so he dived under the surface to look for one of them until he was practically exhausted and had to be pulled back to the bank. This rescue attempt was sustained for about 25 minutes in icy water and in forcing his way through the sharp ice David received multiple abrasions on body, legs and arms.

WHITEHEAD 379

Thomas Atkinson
Rank/Title: Mr.
Unit/Force/Occupation: Workman at a tar distillers
Other Decorations: —
Date of Gazette: 5 Sep. 1922
Place/Date of Birth: County Tipperary, Ireland — 17 Jul. 1887
Place/Date of Death: Larne, Ireland — 27 Aug. 1973
Place of Memorial: —
Town/County Connections: Sunderland, Co. Durham
Remarks: (EM)

Account of Deed: The stills used at the works of Messrs. Brotherton & Co. Ltd. of Sunderland, tar distillers, were large cylinders two feet in diameter and twenty feet deep. While one of these stills was standing empty, and, it was thought, disconnected from the adjoining stills, a workman went down inside by means of a rope ladder through the small man-hole, fifteen inches in diameter. When he reached the bottom he collapsed and his mate, realising that gas must have accumulated in the still, shouted for help and ran for a rope. Another workman without waiting for a rope attempted a rescue, but was overcome and collapsed. A second attempt was made, the rescuer going down with a handkerchief tied round his mouth and a rope round his body, but he was also overcome and was pulled up. Then Mr. Whitehead made two attempts to reach the two unconscious men, first equipped with a gauze respirator and then with a hood with oxygen pumped into it, but on both occasions he had to be pulled out. By this time the pitch-pipe had been removed from the bottom of the still and air was being forced in, and eventually rescuers reached the two men and they were drawn up, but were found to be dead.

WILCOX 380

Charles
Rank/Title: Mr.
Unit/Force/Occupation: Painter, employed by Birmingham Corporation
Other Decorations: —
Date of Gazette: 30 Sep. 1949
Place/Date of Birth: — 11 May 1919
Place/Date of Death: —
Place of Memorial: —
Town/County Connections: Birmingham
Remarks: (EM); served in Second World War.

Account of Deed: On 23rd August 1949 Mr. Wilcox was engaged with other men in painting a Council House building in the centre of Birmingham. One of the other painters climbed from a ladder on to an arched sill about 18 inches wide and 45 feet above the street. This sill was below a window which he found to be bricked up from the inside, so that there was nothing for him to hold on to. He turned round to get back on to the ladder but could not see it, became frightened and crouched down on the ledge. The foreman painter saw the man's predicament and sent another man to his assistance, but he returned to the ground almost immediately. Mr. Wilcox then climbed up to help and by kneeling on a flat piece of masonry some 18 inches square, was able to support his workmate who was suffering from severe shock. Mr. Wilcox stayed in this position for 45 minutes, in imminent danger of falling had the other man kicked out or made any violent movement. By the time the Fire Brigade arrived he was unconscious but was brought to the ground in a safety belt which Mr. Wilcox strapped on him.

WILD 381

Robert
Rank/Title: Mr.
Unit/Force/Occupation: Workman, D.R. Cotton Mills Ltd., Rochdale
Other Decorations: —
Date of Gazette: 22 Oct. 1926
Place/Date of Birth: —
Place/Date of Death: Rochdale, Lancashire — 6 May 1976
Place of Memorial: —
Town/County Connections: Rochdale, Lancashire
Remarks: (EGM)

Account of Deed: Mr. Wild was awarded the Empire Gallantry Medal in recognition of his bravery in extinguishing with his bare hands the fiercely blazing clothing of a fellow workman which had accidentally ignited.

WILLETTS

382

Michael
Rank/Title: Sergeant
Unit/Force/Occupation: 3rd Bn., The Parachute Regiment
Other Decorations: —
Date of Gazette: 22 Jun. 1971
Place/Date of Birth: Sutton-in-Ashfields, Nottingham — 13 Aug. 1943
Place/Date of Death: Belfast — 25 May 1971
Place of Memorial: St. Mary's churchyard, Blidworth, Nottinghamshire
Town/County Connections: Blidworth, Nottinghamshire
Remarks: —

Account of Deed: On the evening of 25th May 1971 a terrorist entered the reception hall of the Springfield Road Police Station, Belfast. He carried a suitcase from which a smoking fuse protruded, dumped it quickly on the floor and fled outside. Inside the hall were a man and a woman, two children and several police officers. One of the latter saw the smoking case and raised the alarm and he and the other police officers began to clear the room. Sergeant Willetts was on duty in the inner hall and hearing the alarm, sent an NCO up to the first floor to warn those above, and then went himself to the door through which those in the reception hall and office were being hustled. He held the door open while all went safely through and then remained standing in the doorway, shielding those taking cover. In the next moment the bomb exploded with terrible force, mortally wounding him. By this considered act of bravery Sergeant Willetts risked — and lost — his life for those of the adults and children.

WILLIAMS

383

Osmond
Rank/Title: Mr.
Unit/Force/Occupation: Electrical Foreman, Public Works Department, Sierra Leone
Other Decorations: —
Date of Gazette: 29 Nov. 1932
Place/Date of Birth: Bangor, Caenarvonshire, Wales — 20 Jan. 1899
Place/Date of Death: Aber, Bangor, Caenarvonshire, Wales — 4 Mar. 1981
Place of Memorial: —
Town/County Connections: Aber, Bangor, Caenarvonshire, Wales
Remarks: (EM)

Account of Deed: On 15th July 1932, Mr. Williams received a message that a distribution wire had fallen in a street in Freetown and he immediately went to investigate. When he arrived at the spot he saw a woman approaching the broken wire and shouted to her to stop, but she continued on her way and became entangled in the wire. Mr. Williams at once started to free the woman and in spite of severe shocks, succeeded in doing so. He applied artificial respiration until the woman's breathing appeared to be normal and then drove her to the hospital. Afterwards he returned and superintended the repair of the broken wire. The woman subsequently died from the shock which she received.

WILLIAMS

384

Sidney
Rank/Title: Lance-Corporal
Unit/Force/Occupation: 1/6th Bn., The City of London Regiment
Other Decorations: —
Date of Gazette: 30 Aug. 1918
Place/Date of Birth: Lambeth, London — 23 Dec. 1887
Place/Date of Death: Clapham, London — 12 Oct. 1976
Place of Memorial: —
Town/County Connections: London
Remarks: (AM); served with the Civil Defence (Fire-watcher) in the Second World War; Freeman of the City of London.

Account of Deed: On 4th January 1918 in France, a soldier dropped a lighted match in a dug-out which had been used as a store for gunpowder. Although most of the gunpowder had been removed, there was a considerable amount scattered on the floor which caught fire. The soldier was overcome by the fumes, and in spite of the volumes of smoke issuing from the dug-out, Lance-Corporal Williams went in and rescued the soldier, who was then badly burnt and unconscious. The Lance-Corporal, who was severely burnt himself, had to carry the man up twenty steps, and if it had not been for his prompt action, the man would have lost his life.

WILSON   385

Harry
Rank/Title: Mr.
Unit/Force/Occupation: Miner, Harriseahead Colliery, Staffordshire
Other Decorations: —
Date of Gazette: 22 Aug. & 2 Sep. 1924
Place/Date of Birth: — 13 Jan. 1903
Place/Date of Death: Stoke-on-Trent, Staffordshire — 26 Mar. 1986
Place of Memorial: —
Town/County Connections: Stoke-on-Trent, Staffordshire
Remarks: (EM)

Account of Deed: On 10th March 1924 an inrush of water took place at Harriseahead Colliery. Most of the workmen had already left the mine, but one who had been working alone was missing. The manager was told that it was impossible to rescue him, the bottom of the pit being three parts full of water which was still rising, but he called for volunteers. Mr. Wilson was one of five men who responded and descended into the mine by a foot-rail. The rescue party reached a ventilation door which they dared not open owing to the pressure of water behind it and they prepared to go back. The manager, who had followed them, insisted that the man could not be left, so he and Mr. Wilson forced the ventilation door, allowing the water to escape gradually. They then waded to the trapped man, reaching him with great difficulty, and all three were eventually drawn to the surface.

WILTSHIRE   386

Sidney Noel
Rank/Title: Pilot Officer
Unit/Force/Occupation: Royal Air Force
Other Decorations: —
Date of Gazette: 31 Jan. 1930
Place/Date of Birth: Farnham, Surrey — 12 Dec. 1909
Place/Date of Death: —
Place of Memorial: —
Town/County Connections: —
Remarks: (EGM); served in NZAF 1939-44 (Squadron Leader); transferred to Transport Command, RAF 1944-45; returned to New Zealand and worked for Hutchinson Motors Ltd., Christchurch, until 1978.

Account of Deed: On 21st October 1929 Pilot Officer Wiltshire was flying with his instructor at Sleaford in an aeroplane that crashed on landing and at once caught fire. Having extricated himself from the wrecked machine, Pilot Officer Wiltshire found that his instructor's foot was caught in the wreckage, so he re-entered the blazing plane and pulled the man out, badly burnt but alive.

WINTER   387

Gerald
Rank/Title: Mr.
Unit/Force/Occupation: Agricultural worker
Other Decorations: —
Date of Gazette: 28 Jun. 1940
Place/Date of Birth: Heathfield, Sussex — 29 Mar. 1900
Place/Date of Death: — 8 Jan. 1971
Place of Memorial: —
Town/County Connections: Peacehaven, Sussex
Remarks: (EGM)

Account of Deed: On 21st March 1940 Mr. Winter was working in a field in Sussex when an RAF plane crossed the coast east of Shoreham, disappeared over the hills north of Brighton and crashed into a hill-top at Portslade. It burst into flames, ammunition began to explode, and the gorse bushes around it were set on fire. Mr. Winter ran through the blaze, dived into the plane and pulled an airman out from the after-part of the machine. The airman told him that the pilot and the navigator were trapped in the forward cockpit so Mr. Winter climbed into the plane again and tried to pull the two men out. But they were so firmly fixed and the heat was so intense that he was forced to abandon the task.

WOLSEY

388

Hilda Elizabeth
Rank/Title: Miss
Unit/Force/Occupation: Nurse
Other Decorations: —
Date of Gazette: 28 Mar. & 26 May 1911
Place/Date of Birth: — 26 Jun. 1886
Place/Date of Death: Ealing, London — 11 Mar. 1974
Place of Memorial: —
Town/County Connections: Ealing, London
Remarks: (AM)

Account of Deed: On 11th June 1910 a female patient at the Hanwell Asylum, while exercising in one of the airing courts, climbed over the wire covering one of the fire-escape staircases and, reaching the roof of the laundry ward, ran along the narrow guttering at the edge of the roof. Nurse Wolsey followed her over the wire covering of the escape and along the narrow guttering, 25 feet above the ground, making her way by leaning with one hand against the sloping roof and, reaching the patient, held her, at great personal risk, until ropes and ladders were fetched and she was lowered to safety.

WOODBRIDGE

389

Stanley James
Rank/Title: Flight Sergeant
Unit/Force/Occupation: 159 Squadron, Royal Air Force Volunteer Reserve
Other Decorations: —
Date of Gazette: 28 Sep. 1948
Place/Date of Birth: Chelsea, London — 29 Aug. 1921
Place/Date of Death: POW Camp, Burma — 7 Feb. 1945
Place of Memorial: Rangoon War Cemetery, Burma
Town/County Connections: Chingford, Essex
Remarks: —

Account of Deed: Flight Sergeant Woodbridge was a wireless operator in a Liberator bomber which crashed in the jungle in Burma on 31st January 1945. Together with five other members of the crew he was captured by the Japanese. All six were subjected to torture in an attempt to make them disclose information which would have been of use to the Japanese Intelligence Service. When they refused to speak, all except Flight Sergeant Woodbridge were beheaded — the Japanese thought that he, being a wireless operator, was in a position to give them information about wireless equipment, codes and wavelengths. They therefore subjected to him to a further period of most brutal torture, but when all efforts to make him speak were fruitless this very gallant young airman was beheaded.

WYLIE

390

George Cameron
Rank/Title: Sapper (later Corporal)
Unit/Force/Occupation: Corps of Royal Engineers
Other Decorations: —
Date of Gazette: 30 Sep. 1940
Place/Date of Birth: Kilmarnock, Scotland — 25 Dec. 1908
Place/Date of Death: London — 1 Feb. 1987
Place of Memorial: —
Town/County Connections: London
Remarks: —

Account of Deed: Sapper Wylie went with Lieutenant Davies* to recover a bomb which fell in the close vicinity of St. Paul's Cathedral on 12th September 1940. It was a night of heavy raids on London and it was not at first realised exactly where the bomb was. It was Sapper Wylie who discovered it deep down under the pavement in front of the Cathedral and he was also instrumental in removing it to the vehicle in which it was driven away for disposal. (*See also entry for DAVIES, R.)

YADAVA, Bhim Singh — see **BHIM SINGH YADAVA**

YAR

391

Ahmed
Rank/Title: Havildar (later Havildar-Major)
Unit/Force/Occupation: 24th Mountain Brigade, Royal Artillery
Other Decorations: —
Date of Gazette: 19 Nov. 1935
Place/Date of Birth: —
Place/Date of Death: Khushab, Sargodha, Pakistan — 31 Aug. 1986
Place of Memorial: —
Town/County Connections: —
Remarks: (EGM)

Account of Deed: At the time of the Quetta earthquake (31st May/1st June 1935) men of the 24th Mountain Brigade were early on the scene of the disaster, putting out fires and rescuing any survivors they could find. Havildar Ahmed Yar worked for five and a half hours trying to extricate a man who was trapped in a hole 15 feet below a very unsafe wall. During this period there were several further earthquake shocks and there was a grave risk of the havildar being buried, together with the man he was trying to save. He was on continuous rescue work from the time of the 'quake until his battery returned to its lines on the evening of 3rd June.

YATES

392

Philip William
Rank/Title: Mr.
Unit/Force/Occupation: Miner, Bentley Colliery, Yorkshire
Other Decorations: —
Date of Gazette: 30 Sep. 1932
Place/Date of Birth: 3 Jan. 1913
Place/Date of Death: —
Place of Memorial: —
Town/County Connections: Bentley, Doncaster, Yorkshire
Remarks: (EM)

Account of Deed: On 20th November 1931 in the afternoon, a violent explosion of firedamp, followed by fires, occurred in the North East District of the Bentley Colliery. Of some 47 men working at or near the coal face, 45 were either killed or died later. A number of miners rendered heroic assistance at the work of rescue, among them Mr. Yates who displayed great gallantry and perseverance in extricating the injured and conveying them to a place of safety. They had to work in an atmosphere which was hot and vitiated and there was always risk of further explosion. One such explosion actually occurred at 10.30pm injuring members of one of the rescue parties, and this was followed by yet another. (See also entries for ALLPORT, E., DARKER, R.E., SOULSBY, O., SYKES, F. and TEMPERLEY, S.J.)

YEHIA

393

El Imam
Rank/Title: Police Constable
Unit/Force/Occupation: Khartoum Police
Other Decorations: —
Date of Gazette: 1 Jan. 1932
Place/Date of Birth: — 1912
Place/Date of Death: Omdurman, Sudan — 16 Feb. 1987
Place of Memorial: —
Town/County Connections: —
Remarks: (EGM)

Account of Deed: An unusual incident in Khartoum in 1931 earned Police Constable Yehia El Imam an EGM. Having failed to kill with his baton a rabid dog which was attacking a man, he strangled it with his bare hands, being severely bitten in the struggle. There is no doubt that by his prompt action and courage he saved a number of people from contracting rabies.

YOUNG

Archibald
Rank/Title: Mr.
Unit/Force/Occupation: Workman, Roslin Explosives Factory
Other Decorations: —
Date of Gazette: 1 Jan. 1917
Place/Date of Birth: — 29 Feb. 1892
Place/Date of Death: — 4 Nov. 1976
Place of Memorial: —
Town/County Connections: Roslin, Midlothian, Scotland
Remarks: (EM)

394

Account of Deed: On 20th June 1916 a small explosion occurred at 10am in a building at the Roslin Explosives Factory, Midlothian. Two men who were aware that four girls were in the building which had caught fire and that the building was full of explosives, ran towards it. As they approached, two of the girls came out and fell unconscious. The building was now blazing furiously, but the two men, who knew the position of the explosives within, used the fire buckets so as to allay the flames in the dangerous quarter and to enable one of them to dash in. He groped through the smoke, which was dense white, found one girl and passed her out to Mr. Young who had arrived meanwhile. He then returned for the second girl, and eventually brought her out, while Mr. Young put the first girl on a bogey which he thrust along the line out of danger, and then returned for the second. During the whole of this time small explosions were continually taking place within the building and immediately after the second rescue a heavy explosion occurred, which flattened part of it. Twelve minutes after the original explosion the whole building blew up.

YOUNG

St. John Graham
Rank/Title: Lieutenant
Unit/Force/Occupation: Royal Tank Regiment, attd. The Central India Horse (21st King George V's Own Horse), Indian Armoured Corps
Other Decorations: —
Date of Gazette: 20 Jul. 1945
Place/Date of Birth: Esher, Surrey — 16 Jun. 1921
Place/Date of Death: Italy — 24 Jul. 1944
Place of Memorial: Arrezzo War Cemetery, Italy
Town/County Connections: Esher, Surrey
Remarks: —

395

Account of Deed: On 23rd July 1944 when in command of a night patrol in Italy, Lieutenant Young realised that they had run on to a mine field and immediately ordered his men to remain where they were until it was light. Some time later a member of the patrol who had been wounded was in great pain and Mr. Young began to crawl forward carefully poking in front of him with his fingers. He located and rendered harmless three Schu mines, and then, deviating from his course, knelt on a mine which exploded, severing his right leg. Despite this he went on, reached the injured man and dressed his wound. For the next five hours he continued giving encouragement to his men. At first light he was carried off the minefield and when the Regimental Medical Officer came to him 30 minutes later he was sitting up and giving orders to his patrol, supervising the evacuation of the wounded. He then lost consciousness and died the same evening. One of the men under his command also received a posthumous George Cross on this occasion. (See also entry for DITTO RAM).

YOUNGER

William

Rank/Title: Mr.

Unit/Force/Occupation: Deputy, Louisa Old Section, Louisa Colliery, Durham

Other Decorations: —

Date of Gazette: 20 Jul. 1948

Place/Date of Birth: — 24 Mar. 1909

Place/Date of Death: —

Place of Memorial: —

Town/County Connections: Durham, Co. Durham

Remarks: (EM); Brother of the Order of St. John; served in Second World War.

Account of Deed: Shortly before midnight on 22nd August 1947 a serious explosion of firedamp and coal dust occurred in the Louisa Colliery. Mr. Younger and two other deputies*, who with their intimate knowledge of the geography of the mine could have made their way to safety, went at once to the scene of the disaster, where they were soon joined by an overman* who came down from the surface. Twenty-four men, all of whom were either injured or incapacitated by carbon-monoxide poisoning, were in the district at the time; 19 of them died and but for the prompt and continuous heroic work performed by the three deputies and the overman, there is little doubt that not one would have survived. The atmosphere was so thick that the beams of the cap-lamps could only penetrate a foot or so, which meant that the rescuers could do nothing to guard against danger from falls of ground, a very real danger after an explosion, and the road in places was almost completely blocked by tubs derailed by blast. (*See also entries for HUTCHINSON, J., ROBINSON, H. and SHANLEY, J.)

Town & County Connections

BIBLIOGRAPHY

ABBOTT, P.E. and TAMPLIN, J.M.A., *British Gallantry Awards* (Guinness Superlatives and B.A. Seaby, 1981)

BISSET, Lieutenant Colonel Ian, *The George Cross* (Frederick Muller, 1963)

HAMILTON, A.D. & CO., *Hamilton's Coin & Medal Despatch,* ed. R.J. Malloch

O'SHEA, Phillip P., *An Unknown Few* (P.D. Hasselberg, Government Printer, Wellington, New Zealand, 1981)

SMYTH, Brigadier The Rt. Hon. Sir John, Bt., VC, MC, *The Story of The George Cross* (Arthur Barker Ltd., London, 1968)

STANISTREET, Allan, 'Gainst All Disaster (Picton Publishing, Chippenham, 1986)

SWETTENHAM, J., *Valiant Men; Canada's VC and GC Winners* (Hakkert, Toronto, 1973)

WIGMORE, L. and HARDING, B., *They Dared Mightily* (Australian War Memorial, Canberra ACT, 1963)

WILSON, Sir Arnold, MP, and McEWEN, Captain J.H.F., MP *Gallantry* (Oxford University Press, 1939)

ACKNOWLEDGMENTS

The Publishers would like to thank the following for their valuable assistance in the preparation of this volume:

The Director and Staff of the Imperial War Museum, London, for allowing facilities for extensive research, in particular the files compiled by the late Canon William Lummis, MC;

Miss Rose Coombs, MBE, until recently Special Collections Officer, Imperial War Museum, for her invaluable co-operation and help from her own extensive archives;

Wing Commander Frederick G. Carroll, for allowing access to his very comprehensive files and in particular his photographic records, which form the majority of all the illustrations used in this book;

Mr. Allan Stanistreet for general information and photographs, in particular with regard to railway employees and also former Albert and Edward Medallists;

Mr. Sydney Cauveren and Mr. Kenneth Williams for supplying additional photographs;

Miss Sandra Koller, of The Central Chancery of the Orders of Knighthood, for her help in checking lists and biographical details;

Major T.A.E. Gibson, MBE, Chief Records Officer, The Commonwealth War Graves Commission, for information relating to dates of death, memorials and graves;

The Victoria Cross and George Cross Association, for biographical information and general help and encouragement. In particular we are grateful to Air Vice-Marshal Sir Laurence Sinclair, GC, KCB, CBE, DSO, and Major General H.R.B. Foote, VC, CB, DSO, for their help in obtaining biographical details relating to Royal Air Force and Army winners of the George Cross; also Mr. Alan A. Martin, Honorary Press Adviser to the Association, for help and guidance;

Regimental Museums, for help over individual awards;

The late Commander D. H. Evans, GC, for his biographical information regarding former holders of the Albert Medal;

Mr. Ronald Biddle, for general information and in particular with regard to police personnel;

The Warden of Soham Village College, Cambridgeshire, for allowing us to photograph the George Cross, awarded posthumously to Fireman James Nightall, for use on our cover;

Finally, Mrs. Nora Buzzell of *This England* upon whose shoulders fell much of the burden of research.